The Queerness of Water

Under the Sign of Nature: Explorations in Ecocriticism
Serenella Iovino, Kate Rigby, and John Tallmadge, Editors
Michael P. Branch and SueEllen Campbell, Senior Advisory Editors

The Queerness of Water
TROUBLED ECOLOGIES IN
THE EIGHTEENTH CENTURY

Jeremy Chow

UNIVERSITY OF VIRGINIA PRESS
CHARLOTTESVILLE AND LONDON

University of Virginia Press
© 2023 by the Rector and Visitors of the University of Virginia
All rights reserved
Printed in the United States of America on acid-free paper

First published 2023

9 8 7 6 5 4 3 2 1

Library of Congress Cataloging-in-Publication Data
Names: Chow, Jeremy, author.
Title: The queerness of water : troubled ecologies in the eighteenth century / Jeremy Chow.
Description: Charlottesville : University of Virginia Press, 2023. | Series: Under the sign of nature : explorations in ecocriticism | Includes bibliographical references and index.
Identifiers: LCCN 2022060365 (print) | LCCN 2022060366 (ebook) | ISBN 9780813949505 (hardcover ; acid-free paper) | ISBN 9780813949512 (paperback ; acid-free paper) | ISBN 9780813949529 (ebook)
Subjects: LCSH: English literature—18th century—History and criticism. | Bodies of water in literature. | Violence in literature. | Masculinity in literature. | Ecocriticism. | Queer theory. | LCGFT: Literary criticism.
Classification: LCC PR448.B59 C46 2023 (print) | LCC PR448.B59 (ebook) | DDC 820.9/36—dc23/eng/20230320
LC record available at https://lccn.loc.gov/2022060365
LC ebook record available at https://lccn.loc.gov/2022060366

Cover art: Background by Photo Junction; font Adobe Stock/242421856

Contents

Acknowledgments   vii

Introduction: What's Queer about Water?   1

1. Taken by Storm   33
   Intermezzo: Teaching Wreckage in Rising Waters   58
2. See Monkeys   67
   Intermezzo: Reading Swift on the Planet of the Apes   97
3. Aqueous Punishment   102
   Intermezzo: Off with Her Head   130
4. Sacrif-Ice   136
   Intermezzo: Freeze!   157
   Conclusion: Sea Monsters   165

Notes   187
Bibliography   215
Index   231

Acknowledgments

Kindness is uncommon and underappreciated in academia. This book, which was once (and possibly still is) a fever dream, is only possible because of a community who refused to concede to academia's vehement, negative affects. Such a realization motivates me every day to shift the terrain of our disciplines and fields to be better, do better, and become more inclusive through teaching, mentorship, and scholarship.

At UC Santa Barbara, my formative ideas were nursed by Tess Shewry, E. Heckendorn Cook, Melody Jue, and Bill Warner. The support of a University of California Presidential Predoctoral Fellowship provided time and support to complete an earlier draft. Candace Waid and Ben Olguín extended guiding lights in the darkness of adversity. Bernadette Andrea welcomed me with respect and care and has offered unparalleled mentorship.

My colleagues and students at Bucknell have inspired me to continue to do my best work. Thanks is owed to Maria Antonaccio, Carly Boxer, Claire Campbell, Michael Drexler, Chase Gregory, Ghislaine McDayter, Jessica Pouchet, Anthony Stewart, and Virginia Zimmerman. Kat Lecky has modeled support and counsel to me both in central Pennsylvania and beyond. I am grateful to Bucknell's Office of the Provost for the continued support of this book's publication.

Friendships have sustained me as I completed this book in the throes of the pandemic. Thank you to Timothy Williamson, Adam Cortez, Doug Nelson, Courtney Kase, Amelia Greene, Michelle Zaleski, and Sandy Williams. Equal thanks to the select few—Aili Pettersson Peeker, Sage Gerson, Maite Urcaregui, and Shelby Johnson—to whom I entrusted chapters of this project that I have long kept breasted. Jolene Zigarovich has nurtured my growth from a neophyte to an emerging scholar; thank you for believing in me and for always pushing me in new queer directions.

University of Virginia Press has made my experience as a first-time author enjoyable and seamless; I know this is rare. Angie Hogan spearheaded this work from the get-go, and the production and editorial teams have been invaluable collaborators. I am honored by the commitment and encouragement that I have received. The two anonymous reviewers offered me comprehensive, rigorous, and constructive feedback that has enriched the final product. Thank you for believing this book was something worth reading.

And lastly to Bonnie, who never read a page of this book, learned to read, or understood a lick of it, but who was my constant companion living her best life on my dime. *We rescued each other.*

My frenzied work has found rare homes at select publication venues. I wish to thank the editors, editorial boards, and editorial teams at *Eighteenth-Century Fiction, Digital Defoe, Resilience: A Journal of the Environmental Humanities, English Language Notes, Journal for Eighteenth-Century Studies, Humanities, Sexualities, Literature Compass, Studies in the Novel, ABO: A Journal for Women in the Arts, Science Fiction Studies,* and *Lateral* for supporting my ideas. In addition, Gena Zuroski, Laura Engel, Declan Kavanagh, George Haggerty, Ardel Haefele-Thomas, Neel Ahuja, Nicole Seymour, Suzanne Guiod, and Julia Oestreich have extended collegial olive branches. I am honored to be in community with you.

A version of chapter 1 was published as "Taken by Storm: Robinson Crusoe and Aqueous Violence" in Bucknell University Press's *Robinson Crusoe after 300 Years.* An excerpt from chapter 2 was published by *Journal for Eighteenth-Century Studies* as "Prime Mates: The Simian, Maternity, and Abjection in Brobdingnang." And an excerpt from the conclusion was included in a special issue of *English Language Notes,* published by Duke University Press, as "Hydro-eroticism."

The Queerness of Water

INTRODUCTION
What's Queer about Water?

> But tell me, tell me! Speak again,
> Thy soft response renewing—
> What makes that ship drive on so fast?
> What is the OCEAN doing?
> —First Voice, *The Rime of*
> *the Ancient Mariner* (1798)

> You'll be back, soon you'll see
> You'll remember you belong to me
> You'll be back, time will tell
> You'll remember that I served you well
> *Oceans rise, empires fall*
> We have seen each other through it all
> —King George III, *Hamilton* (2015)

Catastrophe, cataclysmic destruction, and calamity await in the aqueous bodies of eighteenth-century narratives that envision worlds beyond terrestrial boundaries. Oceans swallow human trespassers whole; storms waylay unlucky travelers; ice sheets fracture colonial enterprise; rivers home aquatic and amphibious creatures unfamiliar and unfriendly; and pools invite, cool, and disarm. Eighteenth-century literary and artistic archives reveal the antagonistic relationships shared among consenting, conscripted, coerced, and enslaved maritime travelers and their liquid landscapes: water's mercuriality manifests in doomed, leaky, or carceral wooden structures. *Warm welcomes are not found in cold waters.*

Consider one submersive model that dives right in: the aqueous tumult recounted by William Falconer's epic poem *The Shipwreck* (1762), which follows the ship the *Britannia* over six days as it is bombarded by political and ecological antagonists.[1] The third canto, the poem's last, highlights the ocean's violent potential to dispossess hubristic and unaware maritime explorers. That the ship is christened *Britannia* identifies these aquatic antagonists as ones with which the nation must also metonymically reckon: "Of BRITANNIA were the gallant crew, / And from that Isle her name the vessel drew."[2] On the high seas of Falconer's poetry we find microcosms of imperialism threatened and worlds of meaning layered and confused:

> The Ship no longer, foundering by the lee,
> Bears on her side th' invasions of the sea;
> All lonely o'er the desert waste she flies,
> Scourg'd on by surges, storms and bursting Skies:
> As when enclosing Harponeers assail
> In Hyperborean Seas the slumb'ring Whale,
> Soon as their javelins pierce his scaly side,
> He groans, he darts impetuous down the tide;
> And racked all o'er with lacerating pain,
> He flies remote beneath the flood in vain—
> So with the resistless haste the wounded Ship
> Scuds from pursuing waves along the deep;
> While, dashed apart by her dividing prow,
> Like burning adamant the waters glow;
> Her joints forget their firm elastic tone,
> Her long keel trembles, and her timbers groan.[3]

In a series of logical inversions, the *Britannia* is beset by the sea's "invasion," and such intrusions transform the ship into a living being: a "slumb'ring Whale." The ocean becomes fantastically anthropomorphized into the assailing harpooner, and the ship morphs into a defenseless cetacean massacred by aqueous barbs. Positionalities are swapped; pronouns get confused. Moments of oceanic intensity alchemize the inanimate into the animate. Materiality comes vibrantly alive. Such a comparison serves to position the crew as Jonah incarnates (swallowed by the ship-*cum*-whale) while also viscerally illustrating the ocean's waves as "lacerating pain" coincident with bodily slashes induced by harpoon. Each saline wave's crest licks at the open wounds it has actuated. As Scott Juengel observes of William Cowper's poetry, which is undoubtedly in conversation with Falconer's, "To fill with water and sink is not limited to ships."[4] Falconer, Cowper, and other hydropoets identify the human, nonhuman, and more-than-human capacities that are commingled and disrupted by oceanic extremity. For Falconer's speaker, the water's glow becomes a Lucifer-controlled hell wrought by the ocean. Case in point: the following stanza alludes to "that rebellious Angel, who, from heaven, / To regions of eternal pain was driven."[5] In the stormy ocean lies a hell realized. Such a realization bears repeating, at least for eighteenth-century narrators and protagonists, who embark with eager hopefulness only to find themselves in an infernal oceanic quagmire. *The River Styx is only the beginning.*

Falconer's poetic illustration of the *Britannia*, and my intense, frenzied close-reading of the poem, index the genres of aqueous, ecological violence that this book charts. While fluid and troubled landscapes are often downplayed as fantastical expressions of personification, setting, and assumedly then strictly creative license, *The Queerness of Water* refuses to write these moments off as literary or stylistic devices meant to exclusively signal flair or sublimity. Bodies of water participate in reframing notions of violence that at once level anthropocentric hubris and supremacy; there are material and embodied consequences to those who hazard the tumult of aqueous sites. *The Shipwreck*'s surges, storms, and bursting skies swell with aqueous violence as a narrative and ecological force that preys upon a long-eighteenth-century literary imagination and extends a *longue durée* of coming to terms with climactic instability.

This book makes headway into eighteenth-century literary and cultural studies, the environmental humanities, and queer studies to indicate how these fields might collaboratively yet contentiously convene. Such a nontraditional constellation highlights how bodies of water queerly construct and deconstruct notions of masculine subjectivity and, even more, concepts of the human and nonhuman. The genres of queerness that this book uploads, and which are articulated more fully below, operate within multiple scales. By pairing queerness and water, I am interested in the fluid terrains of gender, sexuality, and embodiment that appear in literature, media, and theory. I invest in queerness to access and contribute to diverse well-established conversations within gender and sexuality studies that enfold intimacy, temporality, sexuality, and animacies. As Mel Chen reminds us, "queering is immanent to animate transgressions, violating proper intimacies (including between humans and nonhuman beings)."[6] I look to canonical long-eighteenth-century narratives: from Daniel Defoe to Jonathan Swift, from William Beckford to Matthew Gregory Lewis, and from John Gabriel Stedman to Jane Austen and Mary Shelley. This colloquy demonstrates that water's queerness introduces anticolonial possibilities in which white, colonial heteromasculinity and its attendant hetero-reproductive norms are ruptured, disrupted, and waylaid. My use of anticoloniality, which I explicate below, recognizes how environmental interactors can participate in upheaving colonial norms and taxonomies and looks explicitly within—rather than exclusively outside—an eighteenth-century literary canon to do so.

This book rejects the notion that any attention to canon only serves to reify its canonicity. I address fluid fringe moments in each of these narratives to explicitly *unsettle* canonicity. Fluid fringe moments enable unsettling to emerge from within; unsettling and unlearning turns the canon in upon itself. Because these narratives are not centrally about water, the submarine moments I undertake are ancillary, auxiliary, or just plainly unimportant. Or so it would seem. In ancillary and auxiliary inclusion lies vast potentials of queer becoming shaped by violent, aqueous entanglements. Water's queerness enables us to read *with* and *against* canonicity to visualize how environmental interactors undermine linked conceptions of canon, coloniality, and masculine bodies believed inviolable. *The Queerness of Water* offers close readings that are deliberately unorthodox—that develop out of a commitment to truly interdisciplinary *(t)reading*—and intimate to make possible alternative purviews that can enliven an intersectional queer methodology for apprehending environment and its transcorporeal enmeshment with(in) the literary human.

By asking "What's Queer about Water?" I introduce the key concepts that this book will plumb and look to the rich and troubled waters that the eighteenth century provides for literary and theoretical vistas of queer possibility. This introduction poses the following questions: What can the triangulation of water, violence, and queerness tell us about embodiment, narrative, and media in the eighteenth century and its afterlives? How might eighteenth-century literatures prefigure larger discussions of queerness and environment? What can (t)reading water teach us? *The Queerness of Water* lays bare static presumptions of embodiment, masculinity, and environmental enmeshment to advocate for a queer ecology that recognizes aqueous unsettling as vital to the eighteenth century and beyond.

WATER, CRITICALLY

Critical, scholarly attention to the ocean—for example, what Steve Mentz calls "blue cultural studies," John Gillis refers to as "blue humanities," and Hester Blum identifies as "oceanic studies" (there are dozens more)—similarly motivates the currents that *The Queerness of Water* navigates.[7] But this book is not exclusively about the ocean. It is also about rivers, streams, pools, and glaciers. In this way, I recalibrate a focus on the ocean that is inscribed in these theoretically motivated neologisms, to more appropriately account for other bodies of water that invariably contour the "blue" in the blue humanities or blue cultural studies. My investment in water engages what I will call *critical water studies,* which is an attempt to productively galvanize and thereby unify terms that visualize how the humanities and interpretive social sciences explore global, speculative, and historical bodies of water. A critical water studies approach has heretofore been employed by scholars in the water sciences and political ecology, especially those working within and about the Global South, such as in India and South Africa.[8] My use of critical water studies borrows from these intellectuals but is admittedly invested in framing such a concept within environmental humanist thought—that is, centering the humanities with foci such as literature, art, media, and critical theory—so as to magnify the value in parsing out the oceanic from the littoral, the river from the bog, the deluge from the glacial, the wetland from the pond. To echo Steve Mentz, "I seek a blue humanities that responds to water's material complexity and imaginative polyphony."[9]

While the blue humanities endeavors to do something similar, its extant form still relies (too) heavily on the ocean. I want to recalibrate this attention in a gesture that is both inclusive of and specific to watery environs. The diversity of distinct bodies of water (the distinction of diverse bodies of water, too) prevents the facile essentialism of the ocean as what Stefan Helmreich calls, and rightly critiques as, a "theory machine."[10] The specificity of bodies of water enriches my investigation and demands our mindfulness, especially in light of the dramatically shifting liquid landscapes that currently plague contemporary existence alongside glacial melt, sea level rise, and coastal erosion. So too, as I'll show, is this the case for eighteenth-century interlocutors. A critical water studies purview emphasizes specificity to better account for the affective, phenomenological, physical, emotional, and queer rigors that lurk in bodies of water.

While early modernists repeatedly attend to the sea's siren song, we as eighteenth-century scholars have only just begun to scratch the surface of literal and metaphoric wreckages that dwell within and alongside waterscapes and upon their littoral shores.[11] For example, in *The Novel and the Sea*, Margaret Cohen repositions the rise-of-the-novel discourse within a transatlantic maritime culture—"the global age of sail"—to draw attention to the "adventures" of sea fiction, which enfold "life-threatening storms, reefs, deadly calms, scurvy, shipwreck, barren coasts, sharks, whales, mutinies, warring navies, natives, cannibals, and pirates."[12] Cohen's investigation queries the forms of "craft" that circulate in maritime literatures throughout the eighteenth century, to more broadly outline the rise of print cultures and also to invite critics of the novel to *"leave the land and to embark."*[13] As with Jayne Lewis's *Air's Appearance: Literary Atmosphere in British Fiction, 1660–1794*, which grapples with capacious illustrations of what might be deemed atmospheric, Siobhan Carroll's *An Empire of Air and Water* similarly attends to the mesh of elemental thinking—a concern that has received revived favor by environmentally attentive media scholars such as John Durham Peters and Melody Jue.[14] Carroll examines "atopic" spaces within the conjoined eighteenth- and nineteenth-century literary imaginary, specifically locations that rival a situated sense of "place" because they are natural regions deemed "intangibl[e], inhospitabl[e], or inaccessibl[e]" and altogether "hazardous" due to foreboding "bodily disintegrations."[15] In mode with Cohen and with Alain Corbin's *The Lure of the Sea*, Carroll elucidates the imperial politics that accompany an oceanic (Arctic and aerial, too) atopia, especially as represented by cartographic and print culture materials. Margaret Cohen and Killian Quigley have, in addition, proffered "submarine aesthetics" to theorize the undersea as a "vital atmosphere for revising and reorienting aesthetics," which adjusts an oceanic purview that has heretofore eclipsed the eighteenth century and long early modern period.[16] Cohen and Quigley admit the "submarine slippages and strange workings" of aquatic interaction that, as I'll suggest below, subtend a necessary queering of human, nonhuman, and environmental entanglements—a recasting of Mona Narain's invocation of global eighteenth-century "oceanic intimacies."[17]

The ocean's immersive nature has made theorization of it similarly immersive: reducing the planet's largest bodies of water to an aqueous catchall and in so doing, making invisible the unique constitutions and interactions that find home in distinct geographies. In "Wet Ontology, Fluid Spaces," Philip Steinberg and Kimberley Peters focus on thinking *alongside* and *with* the ocean rather than exclusively *about*—the latter a preposition that imposes neocoloniality and voyeurism.[18] As Cecilia Chen, Janine MacLeod, and Astrida Neimanis declare in agreement, to think *about* water is to superimpose and "repeat the assumption that water is a resource needing to be managed or organized."[19] As the chapters that follow demonstrate, this is a Sisyphean task; the literary waters I chart emphasize uncontrollability despite a character's best intentions to rein in such disorderliness. This is precisely what I mean by "troubled ecologies." A troubled ecology is one (or a rhizomatic multitude) that resists anthropocentric containment. Troubled ecologies antagonize, upset, and threaten human interlocutors; they refuse to acquiesce to colonialism's insidious managerial enclosure. A troubled ecology upends narratives of domination to honor the ineluctable messiness in which environmental, nonhuman, and human interactors are insinuated. In *Staying with the Trouble*, Donna Haraway writes, "*Trouble* is an interesting word.... Our task is to make trouble, to stir up potent response to devastating events, as well as to settle troubled waters and rebuild quiet places."[20] What happens, this book asks, when troubled waters—troubled ecologies—refuse to be settled or rebuilt? How might troubled ecologies queer and resist settling and settlers? These provocations motivate my interest in water's radical, anticolonial, subversive ethic.

My use of italicized prepositions gestures towards a queer grammar that *The Queerness of Water* is invested in claiming as a politics of epistemology, authorship, and performance. Eve Sedgwick invokes *besides* as a queer prepositional methodology that realizes the potential for limiting "origin and telos" to uphold planar relations in favor of dehierarchizing (hetero)normative logic systems. Sedgwick's *beside*—like my invocation of *alongside* and *with*—corrupts linear, hierarchical regimes of grammatical subordination (and with them, troubling linear and dichotomous thinking) to instead bring to bear "a wide range of desiring, identifying, representing, repelling, paralleling, differentiating, rivaling, leaning, twisting, mimicking, withdrawing, attracting, aggressing, warping, and other relations."[21] Put simply, our prepositional use always encodes politics and perspective: *our politics are always prepositional*. What we stand *against*, who we advocate *for*, how we move *beyond* telegraph these realities. Steinberg and Peters's formulation of "thinking with water" as an assemblage "in which mobile human and nonhuman (including molecular) elements and affects are not merely passively consumed but imagined, encountered, and produced," comes closest to my illumination of water's queerness, in which bodies of water are crucibles of and participants in the violence of metamorphosed embodiment. The first of the two disembodied voices that haunt the eponymous mariner in Samuel Taylor Coleridge's *The Rime of the Ancient Mariner* (1799) perhaps captures this best: "What is the OCEAN doing?"[22] To which this book responds: queerly unsettling.

WATER, QUEERLY

To recognize water's queerness is to pay homage to how representations and embodiments of queerness resist stasis, reject ontological stability, embolden fluid becomings, and seep *into, through,* and *beyond* commitments to heteronormativity. Water's queerness develops out of queer ecological frameworks pioneered by Catriona Sandilands and Bruce Erickson, Nicole Seymour, Greg Garrard, Greta Gaard, Mel Chen, Stacy Alaimo, Omise'eke Natasha Tinsley, and Timothy Morton, to name just a handful.[23] These frameworks derive from the intersections of feminist, queer, trans, and sexuality studies and the environmental humanities. While traditional arms of queer theory have emerged out of schisms with feminisms and have often defaulted to identity politics (from which my own investment in queer studies has hatched), the queer ecologies that motivate my work here are not strictly identitarian. In other words, water doesn't out, it's not born this way, and it doesn't maintain an inherent queerness—indeed, water has, as I show in chapters 3 and 4, been exploited as a disciplinary tactic that biopolitically manipulates bodies deemed nonnormative. *The Queerness of Water* is invested in thinking *with, alongside,* and *through* queer theories that take up how queerness is a vehicle for imagining alternative modes of temporality, relationality, and intimacy. Each chapter speaks to a different, distinct conversation in queer theory that evidences the wide applicability of water's queerness as not a monolith but a fluid entanglement of theory, materiality, and archive.

In their landmark collection, *Queer Ecologies*, Sandilands and Erickson question the limits of the "natural" (and with it, the normative) to explore the "interrelated conjunctures of sex and nature, oriented to probing and challenging the biopolitical knots through which both historical and current relations of sexualities and environments meet and inform one another."[24] This book reframes these concerns to address how aqueous contact resituates the masculine subject and opens up realms of uncomfortable porosity otherwise thought impossible. Queer ecologies are thus vital to grasping eighteenth-century literature, culture, and masculine subject formation *before, through,* and *following* the Enlightenment. For example, in chapter 1, I approach the storms and waves that predate upon Robinson Crusoe and magnify the enmity he shares with the sea. He writes, "I saw the Sea come after me as high as a great Hill, and as furious as an enemy, which I had no Means or Strength to contend with."[25] Crusoe's admission apes the forms of ecological antagonism later charted by Falconer and demonstrates that the sea's fury drastically reforms and reshapes conceptions of masculine resilience. Defoe imagines new frameworks for apprehending sea power.

The porosity of masculine subjectivity spurs modes of queer being that highlight the fraught tensions between queerness and violence. Queer violence lives on the fringes of queer world building: epistemologies that seek (oftentimes exclusively) benevolence, altruism, and optimism and recurrently assume queer identity as a monolith.[26] In queering violence, I do not intend to exploit the real-lived experience of contemporary violence enacted against LGBTQIA+ individuals, especially as these precarities are ratcheting up as I write this. Such a lived and vivid reality has deeply informed my engagement with violence. This book instead envisions potentialities for queer studies that, as Kadji Amin contends, "might disturb the tendency . . . to equate naming an object queer with claiming, for it [the object], an unequivocally positive political value."[27] The queer violation of narrative waters disturbs unequivocal positivity and imagines horizons (not strictly future-facing ones) for queer environmental thinking.

Water's queer ecopossibilities, fortuitously, have not escaped attention. For instance, Sandilands posits that "the queerness of blue ecologies" resides in queer negativity, proximity to death, and a constant flux of affective interactions and states. Sandilands's poetic thought-process suggests that:

> Blue is worldly depression, not the cruel optimism of neoliberal fantasy. Blue is the compassion that derives from loss, and the networks of care that may spring from the experience: not hearty, organic, muscular, progressive solidarity. Blue is a recognition of fragility, vulnerability, and precarious, ecological enmeshedness in the world. Blue is a political form that does not rush to positivity, but instead lingers in critique for long enough to question the necessity and temporality of growth and expansion. Blue is desire and its limits. Blue is uncertainty. Blue is negativity (but not apocalypticism). Blue is fragility, a move toward dispersion in breath, in the sky, rather than a solid identity, grounded in the earth.[28]

The anti-utopianism reflected here upholds precarity, fragility, porosity, and enmeshedness as vital affects and effects of aqueous becoming. In Astrida Neimanis's words, "water . . . is facilitative and directed towards the becoming of other bodies. Our own embodiment . . . is never really autonomous."[29] The blueness of water, then, exalts queer opportunities to hold desires, vulnerabilities, and ironies in constructive tension. So too is the case in what follows: water's queerness resides in modes of environmental violence that serve as checks of and detriments to ostensibly impenetrable masculinity. In our various entanglements with bodies of water, Elizabeth Povinelli acknowledges, "we see a different kind of [atmospheric] touching, not the contact between difference, but an entanglement of substances that produces difference."[30] Queer aqueous violence makes legible those productions of elemental, embodied, and narrative difference. A queer critical water studies purview enables us to re-view and revisit those understandings of environmentalism, ecocriticism, queerness, justice, and epistemes that have heretofore dwelled on the fringes.

The queer ecologies inaugurated through aqueous queerness anticipate and model a humanistic methodology that can invigorate literary, media, and cultural studies and enfold water into the enigma of queer possibility. Amin Ghaziani and Matt Brim distinguish between a queer method (as noun) that may appear paradoxical given long trajectories of queer theory's investment in destabilization and "queering methods" (a verb) in which tenets of queer theory "tweak or explode what is possible within our existing procedures."[31] *The Queerness of Water* does this tweaking (perhaps twerking too) and exploding to grapple with a queer ecological methodology that reveals how queer world-building is at once constructed and demolished. Again, the queer world-building that attracts me is not strictly Eutopic; queer worlds do not appear exclusively in the rose-colored glasses of optimism.

Queerness resists singularity. Queerness, as I see, embody, and theorize it, enables us to wash away stable signifiers and the regimes of normality that they safeguard. The queerness of water, in turn, is a means to apprehend varying, sometimes conflictual, and sometimes ironic modalities that reject stability. Rather than suggesting a use of queerness so loose that it undermines any deployment of the term, I highlight two primary modalities of water's queerness that recur in the following chapters. One, water's queerness induces the reconfiguration of the male colonist's relationship with self and other through irremediable violence that disorients constructs of masculinity and their attendant hegemonic identity. Two, the queerness of water accounts for potential nonheteronormative relationalities and sexualities that snake their way through an eighteenth-century canon. If as José Esteban Muñoz has excitingly proffered, "Queerness is not yet here,"[32] and as Alaimo has noted, "the Anthropocene is no time to set things straight,"[33] then *The Queerness of Water* wades into the imagined potentiality (like a similar imagined potentiality of what constitutes masculinity and heteronormativity, which I excoriate below), wherein queerness lurks in the entangled relationship with the environment generally and bodies of water (ourselves included) more specifically. Water's queerness visualizes what genres of interaction exist—both constructed and deconstructed—within narratives that locate bodies of water as sites of violent, radical extremity.

ON VIOLENCE

My use of aqueous violence is, quite plainly, an endeavor to understand how *violence queers:* it ruptures, disassociates, and makes legibility opaque. Eroticisms inevitably cohere, but consent and mutualism do not traffic in this particular form of violence. Eighteenth-century literatures document this as they invite us to peer deeper, longer, more pensively into the violent and stormy depths of troubled ecologies. William Diaper's understudied *Nereides: Or Sea-Eclogues* (1712) is one such record. In characterizing the manifold embodiments that reside in submarine zones, Diaper recasts the Virgilian template of the pastoral within simultaneously inviting and turbulent waters. Diaper's Latinate epigraph to his piscatorial *Nereides*, "*Venus orta mari. Sic, sic juvat ire sub undas*" (roughly translating as "Venus rose from the sea, and so I choose to go under the waves"), summons readers to seek out subterranean worlds in search of origin, desire, or knowledge—a tactic *The Queerness of Water* similarly invokes.

In the preface to *Nereides*, Diaper writes, "Besides we know, that the agreeable Images, which may be drawn from things on Earth, have been long since exhausted, but it will be allow'd, that the Beauties (as well as the Riches) of the Sea are yet in a great measure untouch'd."[34] Perhaps unwittingly, Diaper conveys the sea as a virginal "untouch'd" body, abounding with beauties and riches to be explored, mined, and potentially exploited. Accompanying the reminder of Venus's depiction and her consequent lure, this aqueous virginal body is akin to voluptuous femininity, a desire to witness in the sea what Sandro Botticelli canonized in *The Birth of Venus* (ca. 1480s) and an echo of Rachel Carson's origin story of the maternal ocean in

The Sea Around Us (1951). "Beginnings are apt to be shadowy," Carson opens, "and so it is with the beginnings of that great mother of life, the sea."[35] The feminization and accordant subjugation of the sea are not readings that *The Queerness of Water* will abide, because they only further colonial exploitation. The recognition of bodies "untouch'd" and thus unfamiliar to interlopers are a recurrent means to justify intervention, violent contact, and expropriation. Such feminizations of the sea, of which Charybdis and Scylla are mythic icons, likewise run the risk of demonizing feminine embodiments because of allegedly insatiable appetites, wayward passions, and misandrist axes to grind. The monstrosity of feminine waters ironically becomes yet another means to hold harmless violent contact and containment. The dichotomous angel/whore rhetoric, as this suggests, dilutes metaphoric readings of troubled waters, and I do not prefer them here, because they only serve to perpetuate forms of misogynistic oppression that the queerness of water can remedy.

While Falconer's depiction of the shipwreck and Diaper's illustration of the pleasures of the sea may appear opposed, the two poets agree on the mercurial nature of the ocean's waves and the portents of an aqueous violence that awaits sea trespassers. Diaper, Quigley suggests, represents the sea in *Nereides* as "outside structures of knowability."[36] The poetry collection's "submarine conjurings are pleasures as well as curiosities, . . . Diaper sets in motion an incontrollable, and occasionally exquisite, marine poetics, where pastoral encounters a boundary at once fluid and insurmountable."[37] For instance, in "Eclogue III"—a dialogue among a trio of nereids—the aqueous subaltern critique the "avarice" of landlubbers and their ignorant pursuit of the ocean's promise. Drymon, one of the trio, complains: "Tho' they have all that's good, and truly rare, / Yet (envious) think their own too mean a Share: / For foreign Toys they roam to ev'ry Shore, / And bring Disease home unknown before."[38] Characterized by licentiousness and a juvenile desire for "foreign Toys" (commodities, bodies, and cultures previously unknown to them), these insouciant maritime sailors greedily avail themselves with wild abandon. But Drymon tires of their antics, which include a penchant for "endless Wars" that "whets their Rage, and ever makes 'em brave,"[39] and doles out retributive justice:

> Oft have I punish'd that ambitious Wight
> Who thus entrenches on the Mer-man's Right:
> Who born on Earth, yet leaves his native Glades,

And to his own prefers the watry Meads;
Oft have I strove to burst the yielding Planks,
And force the leaky Ship on sandy Banks.⁴⁰

The nereids, as embodiments and agents of the sea, perform a mirrored violence that intends to subvert colonial endeavors to traverse oceanic spaces under the auspices of empire.⁴¹ I return to these modes of mermaid being and interaction repeatedly throughout this book, especially in the intermezzi that reside in between each chapter and most definitively in my conclusion, which further imagines aquatic interspecies intimacies and their volatile and queer futures. As both Falconer and Diaper relay, water's violence taps into mythic and affective states that are conjured alongside and as results of literary warnings that caution the lure of thalassic environs.

The Queerness of Water makes explicit the violent potentialities and entanglements that bodies of water effect. Borrowed from the Middle French *violence/violance*, the early origins of the term "violence" denote an excessive use of force, a meaning that remains captured in contemporary parlance. Between the fourteenth and fifteenth centuries, the Middle French word signified power of a natural force, like a storm, and of physical coercive force, like sexual violence, both stemming from the classical Latin, which underscored an unreasonable use of force, aggression, or passion. The types of aqueous violence traversed here reflect this plural etymology and are attentive to natural forces (as in Robinson Crusoe's unsuccessful navigation of the sea in chapter 1) and aggressions, passions, and sexual violences (as with Gulliver's experience with the simian in voyages to both Brobdingnag and Houyhnhnmland, which I explore in chapter 2).

Violence must be recognized as a fraught category that entangles human and nonhuman actors.⁴² Violence is not securely and solely anthropocentric. Violent relations span the human/nonhuman divide, imbricating both in experiences of brutality, pain, and excess. By figuring violence as a central apparatus by which to view the human-nonhuman relationship, this book engages a longer genealogy of scholarship on violence that has primarily focalized anthropocentric expressions, especially following two world wars and the enduring deployment of chemical and nuclear warfare. Only recently has scholarship begun to weigh how environmental interactors might similarly become enfolded into regimes of violent being and entanglement. William Boelhower, for example, identifies an "ecology of marine violence" that prefigures the "peril and immemorial fright" that the ocean represented for the nineteenth century's "history of wild weather."[43] Rob Nixon's *Slow Violence and the Environmentalism of the Poor* similarly adjusts conversations surrounding violence to envisage "a different kind of violence, a violence that is neither spectacular nor instantaneous, but rather incremental and accretive."[44] Chiefly among Nixon's frameworks for imagining slow violence are issues of climate change, rising sea levels, deforestation, ocean acidification, and the like. My use of aqueous violence differs from the types of wild-weather histories that Boelhower outlines and from the notions of slow violence that Nixon theorizes. However, my use nears Nixon's assessment of "structural violence," which demands "rethinking different notions of causation and agency with respect to violent effects."[45] The descriptions and representations of aqueous violence I trace here are in fact spectacular and oftentimes instantaneous. However, like slow violence they persist under the radar of recognition, either out of willfulness, recalcitrance, or ignorance. *The Queerness of Water* is willful in its attempts to disabuse us of this ignorance so as to highlight fringe moments of aqueous violence.

MASCULINITY AND ANTI/COLONIALITY

The Queerness of Violence unveils violent queer insurgencies that demand a near about-face of the masculine experience, which is not a turn to feminization (that may only double down on an obdurate gender-performance binary) but rather a reconsideration of an unwavering masculine ethos. Not all the masculine characters die. And it is those who do not die—those who survive or embody forms of marred and coerced resilience—that reveal the potential for violence to powerfully and more comprehensively queer relationality, temporality, and intimacy.

Greta Gaard's "Where Is Feminism in the Environmental Humanities?" attests to the necessity of feminist and queer "intellectual honesty" that reconfigures modes of inquiry within the environmental humanities to be more representationally diverse as well as diverse in offering, topic, and epistemology.[46] *The Queerness of Water* is one such offering. Explorations of masculinity within environmental literary criticism are not counterintuitive to ecofeminism but rather in mode with what I envision as a capacious ecofeminist endeavor, which inspires and coheres alongside queer ecology, to visualize how plural genders, sexualities, and embodiments are mediated by environmental entanglement. Whereas early waves of ecofeminist scholarship critiqued the masculinist domination of nature, in the narratives

I undertake below I am more curious about how masculinist domination—that is, empire especially—is undermined, unsettled, or troubled by aqueous landscapes. The subordination of women and other genders is not lost on me in these narratives, and my intermezzi highlight these tensions, but the fragility of masculinity demands our attention too. White, cis-het, masculine subjectivity, as I teach my students, is not a default mode of being; it is not a comparative referent by which all other identity categories are defined. It is our responsibility to unravel the constructedness of all identity categories and their cultural circulations. To assume they are static and unassailing is only to extend legacies of social violence.

In *The Queerness of Water*, I thus practice what I preach. I decidedly make explicit that forms of masculinity articulated by eighteenth-century narratives demand our attention and discerning eye so as to better unearth the lethal ramifications of gendered and sexual normativity, which emerge out of the Enlightenment's "science"—an enduring, epistemological overhaul that has fundamentally shaped embodiment, gender, race, identity, and other taxonomic orders legitimated by *scientia*.[47] If, as Mentz offers in *Break Up the Anthropocene*, we need to displace, "untranslate," and "unweave" the "Old Man" of the Anthropos, then this book accounts for how masculinity's embeddedness within Anthropocene thinking can be unmoored by liquidation.[48] To be certain: masculinity is not a monolith. My use of "masculine" is deliberately capacious and responds to recent currents in eighteenth-century gender and sexualities studies that have addressed how masculinity manifests through political, social, and economic participation.

The emergence of a salient masculine identity throughout the eighteenth century was largely predicated on oppositional identification—an extension of Enlightenment thinking that demanded binarized opposition. The masculine figure was *not* the fop, the lady, the molly, the boy, the effete aristocrat, or countless other gendered archetypes.[49] To bolster an ethos of "manliness," David Kutcha notes, the eighteenth-century masculine individual made "masculinity a prerequisite to political legitimacy and by claiming masculinity as their own, men in power used the label of effeminacy to directly exclude from power all other men—men of other classes, as well as men with alternative sexual practices."[50] The work of Hans Turley, Katherine Arens, and Mary Beth Harris as well as Tim Hitchcock and Michèle Cohen has attended to how frameworks of masculinity in the eighteenth century coalesce around expressions of gender performance *and* sexuality—even if these frameworks may have been unavailable to, or circulated under different nomenclature and affects to, our eighteenth-century interlocutors.[51]

In response, the gestures of masculinity I interrogate here often coincide with heteronormative expressions of indomitability that are the hallmark of a masculine exceptionalism, by which I mean the masculine subject's individual difference from others who do not ascribe to the same normative masculine ideals and expressions. Eighteenth-century masculinities of naval and militarized men are compounded, Julia Banister reasons, by "contingent, malleable and commodifiable construction."[52] In concert, *The Queerness of Water* looks to eighteenth-century masculine indices to clarify how notions of gender and sexuality persist porously. As Neimanis avers of embodied porosity, "as bodies of water we leak and seethe, our borders always vulnerable to rupture and renegotiation."[53] Fluid ruptures and renegotiations induce queer violences. My larger conceptualization of queer violence, queries, first, how environmental interactors participate in shaping human actors rather than simply the opposite, and, second, how aqueous violence demands a reconsideration of that masculinist ethos that is assumed but no longer indomitable, static, or uncorrupted by environmental factors. Put another way, aqueous violence disciplines and undisciplines varying modes of masculinity, thereby queering how displays, embodiments, and enactments of masculinity are negotiated. Violence tests the brittleness of masculine subjectivity, and in so doing unveils precarity, enmeshment, and the limitations of desire.

A note on heteronormativity: *heteronormativity is a fantasy*.[54] It is not an anachronism or a projection of contemporary queer studies on the eighteenth century. It is a culturally constructed—allegedly self-evident—obligation that through social sanction demands normativity in genders, expressions of gender, and embodiments. Ana de Freitas Boe and Abby Coykendall's *Heteronormativity in Eighteenth-Century Literature and Culture* attests to the entrenched means by which heteronormative rhetoric and cultural mandates (strictures of sex, gender, sexuality, family, marriage, and embodiment) maintain inertia and come into their formidable own throughout the eighteenth century.[55] Heteronormativity, in its most inescapable hegemonic form, functions as a pervasive system of cultural norms and compulsions that does not preclude anti- or nonheteronormative arrangements but anticipates, expects, and upholds the bond of biologically reproductive couples and the gendered accoutrements (class, labor, and dress norms) that accompany such coupling.

The polemic of the of heteronormativity does not make its toxicity any less real. Fantasy does not live solely on the peripheries of the imaginary, and whether it is fictive or not matters little. Rather, how fantasy manifests, or is indulged and exalted, reveals the deep capacities of its pertinacity. The problem of norms and what Foucault calls "normation" is an issue well suited to the eighteenth century: both Foucault's *History of Sexuality: Volume 1* and *Security, Territory, Population* pinpoint the emergence of statistical "norms" within the eighteenth century as a result of growing populations and the rise of censuses, which give way to biopolitical modes of control and surveillance.[56] Several of the subsequent chapters return to issues of how biopolitical governance—through the weaponization of bodies of water—dispossesses and eliminates bodies deemed undesirable or, too often, excessively desirous.

But heteronormativity in its contemporary—rather than eighteenth-century—parlance is commonly glossed and broadly applied; I do not use it so broadly. My particular navigation of heteronormativity pertains to implicit narrative frameworks of masculinity and masculine subjectivity, not to downplay other embodiments, identities, or subjectivities but rather to carefully address a facet of heteronormativity that demands further excavation. That these narratives repeatedly center a single masculine protagonist exposes that they implicitly uphold him as the supreme arbiter of modes of being, as with Crusoe, Ambrosio the monk, and Dr. Frankenstein, or as the conduit that brings colonialism and its conjoined gendered and sexual strictures as demanded exports, as with John Gabriel Stedman. The ostensibly proprietary nature of Western racial, gendered, and sexual interactions imports heteronormativity alongside colonialism, and such a realization thus serves to undergird—as Pamela Cheek and Felicity Nussbaum have shown to eighteenth-century studies and as Joseph Massad and Jasbir Puar have elucidated within postcolonial and queer circles—insidious projections and requisites for embodiment and interactive conformity.[57] Aqueous violence fractures the self-sure masculine subject and his stalwart heteronormativity. As a result, aqueous violence as a heuristic realizes the porous nature by which nonhuman intercession penetrates the male subject and lays bare the painful realities that follow such violent reevaluations of self.

Water's violent potentials participate in a process of unknowing and unlearning colonialism and its imposition of masculine strongholds, which I align with anticolonial and decolonial efforts. I employ anticoloniality and decoloniality here with an intention to enrich a deliberate citationality that honors intellectuals working within critical Black, Indigenous, Latinx, and race studies from whom I have learned and with whom I seek to dialogue. I do not use anticoloniality and decoloniality as synonyms. They surface from different epistemological trajectories, lived experiences, and geographic situated knowledges. While decoloniality and anticolonial intentionality and activism share commonalities, to echo Eve Tuck and K. Wayne Yang, "decolonization is not a metaphor" and within the context in which I write and teach, must center the repatriation of Indigenous and Native North American lands, reject white colonial supremacy's continued afterlives, and supplant settler colonialism.[58] Max Liboiron, in conversation, observes that a "promiscuous" deployment of decolonization, even well meaning, serves only to "advance settler and colonial goals."[59]

In recognition, I am not interested in loosening the frameworks of decoloniality to bastardize a liberational politics writ large. Such substitutive logics only reinforce settler-colonial complicities and appropriations and produce an "empty signifier to be filled by any track towards liberation."[60] I remain fastened to anticoloniality, not as a decolonial substitute, but in acknowledgment that resituating an identical decolonial context and activism in the British eighteenth-century (and in direct conversation with a literary canon that most decolonial scholars write from outside) may only exacerbate social violences.[61] Anticoloniality, as I see and engage it, better accounts for a capacious methodology, set of praxes and activist orientations, and pedagogical commitment that refuse to indemnify colonialism's endurant longevities. As Ami Yoon reveals, the poesis of "anticolonial fervor" encodes the possibility of instaurating new ecologies, "both social and environmental."[62] The anticolonial politics of this book, like those offered by Yoon's reading of William Gilbert's *The Hurricane*, envisage new troubled ecologies wrought from water worlds. Anticoloniality holds the possibility of unsettling and actively unlearning colonial systems and (dis)orders that are bound by place or history.

Unsettling, delinking, unlearning, and unknowing proliferate in the chapters that follow. My repeated use of these gerunds pays homage to decolonial theorists such as Catherine Walsh and Walter Mignolo, Aníbal Quijano, María Lugones, Frantz Fanon, and Achille Mbembe, who deploy them with divergent purposes and activist orientations.[63] I join these intellectuals to demonstrate my citational networks and to underline the dynamic connectivities (and contentions) that arise from this scholarly constellation—not to flatten, but to enrich. Édouard Glissant and Macarena Gómez-Barris, who likewise toggle between anticolonial and decolonial thinking, proffer opacity and submergence, respectively, to dethrone hierarchical visualities and their concomitant colonial extractions in favor of renewed modes of perspective and relationality.[64] Together they inaugurate a genealogy of anticolonialism that is predicated on representations, metaphors, and emphatic attention to water, which I continue here. The hydrophilic valences of anticolonialism animate this book, and I set out to make more explicit what might be understood as anticolonialism's elemental affinities.

Whereas Glissant and Gómez-Barris promote a decolonial thought process that honors elemental perspectival alternatives, my exploration works both alongside these existing frameworks and in tension. Like the anti- and decolonial intellectuals and activists I cite, I am invested in critiquing the very foundations of hegemonic structures and norms that have been demanded by colonialism, its co-conspirators, and its ontological complicities. Others lend their voices to this activist orientation as colonized, oppressed, and subaltern peoples whose precarity is evidenced by (neo)colonial systems that reconfigure bare life, or death-in-life. Anti- and decolonial advocacy remedies the erasure of these voices and representations to reject the dispossession instituted by the immersive nature of colonial (dis)order. In the subsequent chapters, I do not pretend that characters like Robinson Crusoe or Victor Frankenstein represent the colonized: they are instead harbingers, beacons, and handmaidens of colonial (dis)order. They are not decolonial cartographers. I'm not interested in recuperating any of them as victims of circumstance; they're not. Water's queerness provides a way of naming the colonial (dis)order these characters manufacture and upsetting the hegemonies they promote—explicitly or not.

I propose, then, a queer anticolonial method of reading that realizes how the intersections of queer and anticolonial thinking can be harnessed through co-collaboration in order to read simultaneously with and against a long-eighteenth-century canon: admitting such a canon within purview and at the same time pushing against its normative readings and colonial commitments. Queer anticolonial praxes envision readings otherwise that emerge unwittingly within the very fabric of these narratives. "If 'another world is possible,'" Catherine Walsh and Walter Mignolo remind us, "it cannot be built with the conceptual tools inherited from the Renaissance and the Enlightenment."[65] My vision of a queer anticolonial methodology that might transcend rather than concede to Enlightenment epistemologies, in other words, *parasitizes* colonial hegemony and its ensuant literary canon.

My use of parasite is deliberate. As Michel Serres reminds us, *parasite*'s etymology characterizes a person eating at another's table and foretells the connection—often the co-constitution—of pest and host. If we understand colonialism to be both a pest and paternalistic host that feeds upon the colonized (their labor and knowledge too), then anticolonialism's relationship to this discourse is chiasmic, as it too becomes pest and host: "not only living *on* but also living *in*—by [colonialism], with [colonialism], and in [colonialism]."[66] Anticoloniality's parasitism, read through Serres, reasons that it can "eat next to" coloniality: "the one eating next to, soon eating at the expense of, and always eats the same thing, the host, and this eternal host gives over and over, constantly, till he breaks, even till death, drugged, enchanted, fascinated. . . . Not a prey, but the host. The other is not a predator but a parasite."[67] Like Serres, a dialectical binary—prey/predator, colonial/anticolonial—interests me little. Serres bespeaks an asymmetrical relational logic that can further contextualize the types of anticolonial politics I seek to set into motion. By offering an anticoloniality that parasitizes colonialism, I intend to look *within* archives long favored as extensions of colonial knowledge and identity, for glimmers of awesome disruption that aqueous violence induces. In Serres's words, "We parasitize each other and live amidst parasites."[68]

My use of parasitism, in this way, is a recuperative gesture, not a dysphemistic one that might only incite indemnifications of violence against those individuals and ways of thinking rendered nonhuman. Parasitism is, after all, a facet of symbiosis, which is facilely believed to be tantamount to reciprocity. This book isn't interested in questions or utopias of reciprocity; instead, anticoloniality's parasitic verve demonstrates that it can live within (rather than exclusively outside) colonialism's and the canon's stronghold and thus endow creative opportunities for reading against the grain. Furthermore, if, as Mbembe contends, colonial systems consign the racialized native, colonized, and "savage" to "just another form of animal life," then I take seriously parasitism's zoomorphic anticolonial potentialities as a mode of liberation—dislocated from necropolitical designation—in which we can reject, repurpose, and obfuscate becoming animal.[69] To recognize anticoloniality's parasitism is to reckon with how colonial structures can be self-destructive: in coloniality's turning upon and against itself, we witness new queer worlds of anticolonial possibility that disassemble anthropocentrism.

Water's queerness becomes a means to locate and assess the ruptures and violations of white, colonial heteromasculinity, which implicitly take to task the supremacy of the human in the humanities and so-called

Anthropocene.[70] Tiffany Lethabo King identifies the most enduring form of European (neo)colonialism as "conquistador humanism," which predicates white, Christian, male dominance on the subjugation of Black and Indigenous bodies.[71] King's goal is to visualize, like Sylvia Wynter before, how this domineering conquistador humanism perseveres today under the aegis of (neo)coloniality. Mignolo, in concert, notes that the invention of the human (as we conceive of it today) spawns from colonial fictions masquerading as ontology.[72] I offer aqueous violence as one framework by which we can begin to see how gestures of white, male colonialism, indicated by conquistador humanism, become subtly effaced and yet still arise out of Enlightenment epistemologies. This is one way to queer the Enlightenment.

Violence thus serves as a mimetic process, not unlike the one proposed by Fanon that both underlines and undermines coloniality. I recognize that Fanon's decolonization as event manifests from the struggle for Algerian independence, which animated liberatory revolutions around the globe, and the chapters that follow push the limits of what emancipatory potentials accompany radical violence. Mignolo, in reflection on Fanon, writes, "Revolution needs vision. The implementation of vision when successful at some point would engender violence because it would introduce a disruption and a crack into the calm waters of 'reality': that is, the commonsense created through coloniality of knowledge and being."[73] The invocation of "calm waters" is of course poesis, but Mignolo's invocation of a liquid disruption that induces violent revisions and revolutions lies at the heart of aqueous violence: a separate radical violence, motivated by queer anticoloniality, that pays homage to Fanon's decolonial rallying call.[74]

Aqueous violence graphically unveils the types of upheavals and deconstructions that bodies of water home, avail, and foment in eighteenth-century literature and beyond. An eighteenth-century attention to water has repeatedly offered the refrain that the ocean was the primary conduit by which colonialism materialized, reminding us of Philip Steinberg's assessment that as a conduit for merchant capitalism "the sea was fought over not as a space to be possessed, but to be controlled, a special space within world-society but outside the territorial states that comprised its paradigmatic spatial structure."[75] An eighteenth-century preface to such a sentiment is captured by James Thomson's jingoistic "Rule Britannia" (1740), in which supremacy over and control of the waves ensures that "Britons never will be slaves."[76] By Thomson's logic, the ocean is complicit with enslavement and the protection of white supremacy.

The Queerness of Water flips that script. Rather than progressing the notion of the ocean's discreet complicity with colonial gain—which is accurate—this book investigates the ways in which bodies of water complicate colonial infrastructure and coincident, gendered performances. As Carroll notes, "many eighteenth- and nineteenth-century literary works portray the ocean as a space that troubles rather than supports Britain's pretensions to imperial power."[77] My close reading of Falconer above makes this evident, and King George III's catchy crescendo, with which I open this chapter, from the Tony- and Pulitzer-winning musical *Hamilton* (2015), records yet another sound bite by which to envision how colonial expansion is implicitly jeopardized by oceanic intercession: "Oceans rise, empires fall."[78] Syntactically, empires fall on the heels of rising oceans; upon the ascension of the ocean comes the descent of empire. Pairing Thomson and *Hamilton* bespeaks a type of oceanic and imperial mercuriality (and temporal switchbacking), which inspired this book.

But it is not just the ocean that triggers the vulnerable pretensions of empire. The aqueous spaces of eighteenth-century literatures participate in anticolonial processes. Put simply, *queer waters contest Enlightenment agendas*. Ariella Aïsha Azoulay has addressed how "unlearning imperialism" uncovers the exploitive and violent technologies of imperialism, under which "there is no longer a common world to care for but only scattered enclaves to protect."[79] Whereas Azoulay frames the unlearning around the shutter of photography, I suggest water—as yet another untapped technology (the Greek etymon *technē* signifies craft, art, and process of knowing) that can further elucidate and broaden internecine constructions of violence, which both accompany and threaten colonialism. Water is an agentive craft: it is—it lays bare—a simultaneous process of knowing and unknowing that lends itself to rupturing self-sure embodiments of colonial masculinity. Bodies of water, in other words, are not strictly alibis for colonial malignancies; they too reform and inform notions of masculine subjectivity that are not without foundering. The violence of water's queerness induces anticolonial potentiality that dethrones and makes violable forms of Enlightenment and colonial supremacy. This is perhaps one of the greatest risks and affordances provided by my queer readings of eighteenth-century canonicity.

SEMIOTIC AND ENTANGLED TREADING

Having presented ideas from this work over many years, I have come to anticipate and steel myself for a recurring "gotcha" question. It usually sounds like this: "You have addressed various levels of semiotic meaning: on one level you address the materiality of water, and in your close readings you emphasize symbolic value." It usually is just this, a statement not a question. But the "why" is implicit. Why our work matters—something I close with in this introduction—to others is always implicit. With alleged "crises" in the humanities, we are now forced to make such questions and answers explicit. This fallaciously suggests that our work does not stand on its own as forms of self-evidence.[80] If I understand the statement/question (and since it recurs, I'd like to think I do) there seems to be an assumption that an irremediable schism between materiality and symbolism exists. The two are binaries that cannot be mixed, conjoined, sutured, or interwoven. Symbolism is a betrayal of materiality. Materiality is likewise a usurpation of symbolism. We are either literal or figurative. Pick your poison.

Nonsense.

The Queerness of Water refrains from having to choose one side over the other. I advocate for "both/and" rather than "either/or," which only reinforces dialectical binaries that accompany Enlightenment epistemologies. The material and the symbolic work in tandem; one is sometimes subordinated to the other but they remain intimately intertwined. Water is a material-semiotic. The hyphen that connects the phrase cannot be unfixed and illustrates their mutual co-constitution. Chen, MacLeod, and Neimanis likewise weigh in on this inextricability: "Metaphor is a key form through which words and ideas come to be shaped by waters. To recognize the materiality of metaphor, therefore, is to acknowledge language as a more-than-human collaboration."[81] To be clear, when the following chapters take up symbolism, it is not at the expense of water's material body. Despite our fascination with and indulgence of aqueous allegory, in this book the ocean, sea, bath, stream, and ice sheet are not metaphors for absolution, baptisms, resurrections, purification rites, and modes of being hygienically made anew. In Hester Blum's words, "the sea is not a metaphor."[82] Water does not stand in for something. It, instead, stands *between, among, beside,* and *within* the bodies that are pieced together here. Ditto violence.

When this book does turn to symbolism, it is through intimate (usually erotic in resonance) close reading. These readings evaluate how masculinity, identity, and colonialism become reframed, reshaped, and resituated through uncomfortable and unrealized eroticisms. Manifestations of masculinity gesture towards and are always symbolic—this is a central tenet of heteronormativity, which I glossed above. In the literatures I explore, masculinity is itself a symbol, albeit one with material ramifications. This again bespeaks how the symbolic and the material cannot and will not be unbound. For example, when John Gabriel Stedman narrates himself grasping a monkey's tail—a monkey he has unsuccessfully maimed and attempts to kill—he endeavors to reclaim his own tarnished masculinity by eradicating the monkey's affective penetrability. I center this horrifying "natural history" in chapter 2.

To belabor the watery puns that flood this book, I refer to this process as *semiotic treading*, in that what emerges feels like treading water—a process that is energy-expensive and which renders the swimmer between a world submerged and one afloat. To tread in pools of semiotics is to always be coming to terms with variegated, sometimes conflicting, vertiginous expressions of meaning. Mentz has advocated for a "swimmer poetics," which recognizes how "our storm-filled world can generate unsustainable but engaging narratives."[83] "Being in the water," Mentz continues, "means knowing that stability cannot last."[84] Perhaps semiotic treading is likewise unsustainable or unstable, but *The Queerness of Water* invites us to consider how long we can stay afloat and whether we can welcome our fluid becomings.

By floating in fluid materiality and thinking, this book traces what modes of violence bodies of water stage or enact in literary narratives, reflecting the new materialist turn that has taken hold of critical theory, generally, and the environmental humanities, specifically. New materialisms, as I undertake them, emphasize an intersectional feminist and queer lens by which to examine the agential possibilities that exist before, around, and beyond the human. Depriviliging an anthropocentric narcissism and hubris, new materialisms showcase the vibrancy of materiality, or of matter, that can foster, by Diana Coole and Samantha Frost's summation, "intersubjective interactions" that realize new, invigorated, and capacious relations.[85] Neimanis's *Bodies of Water: Posthuman Feminist Phenomenology* in this vein underscores the body's wet constitution to query the confluence of "exponential material meaning" and embodiment.[86] Proposing a wet phenomenology in sympathy with feminist and Indigenous modes of thinking, as a tactic to decenter a masculinist ethos, Neimanis dissects Western anthropocentrisms that might separate the human from its environment: "the human is always more-than-human. Our wateriness verifies this, both materially and conceptually."[87] Coincident with Neimanis's feminist aqueous thinking, Stacy Alaimo's oft-cited "transcorporeality" emblematizes Coole and Frost's intersubjective sharing. Alaimo posits transcorporeality as a new materialist posthumanism that positions the human body within the matrix of environmental interactors that reflect a fundamental blurring, bleeding, and sharing of constitutions and elementality. Transcorporeality "renders the human permeable, dissolving stable outlines," which "discourages us from taking refuge in the fantasies of transcendence and imperviousness that make environmentalism a merely elective and external enterprise."[88] A plenitude of transcorporeal fantasies abound, exclusively without recognition, in the fictions I traverse here, and they elucidate the dissolution of stable boundaries and the violent intercession of nonhumans into the entangled fold of the porous body.

WHAT LURKS AHEAD

The pleasures of exploring the queerness of water arise from encountering moments of aqueous extremity or intensity that have previously or otherwise eluded capture. I undertake four distinct bodies of water (though there are myriad others that beckon our attention and invite us into their midst): the sea, the river/stream, the pool, and the glacier. These sites demonstrate how each body of water is distinctive and so too is what takes place in, about, or near that site.[89] The movements among and evolution of bodies of water serve as the organizing principle for the chapters that follow. This is not, foremost, an exhaustive, encyclopedic catalogue that archives all bodies of water as they seep into long-eighteenth-century narratives. I instead spotlight polymorphic illustrations of bodies of water to invite treading, diving, trawling, navigating, angling, and aqueous exploration of all sorts.

The chapters unfold in watery phases. In this procession from ocean to ice, formations of violence, queerness, and the aquatic crystallize. Oceanic waters participate in the reconstruction of resilience and masculine survival. Riverine or Arctic bodies of water stage viscerally graphic violations of the body. Still, contained bodies of water, like pools, dramatically reframe notions of sexuality through exquisite (putatively risible) violence. Both proximity to and immersion within these tangled bodies of water are equally valuable in conceiving of the performance of violence and its enmeshment in suturing and displacing queered forms of relationality.

Chapter 1, "Taken by Storm," pieces together Daniel Defoe's repeated attention to early modern climate change in *Robinson Crusoe* (1719). The novel's repeated concerns regarding aqueous and environmental antagonists illustrate how the sea and its effects account for the insurmountable impacts of the Little Ice Age. In other words, *Robinson Crusoe* situates a long genealogy of *closeted climate fictions*, which I explore through various genres in this book. Closeted, not only for its queer implications, but because it is not typically read in this trajectory. The violent performances of Defoe's seas, narrative shipwrecks, and storms spur queer temporalities in that the storms become time out of time, where Crusoe grasps for every possible breath that the sea, by his account, seeks to steal from him. The sea is a queer temporality. Aqueous violence is part and parcel of Crusoe's survival narrative and his strange adventures overall; in this way, the sea, its tides, and his interaction with the "cannibals" reveal a queer ecological grammar in which bodies of water participate in writing and being written into Crusoe's retrospective reflections. Chapter 1 thus patterns broader cycles of interconnected environmental and human violence that circulate within *Robinson Crusoe*, to apprehend new modes of sea power, a concept I reconceptualize at the chapter's close.

Between each chapter springs forth an *intermezzo*, a distinctly eighteenth-century word (its etymology is situated squarely within eighteenth-century performance cultures) that accounts for a pleasing performative respite between acts of a play or opera. In a musical work, an intermezzo is the interstitial tissue among movements. So too are the intermezzi that conjoin chapters here. These interludes develop out of conversations in the previous chapter but recast these issues, motifs, and currents beyond the eighteenth century. The intermezzi knit the eighteenth century's queer aqueous apertures to alternative narratives, histories, and temporalities that demonstrate a long, durational tide. The eighteenth century, in other words, makes waves well beyond its historical parameters, and we must look elsewhere to fully grapple with the sinews of our discourses.

As performances in and of themselves, the intermezzi approach pedagogy, praxis, and activism. They speak to how whimsy can inform serious scholarship. They are bricolages that deliberately blend media, narrative, art, visual culture, and genre. They situate intertextual conversations that are often eroded or forbidden because of deeply seated reservations about historicity, disciplinarity, or presentism. While nontraditional in their offerings, the intermezzi are vital components of recognizing water's queerness. To echo an injunction William Beckford penned to his American editor, Samuel Henley, upon nearing completion of *Vathek*, which had, as originally envisioned, included three additional episodes that were not published in full until the twentieth century, "I would not have [them] upon any account come forth without [their] companions."[90] I take up *Vathek*'s curious, censored, and dissected publication history in chapter 3. Where Beckford ultimately failed in the aspiration to attach his literary episodes to his magnum opus, this book will not. The intermezzi are the companions to the four traditional chapters. They read transversally and transhistorically—to extend kinship in its most inclusive form. In other words, water's queerness is not—cannot be—just a distinction that exists within eighteenth-century narratives. I am not interested in pigeonholing water's queer potentialities, which would only serve to re-closet aspects I intend to un-closet here. If this book imagines a network of queer and aqueous connectivities, then the intermezzi represent nodal touchstones that address how water's queerness can enliven the fluid pasts, presents, and futures of cultural theory.

The first intermezzo, "Teaching Wreckage in Rising Waters," explores the submarine apocalyptic futures of Adrienne Rich's poem "Diving into the Wreck" (1972). I teach Rich's poetry collection, by the same name, in my course "Literature and the Sea" on the shoreline of the Susquehanna River in central Pennsylvania. Teaching Rich on a littoral site that will be underwater in thirty years because of accretionary exterior and interior water levels demands we come to terms with the pedagogical and lived realities that the National Book Award–winning collection and its implicit eschatological visions document. In Rich's queer eschatology—what I understand as yet another representation of closet climate fiction—we encounter mermaid forms that harden us against and prepare us for the futures of an environmentally ravaged earth. Mermaids and other aquatic hybrid beings produce pedagogical opportunities that recognize the threat of rising waters and welcome our liquid metamorphoses.

Chapter 2, "See Monkeys," traces an eighteenth-century fascination with simian species that spans naturalist tracts and literary imaginations to enlighten two uncanny moments wherein rivers stage violence between male colonist and monkey. Jonathan Swift's *Gulliver's Travels* (1726) and John Gabriel Stedman's *Narrative of a Five Years Expedition against the Revolted Negroes of Surinam* (1796) offer the river location and the simian as conjoined threats to masculinity. The homophonic puns this book details are always deliberate—this is part of my queer grammar. My use of the homophones see/sea in this chapter emphasizes how brief moments of simian-human violence materialize immediately after moments of misrecognition. Gulliver is unable to properly "read" the female Yahoo's mating ritual despite his polyglot abilities, and Stedman is misrecognized as a simian by the monkey he later maims and murders. In both narratives, moments of misrecognition spur violent entanglement, and rivers become the site of violation. These aquatic arteries—rivers—are locales of phenomenologically threatening experiences that disrupt the colonial mission, especially for Stedman and the masculine colonist more generally, thus positioning Gulliver as an implicit arbiter of a colonial agenda rather than just an unlucky, waylaid traveler.

"Reading Swift on the Planet of the Apes," the second intermezzo, further addresses primatological knowledges by locating the affinities between Swift's *Gulliver's Travels* and Pierre Boulle's *Planet of the Apes* (1963). The violating encounter I magnify in chapter 2, between Swift and the female Yahoo, is likewise intertextually recorded in Boulle's science fiction thriller. For Swift as for Boulle, it is not just the uncanny fantasy of human and simian that titillates audiences; it is also recognition of an aqueous soundtrack and location that spurs concerns over human supremacy, violation, and usurpation. Boulle's much-beloved planet of the apes is none other than Houyhnhnmland by another name.

In chapter 3, "Aqueous Punishment," I investigate the recurrence of aqueous sites in Gothic fiction and the ways they home torture as a means of biopolitical control. I pair William Beckford's *Vathek* (1786) and Matthew Gregory Lewis's *The Monk* (1796) to investigate how water is instrumental to a hegemonic disciplining of Gothic bodies that exceed socially sanctioned and desexualized roles. In *Vathek*, Bababalouk, Vathek's lead eunuch, is subjected to waterboarding in the harem's pool for his (hetero)sexual appetite. Likewise, Ambrosio, the titular monk, is tortured in a running stream at the novel's close to expiate for his lascivious and unrepentant sins. Bodies of water configure sites of castigation for a coterie of male characters I refer to as "desexualized," that is, characters whose occupations or roles within the state or church demand their dislocation from the heteronormative sexual economy. Hypersexualized eunuchs and monks deviate from their normatively desexualized roles, which is to say that they aspire and attempt to participate in the heteronormative economies from which they have been dispossessed. I locate pools and streams as sites of violent punishment that condemn the eunuch or monk for trespassing and thus reveal an internalized justice system articulated by the Gothic novel that maintains and upholds hetero-repronormativity. Aqueous punishment ensures the violation of the sexually deviant body and remands the transgressor back to a socially condoned desexualized role. Water here doesn't provide emancipation but rather becomes harnessed by the state in order to subdue and curtail desexuality.

The third intermezzo, "Off with Her Head," revisits forms of aqueous torture through Hans Christian Andersen's *The Little Mermaid* (1837) and its namesake statue, which is perched on the shore of Copenhagen's city center. Edvard Eriksen's 1913 bronze figure commemorating Andersen's original narrative has been subjected to countless acts of mutilation and vandalism under the auspices of social activism. "The Little Mermaid" and its accompanying statuary serve as social canvases wherein violence against women is both normalized and the means by which political and environmental protest is performed. Aqueous punishment, in other words, takes on revived verve in its political and ecological fervor—once again through the mermaid form.

Chapter 4, "Sacrif-Ice," embraces the ice world as a critical site within the late eighteenth-century cultural imaginary to contextualize the Arctic framework with which Mary Shelley deliberately bookends *Frankenstein* (1818). I focus on the creature's promise of sacrifice as an exemplar of violence that both conjures up and is administered in the novel's ice worlds (the Arctic frame and the glaciers above Chamonix). "Sacrif-Ice" underscores how sacrifice, by Shelley's wielding, is only invoked and made possible near water or upon glacial sheets. Ice becomes narratively and literally inscribed in sacrifice and thus augurs a cryonarratology. The ice world is a biome wherein modes of violence crystallize—like the frozen waters in which they occur—and the foreclosure of and disassociation from familial and heteronormative community is required. Sacrifice, however, queerly fails on all accounts and thus signals the accompanying failures of queer community and attachment that Walton, Frankenstein, and the creature repeatedly seek in proximity to one another.

"Freeze!," the last intermezzo turns to the comic arts to query the various and conflicting origins of Mr. Zero/Mr. Freeze/Dr. Fries, a many-monikered villain introduced by DC Comics in 1959 and later portrayed by Austrian weightlifting darling Arnold Schwarzenegger in *Batman and Robin* (1997). Mr. Freeze's comic villainy stems from his connection with Frankenstein's creature, and just as Boulle rewrites Swift, DC Comics' commitment to reanimating Mr. Freeze for nearly sixty years is yet another cultural nod towards Shelley's literary prowess. This intermezzo recognizes Mr. Freeze's character and nonhuman affiliations as participating in a longer history of closeted climate fiction. Mr. Freeze's desire to inaugurate a new ice age (uttered in his 1959 debut) reaches its filmic apogee in *Batman and Robin*, wherein a climate future that rails against reproductive futurism and its entanglement with the Anthropocene is envisaged.

My conclusion doubles down on representations of hybridity that are tracked from the chapters and intermezzi that precede it. "Sea Monsters" locates an eighteenth-century lore of sea creatures to examine how interactions with hybrid aqueous figures reconfigure notions of the human, the erotic, and the potential to see *beyond, into,* and *through* water. The conclusion plaits together strands of hybrid and mermaid embodiment that propose new horizons for interspecies intimacies that can defang the violence of the Anthropocene. I pair Guillermo del Toro's Oscar-winning *The Shape of Water* (2017) with Jane Austen and Ben Winters's *Sense and Sensibility and Sea Monsters* (2009). Del Toro's equal-parts enchanting and violent love story between a mute custodial worker and an imprisoned sea creature is central to understanding the types of antiheteronormative and antireproductive narratives that the queerness of water affords. Opposite *The Shape of Water,* Winters's creative and warped retelling of Austen's *Sense and Sensibility* (1811), wherein Colonel Brandon becomes a tentacled human-nonhuman hybrid, configures how intimacies among species become queered and germane to an eighteenth-century canon. By closing with *The Shape of Water* and *Sense and Sensibility and Sea Monsters,* I position another potential for water's queerness and aqueous violence: modes of thinking that do not obviate care and can participate in mutually beneficial modes of pleasure.

THE MATTERING OF QUEERNESS/THE QUEERNESS OF MATTERING

As humanities scholars we are constantly held accountable for why our research matters, and importantly, we are tasked with considering to whom this research might matter. *The Queerness of Water* is not singularly the liberation soundtrack for a new wave of queer scholars or individuals who seek a more animated intimacy with troubled ecologies. The goal of this book is not to paint all bodies of water with broad, iridescent, rainbow flag–colored strokes, in a gesture that might look like, at best, a naïve and jejune un-closeting of water or, at worst, a destructive queer colonialism veiled by homonormativity. Instead, I seek to inaugurate waves, ripples, and whirlpools of queer possibility that only water might endow.

The readings offered here matter because they introduce the multifold potentialities for queer theory, the environmental humanities, and literary study to fuck worlds anew. Water's queerness is not the antidote to Anthropocene violences or a woeful resignation to the sea level rise that anthropogenic climate change has and will continue to induce. Water's queerness is not an alibi for troubled ecologies that act with or against us or suffer under what Erika Cudworth terms "anthroparchy."[91] Instead, *The Queerness of Water* is a provocation that dives into the uncertain quagmire of interdisciplinarity and seeks to emphasize plural ways of knowing queerness and of apprehending, reading, and interacting with bodies of water. For the literary characters whose experiences are paramount in the chapters that follow, bodies of water embody and portend a frightening and abrasive reality that is almost unnavigable. For Crusoe, Gulliver, Stedman, and Walton, survival is inevitable, but these narratives of survival are not bereft of the physical, emotional, and psychic damages that accompany their immersive experiences. "The pain of water," Gaston Bachelard notes, "is infinite."[92] For Bababalouk, Ambrosio, and Dr. Frankenstein and his creature, whose deaths conclude their respective novels, the effects of aqueous violence prove too much. The infinitude of aqueous pain meets its cosmic match in death.

The experience of immersion is simultaneously a process of becoming and unbecoming—of knowing the porosity and opacity of the body—and this ushers in modes of violent, queer possibility. Put another way, the queerness of water resides in derangement, defamiliarization, and unlearning that bubbles up from diverse entanglements with bodies of water that, as this archive suggests, induce violent relationalities, futures, histories, and contingencies. In its veriest hope, *The Queerness of Water* plumbs a radical reconceptualization of a saturated process that indelibly marks both the literary subject and our means of apprehending water's queer wake in humanistic scholarship.

CHAPTER 1

Taken by Storm

On the evening of 26 November 1703, a level-three hurricane laid waste to London. With wind speeds of one hundred to 140 miles per hour, the storm destroyed roofs, homes, and retaining walls and uprooted trees. This storm remains, by historian Richard Hamblyn's assessment, "the worst in British history."[1] Eight thousand people perished, the majority of them sailors. Though recovery would take years, the trauma of this environmental phenomenon lingered. Some seven years after the storm, Queen Anne was still responding to financial pleas from widows whose sons and husbands were lost. The storm, Robert Markley argues, "reveals the complex ways in which our understanding of climate—in the twenty-first century as well as the eighteenth—both shapes and is shaped by a range of ecological, socioeconomic, and metaphysical values and assumptions."[2] Daniel Defoe's *Robinson Crusoe* (1719), the central focus of this chapter, like his earlier *The Storm* (1704), which I've explored elsewhere, invariably centers the sea and its storms in ways that imagine the waves and wake of the Great Storm, which together demonstrate a coming-to-terms with early eighteenth-century climate and its portents.[3] In pursuit of this destructive wake, this chapter navigates the queer temporal and relational ramifications of climate instabilities to reckon with the formidable potency of aqueous violence that shifts, magnifies, and elucidates the leakiness of human exceptionalism. In short, through Defoe's pen, we encounter an eighteenth-century climate fiction contoured by queer waters.

ROBINSON CRUSOE: CLOSET CLIMATE FICTION

The culprit responsible for topsy-turvy climate upheavals, emblematized by the Great Storm that opened the eighteenth century, was the Little Ice Age.

With its formative steps taken in the thirteenth century, then emerging in full adolescent petulance through the seventeenth and eighteenth centuries, and ultimately waning around the middle of the nineteenth century, the Little Ice Age was a period of extended cooling, which troubled global transport, imperial conquest, and trade; induced widespread famines; and brought about frightening weather phenomena that hazarded planetary life. The Little Ice Age situated the Global North in the throes of climatological and environmental disarray.

The global climate disruptions effected by the Little Ice Age likewise bled into the human nature-cultures of early modernity. In their assessments of the visceral effects of the Little Ice Age, Dagomar Degroot, David Zhang, and Phillip Slavin have each contended that these widespread environmental upheavals laid bare and became impetuses for what Degroot describes as "intrastate and interstate violence."[4] The durational effects of resource precarity and environmental disarray institute forms of intra- and extra-community violence. The correlative propensity between climate phenomena and violence gives rise to, as Degroot puts it, the fact that "climatic shocks encouraged violence by undermining agriculture: the key source of food, employment, and wealth for most early modern communities."[5] Degroot's invocation of interstate violence is assuredly different than the environmental violences I see manifesting in Defoe's novel. That, however, violence and climate change cohere as a result of the Little Ice Age is unmistakeable. Thus I read *Robinson Crusoe* as a novel that centralizes the rippled effects of climate change (especially the aquatic troubled ecologies it induces) and its violent corollaries. This is where *Crusoe's closet climate fiction* lies. Closet operates on multiple levels: on a superficial one, it identifies the fact that Defoe's works have not been read as participating in a longer genealogy of climate fictions, which I intend to remedy here. On a more intimate level, Defoe's closet climate fiction also realizes the queer potentialities of this genre, especially as it is illustrated by violent, aqueous environs.

The genre of water's queerness invoked in this chapter derives from feminist and queer new materialist frameworks to assess the persistent blurring of human and nonhuman aqueous bodies. For Stacy Alaimo, transcorporeality at sea recognizes that "the human is held, but not held up, by invisible genealogies and a maelstrom of often imperceptible substances that disclose connections between humans and the sea."[6] The use of maelstrom engenders both metaphoric, as it is for Alaimo, and literal considerations. Violence, I offer, makes evident the types of queer distortions that accompany the bleeding of human and aqueous bodies and thus instigate bodily, autonomic, and masculine dissolutions. In approaching water as a queer archive, Astrida Neimanis suggests that "we must learn to live with our dissolutions with whatever grace we can muster—and sometimes even embrace them. We must also learn to read in watery archives the politics of erasure as a way of approaching differential mattering in the Anthropocene."[7] While Crusoe may not abide his watery dissolutions and the threat of bodily intercession that accompanies his stormy experiences, his narrative epitomizes a watery archive that gestures towards alternative erasures paved by environmental violence and troubled ecologies.

The violent interrelationality between aqueous sites and Crusoe configures the ocean and its aqueous kin (rivers, shorelines, etc.) as antagonistic; that the sea grasps hold of Crusoe and seeks to draw him into a deathly abyss is unmistakable. He details, "I saw the Sea come after me as high as a great Hill, and as *furious as an Enemy* which I had no Means or Strength to contend with."[8] Even more shocking, Crusoe suggests in repeated fashion that the ocean's waves intend to "swallow" him whole— an evocative personification that reinforces the sea as a violent, embodied force that muddies anthropocentrism. Indeed, the word "violent" occurs, by my count, eighteen times in the novel. It is exclusively used to refer to moments of affliction: either environmental circumstances or situations that plague Crusoe's health. The first use of the word, which refers to the sea storms, exemplifies this claim and operates as an aperture by which to see other moments of violence that I magnify here. Crusoe breathlessly relates: "However, the Storm was *so violent* that I saw what is not often seen, the Master, the Boat-Swain, and some others more sensible than the rest, at their Prayers, and expecting every Moment when the Ship would go to the Bottom."[9] Here, the protagonist conceives of the sea and its corresponding storms as so powerful a force that it could kill. Aqueous violence transforms veteran sailors into suddenly devout believers preparing for end times. Aqueous violence thus becomes an immersive, unrecognizable force that opens new phenomenological experiences of visuality and pain. Scott Juengel realizes something similar by suggesting that in *Crusoe*, "to stray into open seas is to hazard subjectivity in its most naked form, one wherein the subject is exposed to both the elements and the limits of human perception."[10] This is precisely what aqueous violence accounts for. To recognize aqueous violence, as Crusoe does, is to rewrite human subjectivity as it is informed by oceanic entanglement.

As readers of *Robinson Crusoe* are certain, experiences with violence multiply perniciously. Friday's cruel and forced assimilation is assuredly an extension. This chapter moves from the anaphoric sea storms to Crusoe's shipwreck on the Island of Despair and then demonstrates that the violent relationship with the cannibals, like the shipwreck motif, remains contingent on liquid ripples of the sea and its storms. In so doing, I look to this connected constellation of violent intentionality, which, I contend, stems from aqueous interaction rather than potentially unique moments that are distinctly enfolded in a longer narrative.

Violence in *Robinson Crusoe* is contagious: a word that even in its etymological evolution from Latin to Middle English to French continues to underscore contact, togetherness, and—invaluably—touch. Crusoe bears the marks of a violent touch, and he exercises this contagious touch on Friday and the cannibals. As Priscilla Wald, Nancy Tomes, and Lisa Lynch show, contagion lexically operates as a synonym for culture.[11] *Robinson Crusoe* demonstrates that violence is contagious and engenders a violent culture by which admixtures of human and nonhuman communities comprise varied modes of violent being. To be clear, I do not use "contagious" strictly metaphorically, and I do not intend to evacuate it from the sociomedical contexts, specifically the twentieth century's bacteriology, with which it is most associated. Violence is not a disease in the same way that most contagious actants are, but violence is catching, often retaliatory, and embodied.[12]

The violences I constellate here are both environmental and imperial. I connect them in acknowledgment of the colonial relations that circumscribe Crusoe's narrative, which require that we understand Crusoe and his narrative as embodied and textual representations of empire. His maritime aspirations (and consequent shipwrecks) are entwined with imperial ones. Whereas Crusoe's own tribulations with enslavement and his later desertion may serve as contradictory examples of him as a bellwether of imperialism, his narrativized actions on the Island of Despair, participation in enslavement and plantation economies, and his early desire for a seafaring life that is invariably enfolded in regimes of British naval supremacy clarify that his colonial aspirations are realized. Put another way, as early eighteenth-century protagonist and hero, Crusoe is colonialist par excellence: his colonization of the Island of Despair and its flora and fauna, enforced servitude of Friday, and violent endeavors to safeguard the island as if "private property" represent all the vestiges of an immersive Eurocentric colonial stronghold. In addition, the literary deployment of early modern shipwreck, as Defoe authors it and as Steve Mentz has identified, becomes a convenient means to accelerate imperial expansion through survivorship and its attendant narratives.[13] Crusoe's recurrent attention to shipwreck further instantiates Mentz's claim.

The anticolonial reading I mobilize here identifies Crusoe as colonizer and looks to ecological patterns by which this brand of colonization is troubled. As Frantz Fanon insists in *The Wretched of the Earth*—where Crusoe and Friday are foundational examples—the process of colonization is an enactment of violence that must be radically combated with an equal if not greater violence to dispel the colonial legacy and stronghold on the minds of those subjected to colonization. Of Crusoe and Friday, Fanon writes: "their first encounter was marked by violence and their existence together."[14] Whereas Fanon emphasizes the *contagious nature of violence* in the colonial sphere, which reveals that absolute violence, resultant from the enduring tragedy among colonizing and colonized forces, is also emancipatory—I investigate the *violent contagion of nature* to similar anticolonial ends.[15] I thus seek to hold in tension different—not identical—modes of violent interrelationality that seep among humans, those rendered as nonhuman, and environmental bodies.

STORM TRACKING

Eight storms punctuate *Robinson Crusoe*. The recurrence of storms and their immersive propensities situate narrative patterns, marking the sea as the arbiter of violent distortions that induce disjointed time—both Crusoe's apprehension of time and formal, narrative divisions. Put simply, the storms and their accompanying waves lay siege to embodiment, relationality, and temporality in one fell swoop.

The "temporal turn" has recently exploded in eighteenth-century criticism as it has in critical theory more broadly. This section contributes to what Jesse Molesworth identifies as "a favored topic for interdisciplinary research on the long eighteenth century" so as to make sense of how Crusoe's aqueous encounters resist what Elizabeth Freeman terms "chromonormativity," or the normative ways in which bodies are constructed in order to comport max (re)productivity.[16] In *Beside You in Time*, Freeman doubles down on claims of chromonormativity to orient "sense-methods," or the "foregrounding of time as a visceral, haptic, proprioceptive mode of apprehension—a way of feeling and organizing the world through and with the individual body, often in concert with other bodies."[17] The queer effects Freeman espouses as underlining temporal "sense-methods" are apposite and revisited here to account for the violent sinews of temporality and embodiment radically reoriented by the sea storms. The demonstrable distortions begat by the sea storms register temporal and embodied violences that tether human and nonhuman aqueous bodies in uncomfortable chromo-nonnormative ways. *Crusoe*'s oceanic extremity, in other words, can forge new pathways by which to account for the temporal turn—both in its redress by eighteenth century scholars and as a queer ecological methodology. *It's about time.*

Because of *Crusoe*'s lack of a regimented chapter structure, for the first half of the novel (before the journal sets in), the sea storms can be read as the narrative divisions ostensibly missing: they telegraph the marking and passing of narrative time. Such a realization accords Peter Miller's poetic insight in *The Sea*: "The ocean is the grand narrative, seas the microhistories."[18] This is undoubtedly the case for *Robinson Crusoe*. In introducing the first two storms, Crusoe narrates: "All this while the Storm encreas'd, and the Sea, which I had never been upon before, went very high" and "by this Time it blew a terrible Storm indeed."[19] Each new storm brings "encreas'd" narrative recounting. Case in point: the first storm begins and ends in two paragraphs. On the heels of the first, the second storm extends over six paragraphs. The multiplicative nature of the storms compels further narrative recognition. Therein lies Defoe's econarratology, in which environmental intensity induces narrative reproduction. Whereas Margaret Cohen asks for a reconsideration of the novel to realize the necessity of the maritime to the genre's growth and legacy, I explore how *Crusoe*'s sea storms and their narrative structures invite us to consider what happens when the sea as an environmental interactor participates in (or compels) writing the novel.[20]

As each storm throws Crusoe and his sailing companions deeper and deeper into the tumult of the ocean, the narrative grows longer, mirroring the length of oceanic immersion. The storms belie containment; immersion becomes impossibly narrativized. Of the first storm, Crusoe reveals:

> The Ship was sooner gotten out of the Humber, but the Wind began to blow, and the Waves to rise in a most frightful manner: and as I had never been at Sea before, I was most inexpressibly sick in Body, and terrify'd in Mind: I began now to seriously reflect upon what I had done, and how justly I was overtaken by the Judgment of Heaven for my wicked leaving my Father's House, and abandoning Duty; all the good Counsel of my

Parents, my Father's tears and my Mother's Entreaties came now fresh into my Mind, and my Conscience, which was not yet come to the Pitch of Hardness to which it has been since reproach'd me with the Contempt of Advice, and the Breach of my Duty to God and my father.[21]

Crusoe's rambling epitomizes how the novel situates the storm—it is only one sentence—as an experience of nature that is frantic, frenzied, and unyielding. Even the overuse of colons seems to follow the undulating motion of waves that lash at Crusoe and instill mental and embodied sickness, corresponding with P. N. Furbank and W. R. Owen's and Cynthia Wall's analyses of Defoe's prose style, which, they argue, superimposes behavior and meta-intent over narrative.[22] While neither Furbank and Owen nor Wall address *Crusoe*'s oceanic narratology, their insights collectively relay how Defoe's narrative authority can inform metanarration in which form and content become performatively mirrored. The method of storytelling characterizes the sea's behavior. The sea's behavior impels storytelling.

Readers are brought along on this turbulent journey. Each wave amplifies Crusoe's uncertainty and pushes him deeper and further into melancholic self-reflection. Those who opt to read this passage aloud—a fascinating pedagogical experience I invite my students to embrace—undertake a tiring feat. Despite the colons, semicolons, and commas, one gasps for breath while reading it, reliving the experience of storm that so much troubles Crusoe here. We experience the storm in situ. In reading this aloud, we don a Crusoe mask, feel the anxiety on our tongue, and attempt to gather ourselves in moments of maelstrom. This is part and parcel of being taken by storm.

By being taken by storm, Crusoe's narrativized sea storms muddle apprehensions of time, invariably spurring queer effects. This results exclusively from their considerable violence recast on human bodies. The storm's violence proves to distort time by, first, threatening to erase—or literally destroying—a past; two, offering a terrorized present; and three, avowing a future that reacts to the sea's mercurial qualities and renounces a life at sea. As Paul Alkon reveals, Defoe's "temporal settings, whether past, present, or future, become more important than chronology."[23] By waylaying temporality and elucidating the cuts that exist between past, present, and future in stormy phenomena, the storms deter from a chrono-logic that demands linear progression. In so doing, the storms participate in what Sara Ahmed characterizes as queer orientations, or the ways in which queer subjects (and objects) do not and cannot participate in the reproductive futurist narrative and thus embody trajectories that are queered in the rejection of chromonormativity.[24] While I'm not interested in outing Crusoe as a queer subject—an identity-based notion that Ahmed directly addresses—I am interested in the queer temporality and resulting queer effects that the storm's queer orientations induce. Ahmed offers "moments of disorientation [as] vital. They are bodily experiences that throw the world up, or throw the body from its ground."[25] Crusoe's invocation of the sea and its intent to swallow him, which I take up more explicitly later, identifies the queer disorientation that accompanies emesis—throwing the world up.

The textures of temporal distortion that I have so far traced are further exploited by Crusoe's narrative attention to the first storm: "All this while the storm encreas'd, and the sea, which I had never been upon before, went very high, tho' nothing like what I have seen many times since; no, nor like, what I saw a few days later. . . . in this agony of mind, I made many vows and resolutions, that if it would please God here to spare my life this voyage, if ever I got once my foot upon dry land again, I would go directly home to my father, and never set it into a ship again while I liv'd."[26] Crusoe realizes the sea's power retrospectively: this first storm was not the worst and not even the last to experience within a few days' time. Whereas "all this while the Storm encreas'd," recounts the power of the storm in the past as Crusoe's reflective narration is fain to do, "nothing like what I have seen many time since" reflects on the potent storm from a present position. "Nor what I saw a few days after" returns the narrative to the past. He then quickly moves to the conditional spurred by the "agony of mind" prompted by his interaction with the storm. This agony allows Crusoe to abnegate any sense of responsibility for his actions by placing his future within the framework of God's pleasure. The conditions of both the storms and the narration seek to rectify Crusoe's petulance and reconcile him with his parents, who have disavowed his maritime aspirations. In other words, Crusoe's conditional prose here exemplifies the conditions of the sea and its storms that he must abide. The sea rewrites and upholds these conditions, which Crusoe, his embodiment, and mental machinations must heed. Aqueous violence is the ultimate condition for Crusoe, and simultaneously a conditional grammar that discloses the storm's queer effects.

Just like the peppered semicolons and commas, this vertiginous narrative movement of past–present–past–conditional is moderated by and functions like the undulating sea. This reflection of aqueous mobilities reveals the trauma enacted by present and past storms that, in turn, serves as a check on Crusoe's future. In fact, Crusoe's expectation that "every Wave would have swallowed us up" plays with a possible future foreclosed by drowning. The threat of being consumed ushers in the realization of the sea's predation: Crusoe and his inveterate sailing cohort are the prey—a pattern that Falconer emulates in *The Shipwreck*. Crusoe's future cannot be removed from an aqueous past that instills itself as a threat to his (present and future) existence. The temporal distortions modulated in these moments correspond to both Alkon's suggestion of the uneasiness of temporality and chronology in Defoe's works, as well as Rob Nixon's discussion of environmental violence and its "calamitous repercussions [that] play out across a range of temporal scales."[27] For Nixon, these temporal reverberations are both environmentally and bodily felt across broader spectra of time, and yet Crusoe heightens and distills the potency of those reverberations into his account of the sea storms. We witness corruptions of temporality in each stormy sentence. And while the sea links Crusoe to the uneasy mesh of his past and future, the future of the sea storm, as conceived by Crusoe, is only more sea storms.

MAKING WAVES

Defoe's use of waves to reinforce notions of violent relationality anticipates yet diverts from other hydraulic metaphors that arose later in the eighteenth century to determine the extent by which natural phenomena could mask human intercession, especially with regards to the New Science and emerging epidemiology. *Robinson Crusoe* participates in this trend, which recognizes the imbrication of Enlightenment science and the rise of the novel. As David S. Jones and Stefan Helmreich observe, the use of the wave metaphor in nineteenth-century medicine and pathology (with regards to outbreaks, pandemics, etc.) reinforced the notion that waves could be apprehendable and thus controllable.[28] Such an epistemological bent derived from the fact that, as Phillip Steinberg and Helen Rozwadowski have both addressed, British imperialism, especially during the seventeenth and eighteenth centuries, was predicated on employing the ocean and its waves as the primary conduit by which to realize exploitative gain—a neo-Roman gesture that recasts "mare nostrum," or an indication of "our sea" as something possessable and surveillable.[29]

As *The Queerness of Water* clarifies, this flattening of the ocean as a central conduit to colonialism limits the imaginative and realized powers of bodies of water throughout the eighteenth century. The ocean, in other words, is not singularly an accessory to the crimes of colonialism brought about by eighteenth-century travel, transport, and trade. This does not excuse such violences; rather, it tells only one narrative in desperate need of revision, especially alongside the emergence of new materialisms. That history is ostensibly penned and colored by victors also suggests that Euro-colonial endeavors (in their enactment of domination) conveniently downplay moments of disruption or failure; literary bodies of water, in contrast, make obvious these colonial fractures. Whereas, by Jones and Helmreich's assessment, wave representation and imagery can be controlled by human agency, in *Robinson Crusoe*, they work in contradiction to human agency, and in fact prove to dispossesses mental and embodied faculties. The storms and their attendant waves thus reject graspability, containment, and management, which reckon with an anticolonial praxis replete with unlearning and unlinking potential. The immersive nature of waves cannot be controlled; waves resist stasis. Crusoe's experiences with the waves realize that they seek to break him, and with him, the coloniality that his maritime life seeks to extend.

The storms' anticolonial waves bring about violent distortions that ultimately stay Crusoe's development and usher in queer durational effects. The trauma recuperated by the temporally unwieldy narrative functions as a gesture of loss. The sea is thus bound up with loss: Crusoe's past and his former ways of being. *The sea is loss.* Heather Love's conception of queer time proves especially fruitful in visualizing the queer valences of Crusoe's loss and its connection to aquatic bodies. For Love, all queer pasts, especially historical ones, are reclaimed as a gesture of loss.[30] Love's intent is not to uncover the more capacious form of queer temporality and its environmental corollaries that I admit here; in its focus on queer affect, *Feeling Backwards* reclaims forms of same-sex impossibility throughout aesthetic modernism that result from erasure, queer suffering, and social exclusion. However, the queer temporal strokes that Love paints with are similarly recast on Defoe's troubled ecologies.

The queer pasts that Crusoe orients in his experiences with the sea storms do not remand him to the same sexual identity politic that Love excavates, and yet the conditional framing of the storms again recognizes forms of loss through temporal scales. In Love's words, "the history of queer damage retains its capacity to do harm in the present."[31] The genres of loss instilled in Crusoe by the sea storms—temporal apprehension, his family and sailing companions—clarify how environmental interactors continue to bubble forth as he ultimately becomes shipwrecked on the Island of Despair.

But the threat of these losses is as real for Crusoe as his sailing companions, one of whom mumbles during the following storm: "Lord be merciful to us, we shall be all lost, we shall be all undone."[32] Loss incited by the storm is not only a singular experience for Crusoe, but one that contagiously spreads in its aqueous affinities to his colonial compatriots. *Loss makes waves.*

These losses amount to further relational divides as the storms continue to pummel Crusoe and saturate his narrative: temporality, relationality, and narrative are uneasy bedfellows on *Crusoe*'s high seas. The second storm, hinted at by Crusoe's return to the past in the previous passage, immediately follows the first. It is an echo chamber that ushers in Crusoe's final warning against a life at sea: "The Sea went Mountains high, and broke upon us every three or four Minutes: When I could look about, I could see nothing but Distress round us."[33] The chaotic scene that Crusoe cannot fully imagine for us demonstrates, once more, the sublime qualities of the mountainous waves and their accompanying distress. The breaking of the waves serves to break human trespassers and, inevitably, genealogical lineages. For example, the second of only four fathers found in the text—the first is Crusoe's, the second a sea captain, Friday's father is the third, and the fourth Crusoe, himself, at novel's end—cautions Crusoe from pursuing the alluring call: *"Young Man, says he, you ought never to go to Sea any more, you ought to take this for a plain and visible Token that you are not to be a Seafaring Man . . . And young Man, said he, depend upon it, if you do not go back, where-ever you go, you will meet with nothing but Disasters and Disappointments till your Father's Words are fulfilled upon you."*[34] These paternal warnings function as two strikes against Crusoe, and the sea becomes the immersive omen by which paternal admonishments are fulfilled. The storms ironically suture filial connection while simultaneously threatening to dislocate it. The sea captain's reminder of the storm and sea as a token calcifies the agentive possibilities that characterize the sea. For Jane Bennett, the agent of new materialisms is "neither an object nor a subject but an 'intervener,'" and the sea captain's invocation is one such revelation.[35] But Crusoe refuses to yield to this token. He confesses: "But my ill Fate push'd me on now with an Obstinancy that nothing could resist . . . I know not what to call this, nor will I urge, that it is a secret over-ruling Decree that hurries us on to be the Instruments of our own Destruction."[36] In an attempt to recuperate the environmental threats his body has been forced to heed, Crusoe identifies, yes, the lure of the sea, but more importantly that he is responsible for his own destruction. He seemingly attempts to erase the violating potency of the sea in a gesture that relegates environmental interactors to mere objects while upholding his own untarnished subjectivity. The queerness of water, in this moment, highlights the conditions by which we realize the fallible nature of Crusoe's masculine subjectivity at the hands of oceanic violence.

But his sailing companions, who have borne witness to these traumatic storms, do not buy such egocentric bravado or recalcitrance, which likewise threatens to undo them. They acknowledge an unsettling, eldritch connection between Crusoe and the sea: the spread of violence accompanies the twinned appearance of the storms and Crusoe. Whereas Crusoe's desire to remain at sea will not be staunched, those with whom he sails fear this desire to remain at sea. Seemingly, they realize he carries a curse: "You made this Voyage for a Trial, you see what a Taste Heaven has given you of what you are to expect if you persist; perhaps this is all befallen us on your Account."[37] Crusoe becomes like the token articulated by the sea captain. He becomes a didactic semaphore to the sailors as much as the sea becomes a didactic semaphore for him. Their entangled natures represent an agentive mutualism, which bungles conceptions of subject, object, and intervener. Indeed, in conjunction with the conditional syntactic structure and temporality yielded by the storms, so too are notions of subjectivity conditional. Inasmuch as the sailors identify Crusoe to be like the sea, then we must plumb the extent by which this entwinement realizes aqueous becoming, which underscores what Neimanis pinpoints as a "more-than-human hydrocommons," in which "the flow and flush of waters sustain our own bodies, but also connect them to other bodies, to other worlds beyond our human selves."[38] A Defoean hydrocommons reasons that the contagion of aqueous violence thus becomes homed in Crusoe's body and he, as a result, embodies yet another conduit by which to realize the portents of aqueous violence. He too is a stormy body of water.

The shared compatibilities between Crusoe and the sea engender a new materialist realm by which each participates in the other's autonomic process to model a shared autonomy. In "Agency at the Time of the Anthropocene," Bruno Latour contends that because of the stakes of the Anthropocene, "to be subject is not to act autonomously in front of an objective background, but *to share agency with other subjects that have also lost their autonomy.*"[39] For Latour, these gestures of shared and lost autonomy derive from the destructive and immersive tendrils by which humans have coopted and subjugated every aspect of planetary life—of course, this cooptation and subjugation comes at the hands of only certain humans, which the term Anthropocene often conceals. However, Defoe's seas and storms subtly reinforce and reject these anthropocentric paradigms, and the type of shared autonomy I account for here is not exclusively a depiction of anthroparchy that necessitates, or forces the hand of, the sharing of autonomy. As Crusoe uncannily narrates, the sea participates in these notions of supremacy, which inevitably cast dominion over human subjects too. Water's queerness befuddles and realigns regimes of supremacy to account for new modes of shared agency that can upset the Anthropocene.

Even more, the forms of dominion that Crusoe engineers on the Island of Despair stem, incredibly, from the forms of didactic violence that the sea and its storms inaugurate. In the first storm, we begin to witness this acculturation. Upon commencing his seafaring life, Crusoe becomes overwhelmed with sea sickness: "As I had never been at Sea before, I was most inexpressibly sick in Body, and terrify'd in my Mind: I began now to seriously reflect upon what I had done."[40] Crusoe's realization of what the sea can do forces him to pause for reflection. But before reflection, he becomes "inexpressibly sick." The sickness apparent here is a violence on the body, but one that has also been internalized within him in terrifying his mind. Crusoe reveals that violence is as much stamped on the mind as it is on the body, thus confirming aqueous violence as more than just a flesh wound—it becomes internally and externally comprehensive. *Nausea* and *nautical*, in fact, derive from the same Greek etymon, *naus*.

The sea situates itself within Crusoe, and his response is to vomit it outward—and emesis will return later when he discovers the cannibals. The emetic process serves here both to admit the sea's attempts to overtake Crusoe's body and to simultaneously jettison this uncomfortable intercession. Emesis typifies the purgative distortions that he continues to encounter with each subsequent storm and sea voyage. As it was for Ahmed, emetic behavior is a hallmark of disorientation and distortion, here begat by the sea and its storms, one that tests the limits of the body and Crusoe's survival. This dangerous potency alters Crusoe's identity insofar as the sea has embedded itself within him, no matter how much Crusoe attempts to eject it outward. That Crusoe narrates his inexpressible sickness documents the lasting effects, by way of self-reflection, the sea instills upon him. The phenomenology of the sea cannot be forgotten; it instead becomes (in)scribed.

Put another way, despite Crusoe's intention to uphold himself as the bellwether of exceptionalism, the novel makes clear that autonomy is socially constructed and dependent. Autonomy, by *Crusoe*'s wielding, then, becomes anticolonized. If Euro-coloniality assumes and pressures autonomy to be individualistic and separable, then the anticolonial autonomy revealed here is a social assemblage compiled of heterogeneous subjects, objects, and interveners in recognition of and yet blurring with other autonomies. A caveat though: to pinpoint a shared agency is not to collapse or conflate identities. That is, while Crusoe may become violent like the sea, he is not sea, and the sea is not Crusoe. Shared autonomy, as Latour might suggest, is about *becoming like* the other, which points to the entangled connections of violent and violable subjectivity, while still maintaining residual autonomy. Shared autonomy does not efface the subject, object, or intervener. Rather it provides an epistemological vista by which to reimagine structures of autonomy that, in colonial and neocolonial fashion, are predicated exclusively on singular exceptionalism. *Crusoe*'s radical individuality evidences shared autonomy as a reframing of individuality that is entangled, assembled, and conjoined.

DELIVER AND STAND

The two subsequent storms further illustrate Crusoe's contingency upon aqueous bodies for both sustenance and durance. But like the other storms he encounters, Crusoe is constantly the only survivor. His exceptional isolationism is often the justification for recognizing Crusoe as the paradigm for an eighteenth-century radical individuality. For Ian Watt, Crusoe engenders a form of "economic individualism" that imposes the distinct rise of modern capitalism into the very structure of the rise of novel.[41] Caitlin Charman links Crusoe's radical individuality to his deployment of managerial capitalism, modeled by animal husbandry, gardening, and technological penchants; Charman thus binds Watt's articulation of *homo economicus* to Cohen's articulation of Defoe's novel as maritime craft.[42] Additionally, Peter Hulme articulates Crusoe's radical individualism as that which "staggers backwards into the future, lacking in self-understanding, full of guilt, self-contradictory, tearful, violent."[43] Hulme's corresponding definition of radical individuality here aligns itself with both the temporal shifting noted in the previous storms as well as modes of violence that accompany the radical individual. While Crusoe's radical individuality is prompted by the sea and accompanying shipwreck, which repeatedly dislocate him from human community, this emphasis devalues forms of nonhuman and environmental community that accompany Crusoe on, leading up to, and beyond the Island of Despair, for which Charman also accounts. I submit then that the phantom, presumption, and fallacy of Crusoe's radical individuality is reliant upon his experiences with the sea and its storms. The novel's disclosure of temporal admixtures and their accompanying violent relationality that subtend radical individuality remains fixed to the influx of bodies of water—a phrase that reminds us of the whirling and bleeding of oceanic and human bodies, which further the dispossession of (strictly) anthropocentric autonomy.

The third and fourth storms elucidate the repetitive nature of the sea's voice and further clarify that Crusoe recognizes the sea as a nonhuman body gone rogue. *To death,* it seems to repeat and call to Crusoe. This siren call is translated by Crusoe in the fourth storm, "I need not say, that I expected every day to be swallowed up, nor indeed did any in the ship expect to save their lives."[44] As Crusoe and his fellow sailors attempt to flee from the storm, the sea's effective power becomes abundantly clear: "In a word, it took us with such a Fury, that it overset the Boat at once; and separating us as well from the Boats, as from one another, gave us not the time hardly to say, O God! for we were all swallowed up in a Moment."[45] The repeated invocation of swallowing harkens back to the emetic process described above and additionally notices the sea as an entity that seeks to take possession of human trespassers—coincident with swallow's late seventeenth-century etymology meaning "to take for oneself, or into itself, as a territory or other possession; to absorb."[46] The sea, then, operates as a voracious maw that swallows, satiated only by destruction and human offerings, a signal repetition we will see return in chapter 3, wherein Gothic bodies and aqueous chasms participate in sacrificial, pederastic cannibalism.

The sea hungers for the deaths of Crusoe's sailing companions. Such voracious aquatic appetites, sated only by the deaths of fellow sailors, forcibly exile Crusoe from human community and familiarity. None can survive but him. Alongside the excision of human community, the sea's demonstrable power emphasizes the queer corruption of time in that there was "not the time" to speak, which is followed closely by the sea's giant gulp. Queer time is time out of time; it is time consumed. Human voices are muted in this moment, and the only voice/mouth allotted is the sea's.

The sea, however, resists expelling Crusoe and, more compellingly, Crusoe realizes it:

> Nothing can describe the Confusion of Thought which I felt when I sunk into the Water; for tho' I swam very well, yet I could not deliver my self from the Waves so as to draw Breath, till that Wave having Driven me, or rather carried me a vast Way on towards the Shore, and having spent it self, went back, and left me upon the Land almost dry, but half-dead with the Water I took in. . . . I got upon my Feet, and endeavoured to make on towards the Land as fast as I could, before another Wave should return, and take me up again.[47]

The sea preys upon Crusoe's confusion, which in turn vacates his abilities altogether. It forces him to recognize his own shortcomings, which serve to tarnish his conceptions of radical individuality that would otherwise give way to a hubristic masculine patina. His invocation of being "half-dead with Water" reminds us yet again of the sea's intention to insinuate itself within his very body—a liquid intercession that does not sit well with Crusoe.

Crusoe cannot evade the waves and remains incapable of "delivering" himself from them, which endows a suggestive turn of phrase that harkens back to the initial title page, wherein Crusoe is "deliver'd by Pyrates," while simultaneously reinforcing obstetric associations. David Marshall argues that *Crusoe* is replete with "autobiographical acts" that "account" for the protagonist's attempts to negotiate his myriad losses by way of artifice; the novel becomes his artifice. Marshall reasons, "The island is his novel—a work of realism and verisimilitude, however far-removed from everyday life—and in this sense we can rediscover *Robinson Crusoe* as an autobiography in another sense: a self-portrait of the artist as fabulous artificer."[48] While I agree with Marshall that Crusoe's repetition of his various deliverances/deliveries can be felt both religiously and philosophically, by reading the deliveries as strictly a mode of autobiography, we fail to realize how Crusoe's stalwart sense of self—located by autobiography—is jeopardized by nonhuman interactors that likewise induce modes of literal delivery. From at least the mid-sixteenth century, *delivery*'s etymology reinforces its common use today as referring to the process of giving birth or of being born. At the same time, to deliver is also to manumit, to free, to release from possession. The experiences with the sea and its waves invoke both uses. Crusoe's inability to deliver himself from the sea underscores how his attempts at autobiography actually fail to stand on their own. His delivery from the sea remains affixed to the sea's ability and willingness to release him, rather than any semblance of self-governing autonomy that he ultimately fails to achieve.

Crusoe's attention to "delivery" identifies his tribulations in the sea as an experience in utero that forestalls his attempts to self-liberate. In an aside, Marshall gestures to the above moment of delivery as one wherein Crusoe "must deliver himself, deliver his self, from the womb of the ocean."[49] Such a poetic description gives Crusoe too much unearned credit. Crusoe's delivery is, by his own admission, resultant exclusively from the waves that "drive" and "carry" him and then "leave" him on the shore. This oceanic delivery alludes to long-held misogynistic associations of Scylla and Charybdis, which are repeatedly conjured as aqueous *vaginae dentatae* that position sailors on the chopping block of insatiable feminine appetites. Of the mythic pairing, Marilyn Francus writes, "Scylla threatens masculinity, not through compelled penetration of a watery womb/tomb like Charybdis but through submission to insatiable maternal power and the monstrous sexuality and progeny that it perpetuates. The lethal choice of Scylla and Charybdis represents male disgust with (and fear of) sexuality and reproduction, and the Christian tradition continued this negative reading of female fertility."[50] Defoe captures this "lethal" depiction as yet another challenge to which Crusoe must rise and ostensibly conquer.

By Marshall's assessment, Crusoe, inconceivably, is able to free himself of these maternal and oceanic fetters through self-narration. Crusoe's account reveals otherwise; he dictates, "I could not deliver my self." Herein lie the problems of Crusoe's radical individuality, which readers and scholars assume almost in contradiction to the narrative. It operates, then, as a projection of desire—a trope of colonial hubris that ingratiates readers to notions of alleged superiority, independence, and resilience. While Marshall and I are both interested in the obstetric imagery evoked by this passage, we diverge in our understandings of what this portends. Though Crusoe may flee the sea's thirsty tendrils, his articulated failure to properly deliver himself operates as a reminder of an invisible aqueous umbilicus that he likewise fails to snip. That the sea continues to inundate him and the waves repeatedly endeavor to swallow him whole recognizes not his autobiographical development but rather his inability to be reconciled with an oceanic body that has nurtured his violent growth. Do not misread me: I am not interested in rewriting Crusoe's genealogy and replacing his birth mother with the ocean, which would only reinstitute a heteronormative logic. Rather, I magnify the admission of failed delivery to account for the embodied tactics that Crusoe's narrative endows in the sea—as a source that is clearly feminized and demonized in its violence (a "monstrous mother," as Francus might say) and yet invariably embodied and connected to his story, autonomy, and relationality.

The embodiment of the sea plagues Crusoe and predates on his mental capacities: like the invocation of Scylla, Crusoe narrates his concerns regarding the antagonistic sea that wishes to swallow him whole. Steve Mentz and Martha Elena Rojas distinguish such an intention as one that characterizes a "hungry ocean" that "creates an alternative ecology, inhuman but alluring."[51] Hungry oceanic ecologies demonstrate the corrosive effects of shared subjectivity, which Crusoe admits. For instance, in the moment that follows his failed delivery, Crusoe reveals, "I saw the Sea come after me as high as a great Hill, and as furious as an Enemy, which I had no means of Strength to contend with . . . my great Concern now being, that the Sea, as it would carry me a great Way towards the Shore when it came on, might now carry me back again with it when it gave back towards the Sea."[52] Crusoe graphically underscores the transportive horrors of the sea that at once and the same time "carry" him to the shore and also threaten to "carry" him back. On the heels of the gestational model he implicitly aligns with his "delivery" from the ocean, Crusoe's "great Concern" is that he might be swallowed, carried, gestated once more, in a way that recognizes these maternal associations with the sea as "furious" and filled with enmity.

This fear is amplified in that the subsequent wave actually attempts to reconcile Crusoe with the waves that have begotten his isolation:

> The Wave that came upon me again, buried me at once 20 or 30 Foot deep in its own Body; and I could feel my self carried with a mighty Force and Swiftness towards the Shore a very great Way; but I held by Breath, and assisted my self to swim still forward with all my Might. I was ready to burst with holding my Breath, when, as I felt my self rising up, so to my immediate Relief, I found my Head and Hands shoot out above the Surface of the Water; and tho' it was not two Seconds of Time that I could keep my self so, yet it reliev'd me greatly, gave me Breath and new Courage.[53]

In his commitment to what Marshall might identify as a self-delivery, the narration envisions an enormous, monstrous body of the sea that gives way to a reborn Robinson Crusoe whose "Head and Hands shoot out above the Surface of the Water." While Crusoe breaches the sea's confining waves, he assures us that *he* is not breech.

The sea remains, by Crusoe's account, an antagonistic body determined to bring the invocation of "half-dead with Water" to fully dead fruition. Taking baby steps on the littoral, Crusoe confesses "neither would this deliver me from the Fury of the Sea, which came pouring in after me again, and twice more I was lifted up by the Waves . . . The last Time of those two had well near been fatal to me; for the Sea having hurried me along as before, landed me, or rather dash'd me against a Piece of Rock, and that with such Force, as it left me senseless, and indeed helpless, as to my own Deliverance."[54] Like the vertiginous waves that literally punctuate his stormy experiences, Crusoe, as he nears shore and putative safety, returns to an unwieldy narration that vacillates back and forth between aqueous attachments and failed deliveries. That is, while he continues his attempts to evade the sea's grasp, he reminds readers that this evasion is yet another repeated failure. The oceanic body seeks to consume him as it has the other sailors who hazarded the maritime voyage: "I cannot describe, reflecting upon all my Comerades that were drown'd, and that there should not be one Soul sav'd but my self."[55] The sea's consuming penchant reflects the word's etymological root, *consumere*, meaning to lay waste, wear down, or devour. These consuming qualities underscore, first, the sea's body—in that it can consume—and, second, the effects of this consumption on Crusoe's body—in that the sea consumes him and in turn initiates a violent contingency wherein his survival, resilience, and relationality remain indebted to sea power.

ENTER THE CANNIBAL

As I have demonstrated so far, the sea and the sea storms participate in reframing notions of violence and, in doing so, account for the broader matrices of violent entanglement that saturate Defoe's novel. Recognition of an oceanic body and its queer temporal and relational admixtures provides one means by which to imagine this matrix. This section pivots to interrogate Crusoe's violent relationality with the cannibals on the Island of Despair, and their ostensible kinship with the sea's currents. By moving from environmental to cannibal violence, I investigate how Crusoe's identification and fears of nonhuman violence plague his very existence, yet all the while he maintains affinities with water. In truth, Crusoe does not recognize either the cannibals or Friday as belonging to the same vectors of humanity by which he understands himself. The connection Crusoe implicitly forges between the sea and the cannibals thus serves to pinpoint how nonhuman modes of violence penetrate Crusoe's narrative and threaten to undo him altogether.

The littoral space, home of the footprint, Crusoe's shipwreck, and the first interaction with the cannibals, becomes the arena for additional violences to unfold. Crusoe recognizes the shore as the cannibal's territory, "for certain it is, that these Savage People who sometimes haunted this Island, never came with any Thoughts of finding any Thing here; and consequently never wandered off from the Coast."[56] He delineates the cannibals as exclusively belonging to and operating upon the shoreline, and thus his interactions with them reposition this geography as one teeming with violent altercations and machinations. The sea's violence and the potential cannibal violence are, then, different sides of the same coin, especially given that the cannibals only body forth from the shore: "They had two Canoes with them, which they had haled up upon the Shore; and as it was then Tide of Ebb, they seem'd to me to wait for the Return of the Flood, to go away again; it is not easy to imagine what Confusion this Sight put me into."[57] Not only do the cannibals seem to punctuate the shore—amplifying both Crusoe's fear of the littoral and its connection to loss—but their ability to navigate the tides and sea mystifies Crusoe.

The cannibals' ability to decipher the tides and use them to their favor suggests a familiarity with the sea and its currents that Crusoe cannot apprehend. In a bewildered aside, Crusoe later characterizes Friday as "an expert Sailor" despite his inability to understand a compass.[58] Notions of colonial maritime expertise and technological supremacy dissipate in front of Crusoe's very eyes. Crusoe's fear of the cannibal is, then, not exclusively enshrouded in the potential violence they may or may not enact against him, but also in an ability to read the tides in a way that he cannot. This oceanic familiarity suggests a navigational superiority that does not sit well with Crusoe, especially given the failures of his own navigational prowess. For example, having completed construction on his boat, Crusoe sets out away from the Island, "when even I was not a Boat's Length from the Shore, but I found my self in a great Depth of Water, and a Current like the Sluice of a Mill: It carry'd my Boat a long with it with such Violence, that all I could do, could not keep her so much as on the Edge of it . . . Now I began to give my self over for lost."[59] Once again, Crusoe's characterization of the sea as possessing "violence" waylays his plans, intentions, and potential survival. Why then should the cannibals be so adept where he stumbles?

In *Waves of Knowing*, Karin Amimoto Ingersoll offers a "seascape epistemology" as an Indigenous knowledge about the interweaving of elemental entities—sea and wind—"that allows for successful navigation of them."[60] Ingersoll's seascape epistemology "organizes events and thoughts according to how they move and interact, while emphasizing the importance of knowing one's roots, one's center, and where one is located inside this constant movement."[61] Whereas Ingersoll's project sets out to critique and engage the neocolonial surf cultures that have made Hawaii an ecotourism hotspot, I see the framework of a seascape epistemology that honors modes of indigeneity recast in Crusoe's narration of the cannibals with a deeply ulterior valence. To be certain: *Indigenous* and *cannibal* are not synonymous or even adjacent identities. I do not seek to collapse them. Yet the types of seascape epistemologies that Ingersoll contends stem from Indigenous and Native modes of performance and experience are precisely the modes of alternative knowledge that ail Crusoe.

Upon finally witnessing the cannibals in action, Crusoe reveals the similarities between these different kinds of violence: one, the sea's and thus a seemingly "natural" one, and two, a separate "natural" violence that seems immanent in the cannibals. Violence becomes, in other words, doubly naturalized. Crusoe narrates: "in short, I turn'd my Face from the Horrid Spectacle [the consumption of human flesh]; my Stomach grew sick, and I was just at the Point of Fainting, when Nature discharg'd the Disorder from my Stomach; and having vomited with an uncommon Violence, I was a little reliev'd."[62] Crusoe reenacts his previous emetic behavior with the goal of relief—a goal that likewise proposes to differentiate his sense of conduct from the cannibals. Yet, this aping of projectile vomiting bespeaks the slippage—the fluidity—between his body and other bodies. In vomiting "the Disorder," Crusoe mirrors the sea's consumptive and emetic habits. Crusoe, in other words, responds to, replicates, and models expressions of emesis that recur. To vomit outwardly signals modes of failed and shared autonomy. Connection is inexorably situated through vomit. Indeed, Crusoe identifies this emetic behavior as an opportunity for him to relieve himself through "uncommon Violence." The cannibal violence he surveys is too much to bear for Crusoe. The witnessing of this mode of violence necessitates his own embodied form of violence—vomiting—which extends the ramifications of violent contagion.

The revolt that Crusoe literally bodies forth comforts him and distinguishes the allegedly superior colonizer from the forces that ostensibly demand colonization. He narrates, "I look'd up with the utmost Affection of my Soul, and with the Flood of Tears in my Eyes, gave God Thanks that had cast my first Lot in the Part of the World, where I was distinguish'd from such dreadful Creatures as these."[63] As I have discussed elsewhere, Crusoe's repeated use of "creature" intends to signify hierarchies of animal, nonhuman, and racialized subjection to white, Anglo supremacy.[64] The invocation of the cannibals as "dreadful Creatures" seeks to categorize, dehumanize, and differentiate himself from modes of naturalized violence. The use of prayer in this moment consolidates this superiority and yet masks the violent measures that he intends to enact. His narrative voice reveals that certain forms of superiority and violent behaviors are more acceptable to God than others, which serves to indemnify himself of any responsibility to which God consents. However, even in his abilities to successfully expel the violent experience, what remains is the trace of violence. Violence then continues to define him wherein it allows for opacity between his exterior and interior selves.

Though the cannibals do not return to the Island of Despair for eight more years, the thought of them remains at the forefront of Crusoe's obsession with both self and other, and he repeatedly invokes the littoral as an arena for bloodshed. He narrates, "When going down to the Shore, I could see the Marks of Horror . . . The Blood, the Bones and part of the Flesh of humane Bodies, eaten and devour'd by those Wretches, with merriment and Sport: I was so fill'd with Indignation at the Sight, that I began now to premeditate the Destruction of the next that I saw there, let them be who, how many soever."[65] Crusoe justifies such violent plotting in bearing witness to and sympathizing with the trauma of "humane Bodies." The typographical addition of the "e" to human is significant. Of course, Crusoe means human bodies, but the deployment of *humane* suggests a binary of human and nonhuman. Katherine Quinsey argues that throughout the eighteenth century, concepts of humanity and the humane become mutually informative, wherein the former came to reinforce notions of an "emotional sense, [and] privilege compassion and sensibility."[66] For Quinsey, these previously competing concepts become entangled in the eighteenth century's parallel tracks of human and animal rights. The inclusion of the "e" following human reinforces Quinsey's reading and likewise superimposes two uncanny connections. First, that the human(e) body is the victim of cannibalistic (nonhuman) violence removes the victims of the cannibals from their Carib kinship networks and aligns them more closely with Crusoe's sense of victimhood. Victimhood is then imbued with absolute humanity, and with ironic twist, Crusoe uses this to condone violence against the cannibals. Categories of both human and nonhuman "wretch" are thus vexed by violent assemblages, and Crusoe deploys this logic to hold harmless his assault. The cannibal cannot be victim, even to Crusoe, because of their complete rejection to observe the colonial sanctity of "the Flesh of humane Bodies." Second, Crusoe aligns the consumed body with humanity—yet another signal tie by which his experiences with the sea and its swallowing habits seem to undergird notions of the human. Through Crusoe's narration we witness uncomfortable yet informative parameters of humanity, engineered to mitigate the violent offensive of his self-preservation.

In *Robinson Crusoe*, violent thinking is both the fear of being violated and the desire to violate. Violent immersion stems from a maritime relationship and bleeds into Crusoe's obsession with the cannibals, whose cognizance of a "seascape epistemology" bests Crusoe's colonial preponderance. Crusoe's obsessive fanaticism is not just reliant upon seeing and anticipating the return of the cannibals—a clear tie to the experience and anticipation of storms—but the justified violence that he can inflict on the cannibals in their return. Unmistakably, Crusoe aligns his violent mental machinations against the cannibals with a reminder of the violating power of the storms. The thought of violating the cannibals thus rings with the memory of stormy violence. Crusoe confesses to this obsessive thinking: "The Perturbation of my Mind . . . was very great; I slept unquiet, dream'd always frightful Dreams . . . In the Day great Troubles overwhelm'd my Mind, and in the Night I dream'd often of killing the Savages, and of the Reasons why I might justify the doing of it."[67] At the close of this paragraph, the sea and its storms inevitably reappear: "It blew a very great Storm of Wind, all Day, with a great deal of Lightning, and Thunder, and a very foul Night it was after it; I know not what was the particular Occasion of it; but as I was reading in the Bible, and taken up with very serious Thoughts about my present Condition, I was surpriz'd with a Noise of a Gun as I thought fir'd at Sea."[68] Violent thinking (and as with earlier violent experiences) becomes the impetus for and interweaves itself into the very ecological fabric of Crusoe's narrative. He grasps for apprehension of the stormy weather that follows him from nautical to deserted life. The storms represent an ineffable quality similar to the ineffable violence that overwhelms his conscious and unconscious mind. The thought of killing the cannibals is compounded by the sound of the gun "thought fir'd at Sea." This admission promptly closes the paragraph. Crusoe, in this way, narratively models the interconnected modes of weaponized violence that ineluctably vacillate between aqueous antagonists and cannibalistic ones.

The entanglement that Crusoe visualizes here is also the commencement of the eighth storm—the last of the narrative's stormy moments—which is responsible for yet another shipwreck. Upon reaching the Spanish ship, Crusoe summarizes the wreckage: "I concluded, as is indeed probable, that when the Ship struck, it being in a Storm, the Sea broke so high, and so continually over her, that the Men were not able to bear it, and were strangled with the constant rushing in of the Water, as much as if they had been under Water."[69] The last storm captures all the effects of the previous storms Crusoe has been forced to weather. The sea, which Crusoe characterizes only moments before as "run[ning] on with great Violence," becomes further animated as an entity that, by Crusoe's imagination, strangles. Like the aqueous tendrils that attempt to "swallow" Crusoe and drag him back with every tidal wave, so too do the mariners meet a graphic end at the hands of the sea. The sea's immersive power leaves none alive, except a dog, a "poor Creature" who when provided fresh water "if I would have let him, he would have burst himself."[70]

SEA POWER REVISITED

At novel's end and having departed the Island of Despair, despite Crusoe's familiarity with the sea's turbulent and mercurial nature, his residual fear remains: "I had been accustom'd enough to the Sea, and yet I had a strange Aversion to going to *England* by Sea at that time; and though I could give no Reason for it, yet the Difficulty encreas'd upon me so much."[71] His gut instincts take over: "I had been very unfortunate by Sea, and this might be some of the Reason: But let no Man slight the strong Impulses of his own Thoughts in Cases of such Moment."[72] There's good reason too. Crusoe reveals that both of the ships "miscarry'd": one overwhelmed by pirates and on the other "all the People drown'd except three."[73] Such miscarriages remind us of Crusoe's failed autobiographical acts and the means by which the sea hazards deliverance.

Sea power has long been deployed as a commercial or naval concept by which to grasp the fullest extent of empire's sway over maritime environments, colonial commodities including trade and enslavement, and other imperial interests. As A. T. Mahan writes in *The Influence of Sea Power Upon History, 1660–1783*, "The history of sea power is largely, though by no means solely, a narrative of contests between nations of mutual rivalries, of violence frequently culminating in war. . . . The history of sea power, while embracing in its broad sweep all that tends to make a people great upon the sea or by the sea, is largely a military history."[74] Mahan's definition is similarly recorded by Philip Steinberg, Alan James, and Christopher Storrs to further imagine the interstices of sea power and merchant capitalism, political legitimacy, and religio-cultural ideology, respectively.[75] Phillipa Hellawell, too, notes that late seventeenth-century aspirations of sea power were alternatively mapped onto those of science, thus gesturing towards how empire and science mutually inform "aspiration[s] to human dominion."[76] Sea power, yet again, becomes a means by which ecologies are commandeered by human supremacy.

I want to recalibrate that definition, if only momentarily. As this chapter reveals, conceptions of sea power are not exclusively fettered to notions of imperial expansion and naval history. Sea power can resist colonialism; sea power can rewrite naval and narrative histories. If *Robinson Crusoe* is indeed climate fiction, then Defoe's novel provides an opportunity to reconsider how sea power is a mode of actant possibility bestowed upon and extended from the sea. Sea power is, in other words, not strictly an anthropocentric category by which imperial agendas and the manpower indebted to bringing such agendas to fruition are bolstered. By Crusoe's handling, sea power necessitates that we come to terms with the violating potentials that aqueous environments and their stormy comrades make available. Violence, I'll repeat, is not strictly an anthropocentric arsenal to exercise.

Sea power recognizes the alternative, troubled ecologies of violence that Crusoe pens. Defoe's sea power is a new materialist opportunity to swallow, to strangle, to grasp, to behold human interlocutors, and to slash anthropocentric hubris at the knees. Sea power provides platforms to herald modes of embodiment shared between human and nonhuman. With the closure of the novel and Crusoe's return to England, he initially refuses to travel by sea any longer. He resigns himself to sea travel only between Calais and Dover—"resolv'd to travel all the Way by Land"—and, in so doing, consolidates his sea aversion: "In a Word, I was so prepossess'd against my going by Sea at all."[77] Crusoe's prepossession with the sea materializes as horror, disgust, fear, and loathing. The sea frightens Crusoe because it can do damage, both immediately and gradually, and such immersive processes are wholly transformative. Truly, this is sea power reimagined.

INTERMEZZO

Teaching Wreckage in Rising Waters

Ashore the Susquehanna River (the longest river on the East Coast), which in pursuit of the Chesapeake Bay cuts across Maryland, Pennsylvania, and New York, I bring my students to read poetry. This littoral zone, the Bucknell Landing, is littered with remnants of small bivalves—indeed the word *Susquehanna* may derive from the Lenape people's word *Sisa'we'hak'hanna*, which translates to "Oyster River"—oleaginous runoff, and literal garbage. Abandoned and strewn tires are perhaps the most recognizable nonhuman found in taking in the Susquehanna. These rubber riparian punctuation marks make the river feel too often more like a chop shop than a body of water central to the success and failure of central Pennsylvania.

Follow the river south and you will approach Harrisburg. The Susquehanna River that circles Pennsylvania's state capital is home of the 1979 Three Mile Island nuclear disaster, which, now a distant half-century memory, has recently received renewed concern by environmentalists as they continue to trace the durational effects of radioactivity in nonhuman aquatic life. In 2014, for instance, a smallmouth bass with a tumorous facial growth was caught—an occurrence that has been documented in the Susquehanna since 2005.[1] The Environmental Protection Agency reminds us (read: gaslights us into believing) that there is insufficient evidence for alarm, even though environmental activist groups have since 2005 declared the Susquehanna "America's Most Endangered River." The EPA was founded in 1970, on the heels of Rachel Carson's *Silent Spring*—her genre-bending exposé of dichloro-diphenyl-trichloroethane, or DDT, and its widespread, micro- and macro-scale effects on the environment. Carson, a Pennsylvania native, would balk at the sight of the EPA today, especially its dereliction of the Susquehanna. Upon my arrival to central Pennsylvania, one of the first things I was told was to neither swim in the river nor eat any of its contents. I have heeded these warnings.

In "Literature and the Sea," my students and I approach the Landing to read, reread, and read aloud poems from Adrienne Rich's National Book Award–winning collection *Diving into the Wreck: Poems 1971–1972*. Together we alternate reading stanzas from the poem that has given name to the collection. The poem is a microcosm of our course. "Diving into the Wreck" is a prescient, poetic closeted climate fiction, unlike and yet like that offered by Defoe. *Closeted* works in manifold ways here, especially for those familiar with Rich's "lesbian continuum" and her literary reclamation by feminist and queer scholars. To read Rich upon the Susquehanna River's rising waters is to teach us how to dive into poetry, to behold the wreckages of ecological collapse, and to hear our voices beside the polluted waters of a river that threatens us. But as my students and I learn alongside the Susquehanna's accretionary water levels, the queer aqueous futurity of Rich's poem lies in the rich possibility of approaching our own interconnected nonhumanity.

The Landing is a nexus of settler colonialism, elite privilege, and environmental toxicity. We rest ourselves there and swat at mosquitos as a volunteer reads:

> I go down.
> Rung after rung and still
> the oxygen immerses me
> the blue light
> the clear atoms
> of our human air.
> I go down.
> My flippers cripple me,
> I crawl like an insect down the ladder
> and there is no one
> to tell me when the ocean
> will begin.[2]

With Rich, we go down. Not down the ladder of the speaker's descent into the ocean. We instead go down the hilly geography atop which the university sits. We go down in the late summer humidity. We go down to bear witness to the Susquehanna that unveils itself in its current form—constantly in flux and rapidly evolving.

I do not highlight for my students the eroticism of Rich's stanza. This is theirs to find on their own, *as they go down*. I let them conjure this stanza's repetition of "I go down," a sultry invocation of oral sex that, here, accompanies submersion. To go down into and upon queer waters is to participate in worlds of polymorphic pleasure. The possibility of descent likewise triggers vast becomings of nonhuman life: going down spurs intimate entanglements of humans and insect lives. "I crawl like an insect" as I go down. In our descent, we erotically metamorphose, reforming the body and its prostheses. But my students and I pine over the invocation that "there is no one / to tell me when the ocean / will begin." Loneliness, uncertainty, isolation—all these things my students realize lurk in Rich's stanza. These things my students know firsthand.

While the Susquehanna bleeds into the Chesapeake Bay and shortly after the Atlantic, it may ostensibly appear to be unaffected by the types of sea level rise that will inundate coastal cities like San Diego, New York, Miami, or Seattle. This myopia erases arterial waterways, which, in similar fashion, will be drastically redrawn and redistributed alongside sea level rise. To assume that sea level rise will stop at our coastlines is an egregious fallacy—our bays, rivers, streams, and other interior waterways will unquestionably also be affected, buoyed, and saturated. These interior waterways will be forced to welcome additional seepages beyond containable borders. *They will go down.*

As the Union of Concerned Scientists reported in their 2008 climate impact assessment of the Keystone State, "Pennsylvania's climate is becoming wetter."[3] The report documents that over the twentieth century, Pennsylvania has experienced an increase in precipitation varying from a 5 percent increase in some areas to 20 percent in others. Unchecked climate response solutions will be responsible for a continued 5–12 percent increase on those already amplified rates. "Should the state follow the regional trend," the document concludes in the authors' evaluation of precipitation changes, "extreme rainfall events would be expected to produce more flash flooding, which threatens lives, property, and water-supply infrastructure such as dams."[4]

The conditionality of "would be" anticipates a climate future. Yet, the Susquehanna lingers, with scars of violent storms already endured by the exigency of the Anthropocene. For example, in June 1972, Hurricane Agnes devastated the East Coast, bringing with it roughly fourteen inches of rain to the Susquehanna Valley. Nearby cities like Wilkes-Barre were deluged; people, loved ones, property, and memories were literally washed away. With floods and extreme rain events now commonplace, the threat of this washing away is also becoming commonplace. Too often we justify these washing-aways as curatives. No one who experiences such trauma thinks of it as a resurrective baptism: paradise is never built in hell.

Consider two images captured by the archive, which give insight into the havoc wreaked by Agnes—the "A" a reminder that this was the first storm of that season. The first image documents the flooding in Wilkes-Barre, taken from the Pittston Hospital School of Nursing, which looks out over the Susquehanna. Scale is difficult to decipher here, but standard utility poles, like the one still erect in this photo, stand forty feet above ground. Likewise, the second image of the oversaturated agrarian landscape in Union County

Susquehanna River rising from Pittston Hospital School of Nursing (1972). (Photographer unknown; Misericordia University Center for Nursing History Collection)

Flooding of the West Branch of the Susquehanna River following Hurricane Agnes (June 1972). (Photographed by William B. Weist; Elaine Langone Library, Bucknell University, and the Weist Family)

(Bucknell's home) further demonstrates the problem of scale. While the railroad tracks sit mostly unaffected by the rising waters, the structure immersed in the image is a greenhouse. The symbolism is painfully prescient.

My students mostly hail from Pennsylvania, New Jersey, New York, and other parts of the Eastern Seaboard, and even in their short lives, they have borne witness to the formidably destructive powers of violent storms and immersive sea levels. My students often point to Hurricane Sandy, which made landfall in late October and early November 2012, as a memento that has radically shifted their conception of environmental violence. Hurricane Sandy is yet another permutation of aqueous violence, one that makes evident the power of the ocean to dismantle the infrastructures and hierarchies of the human. Hurricane Sandy as aqueous violence makes available the threat of being washed away—again, no cures, baptisms, or hygienic resurrections. The aqueous violence of Hurricane Sandy recasts the lived experience of climate change and rising sea levels, from which there is no respite. Students recount their experiences of being without power, of seeing their schools or towns decimated by winds and waves, of piecing through the storm's detritus. My students know aqueous violence by a different name: they already have the language, based on encounter.

They know aqueous violence because it lives on in their first memory of environmental havoc.

These memories lurk and surface as another volunteer lends their voice to the poem:

> First the air is blue and then
> it is bluer and then green and then
> black I am blacking out and yet
> my mask is powerful
> it pumps my blood with power
> the sea is another story
> the sea is not a question of power
> I have to learn alone
> to turn my body without force
> in the deep element.[5]

We ventriloquize Rich's narrator. My students know the experiences of the vertiginous stormy encounter that whirls with immersive color until there is widespread blackout. In other words, I don't need to convince them to apprehend the threats posed by sea level rise. "The sea is not a question of power" sounds as if it has slipped from the lips of Robinson Crusoe.

In recent years, Bucknell has begun to imagine what it will look like in 2025. This is prior to COVID-19, which seems to have waylaid these utopian imaginaries and ushered in apocalyptic visions of austerity presents rather than endowed futures. With the premonition of interior waterways deluged because sea level rise will not remain exclusively seaside, universities of 2025 may very well be forced to reckon with encroaching aqueous tendrils that reclaim lands that were never theirs to begin with. Aqueous borders don't recognize property—private property, even less. *Can environments be trespassers?* Universities will instead turn to flood insurance: a shockingly awful sum of money doled out regularly that seeks not to heed rising interior waterway levels but rather to proactively expect that these rising waters will go unchecked and lay waste. Roadways will fall into the Susquehanna. Newly commemorated dorms will become littoral sites where the need for a recreational pool will become moot. Offices will be deluged. Classrooms will become unusable. The pristine small-liberal-arts-college aesthetic will flood, and the University will seek to recoup the loss with flood insurance.

Flood insurance doesn't tackle rising waters. Instead, flood insurance sits atop swelling riverbeds avariciously shifting its hands together.

Rich's poem unwittingly affords us an opportunity to envision what that will look like here in the Susquehanna Valley. The aural/oral prescience of the speaker's words is enough. The wreckage Rich's speaker explores runs parallel to the wreckage homed by the river. Our reading implicitly knits these together. The river isn't merely a soundtrack or ambient noise; it is our subject. It is a subject.

> I came to explore the wreck.
> The words are purposes.
> The words are maps.
> I came to see the damage that was done
> and the treasures that prevail.
> I stroke the beam of my lamp
> slowly along the flank
> of something more permanent
> than fish or weed[6]

The wreck that my students and I—that we—encounter is not far off or far under. The wreck we will explore will be the once-remembered Landing that is no longer land and no longer safe for landing. We will seek to recover the names of buildings fallen into the surging Susquehanna. Those words will be our maps as we trace a climate reality that was once a warning and is now a cautionary tale. We come to see the damage that was done. But what treasures will prevail when our fringed existence on the Susquehanna is no longer viable? Do we move more inland? And what if the water follows? What if it becomes "something more permanent"? What does it mean to study place in the middle of nowhere?

> This is the place.
> And I am here, the mermaid whose dark hair
> streams black, the merman in his armored body.
> We circle silently
> about the wreck
> we dive into the hold.
> I am she: I am he

whose drowned face sleeps with open eyes
whose breasts still bear the stress
whose silver, copper, vermeil cargo lies
obscurely inside barrels
half-wedged and left to rot
we are the half-destroyed instruments
that once held to a course
the water-eaten log
the fouled compass

We are, I am, you are
by cowardice or courage
the one who find our way
back to this scene
carrying a knife, a camera
a book of myths
in which
our names do not appear.[7]

My students and I repeat these last three stanzas aloud. Each of us takes a turn feeling these words on our tongue. Poetry is meant to be heard, I tell them; poetry is meant to felt in the mouth, within the ear, beheld by our bodies of water. The sibilant echo of these last three stanzas is like hearing the air punctured from a bike tire or soccer ball, from future dreams perhaps. It is the sound of water leaking in, eking out towards us, following us. This is the place.

To teach "Diving into the Wreck" alongside the Susquehanna is to reckon with the threat of erasure. "Our names do not appear" in this book of myths, not because we are long forgotten but because the opportunity to sit astride the Susquehanna and its polluted body and read poetry aloud is a fixture of the past. If I teach "Literature and the Sea" again, if I teach Rich again, how much will the Susquehanna have swelled? Will the benches we sat upon be just other pollutants in the river? Will there be a landing to return to? The Susquehanna will chase us. *We are, I am, you are* subject to accretionary water levels.

We must don our mermaid forms—hardened and secured by armor—to approach the surfeit of water that will follow us. I do not tell my students to fear. I do not motivate with fear. I ask them instead to envision their mermaid form: an opportunity to realize new genres of being and relationality that accept what we have wrought and visit the wreckage not in search of ourselves but in recognition that we are "half-destroyed instruments." We have fouled the compass. This we must accept.

Onward to our mermaid forms.

CHAPTER 2

See Monkeys

This chapter pivots from the previous by reworking genres of human, nonhuman, and more-than-human interaction that commingle in bodies of water. Where "Taken by Storm" focalizes oceanic bodies, this chapter attends to riverine ones. Water's queerness, here, enfolds rivers located in literary fiction and natural history—two genres that are mutually informative—to imagine how interspecies intimacies and violations, specifically between male colonists and simians, unfurl within aqueous sites. Beginning with Jonathan Swift's literary fiction, *Gulliver's Travels* (1726), and closing with John Gabriel Stedman's diaristic natural history, *The Narrative of a Five Years Expedition against the Revolted Negroes of Surinam* (1796), I retrace two intensely violent moments wherein misrecognition between simians and narrators ultimately reconfigure masculine identity through bodily violation. Both Swift and Stedman situate the entanglement of river and littoral bank to home violent, erotic encounters. Gulliver's experience in Brobdingnag is the impetus for his later interaction with the female Yahoo—where sexual violence is imminent and death a potential. These motifs are carried later into the century, when violation and death become central to Stedman's encounter with a Surinamese monkey. In both, human and nonhuman simian entanglement threatens stalwart commitments to masculinity and accompanies a violent battle for superiority. Such occurrences reify colonial power—the simian-like Yahoo is expelled in Gulliver's account, and the monkey is killed in Stedman's—but also expose serious vulnerabilities that underscore the fragility of colonial masculinity.[1] The riverine site homes and reflects this uncomfortable reality, and this chapter magnifies rivers in the long eighteenth century as crucibles in which to visualize the fraught tensions of colonialism, anthroparchy, and environment.[2]

Two primary goals emerge in the following pages. First, I trace how literary fiction and natural history reinforce and reframe one another as interwoven genres. "Natural history, considered both as a literary genre and scientific pursuit," Robert James Merrett observes, "not only revises traditional views about novelistic procedures but sheds light on current endeavors to remake the novel's history."[3] The two narratives I unite speak to the entwined nature of these ostensibly disparate genres. However, the borders between these genres dissipate through representations and narratives of interspecies interaction. Second, I build on the collective work of eighteenth-century animal studies, especially surrounding the beloved topic of early modern primatology, by centering the aquatic geographies in which the narrativized simian purportedly lurks.[4] While it may appear that this chapter shifts to focus exclusively on animality, the queerness of water here accounts for how fluid environments displace and dispossess the human alongside and because of animal interlocutors. I thus join Greta LaFleur in attempting to recalibrate how environmental interaction informs and animates emergent questions, practices, and apprehensions of eighteenth-century sexuality. In *The Natural History of Sexuality in Early America*, LaFleur "restores the environmental body to the center of studies in sex in the eighteenth century, arguing that like other forms of human variety such as racial difference, diversity in human sexual behavior, and sociosexual organization, and even sexual proclivity, were explained primarily through an environmental logic."[5] This chapter looks specifically to the nonhuman turn in order to better account for how environmental and animal bodies of water mutually yet distinctly inform conceptions of eighteenth-century humanity and its embedded relationship with sexuality.

Gulliver's Travels is perhaps more familiar to readers, especially in slapstick films, for example Jack Black's 2010 recreation as the titular, portly Gulliver that exploits the first voyage (to Lilliput) of Swift's quadripartite novel. My focus here magnifies the second and fourth voyages: in which Gulliver visits Brobdingnag (the inverse of Lilliput, where Gulliver is now miniature) and Houyhnhnmland (an alien land where equines dominate primates). The satire of Swift's novel, which I discuss more fully below, is deeply imbricated in considering environmental effects (as well as affects) and the ways they blur the boundaries of human and animal. While Brobdingnag does not include the river, by pairing these moments I magnify narrative patterns that ultimately come to a head in Houyhnhnmland's watershed.

Stedman will be less familiar to readers, and this is largely because his work as colonial memento is branded as natural history, though we'll see how comparable Swift's literary fiction is to Stedman's putative nonfiction. Stedman's arrival in Suriname as part of a Dutch convoy in February 1773 engenders a colonial effort to protect imperial interests and rein in revolts from enslaved and marooned populations that sought liberation from Dutch and English strongholds. (Case in point: Suriname was not fully emancipated from the Netherlands until 1975.) *Narrative* stands out because Stedman describes, at length, almost all aspects of the colony: infrastructure, language, flora, transportation, the horrors of slavery, and poignantly, Suriname's diverse fauna. He repeatedly documents tortures and flayings of enslaved and Indigenous peoples in which he is complicit. The natural history that Stedman pens in diaristic form is itself a blending of genre: art, narrative, correspondence, and ethology. As an artist, Stedman includes eighty engraved plates that coincide with descriptions from his narrative. Of the eighty, forty-four are dedicated to Surinamese flora and fauna. The other thirty-seven depict either enslaved-enslaving relations or sketches of colonial settlements. If we consider these numbers, which telegraph a type of captured attention, then for Stedman there is something striking about those biotic forms that he encounters in Suriname that require both narrative description and illustration. William Blake, in his early career, would also engrave moments from *Narrative*, positioning it as a contribution to literature, art, and—of course—colonial record and containment. *Narrative* is, like its natural-historical kin, a tome, and while Stedman encounters several simian species, I primarily attend to a single, shocking passage in which the Dutch mercenary maims and murders a monkey in a Surinamese river.

MONKEY SEE, MONKEY DO

As with the other chapters in this book that pinpoint the endemic violence of aqueous sites, this chapter interrogates the types of violence that are fomented by misrecognition, or mis-sight. In Houyhnhnmland, Gulliver misinterprets and misreads the female Yahoo's behavior—despite his polyglot abilities and his similitude with the Yahoo—resulting in his near sexual assault. Stedman's interaction with the monkey similarly results from the fact that the monkey he graphically murders misrecognizes Stedman as a fellow simian. Here, I am fascinated by these moments of catastrophic misrecognition that occur on riparian shores. The failure of sight bedevils the encounters and exacerbates the effects of interspecies misrecognition. As both case studies demonstrate, the misrecognition of the other is, always already, a misrecognition of the self that furthers the markedness of these encounters and requires an uneasy and unwelcome introspection.

These failures of sight are likewise failures to recognize the river as site. *Rivers represent the fluid fringe.* Jeffrey Jerome Cohen posits the river's liminality as an induction of "interstices, mixing, hybridity, autonomy, cogency."[6] It is this characterization of riverine entanglement that marks the river as an immersive, erotic site for Gulliver and Stedman, and the river's body comes to intensify these aqueous and simian interactions by occluding escape or making it altogether impossible. If the queerness of water is about the plurality of experience, trauma, and human-nonhuman mesh, the river becomes a stage for these entanglements to be performed, rather than, as in chapter 1, situated as an active participant. For example, in arriving in Brobdingnag, Gulliver notes that the river's estuary is the locale of many a sailor's death. The river for Stedman is yet another site where his colonizing companions, or enslaved attendants, either drown or are "snap't away by Alligators."[7] The river's illegibility and mercuriality homes nonhuman antagonists—nonhuman, animal, environmental—aplenty. In this way, Swift and Stedman configure the river as an environ of looming doom or violation, and in their repeated attention to this amphibious geography, they ultimately realize that the violence endemic in the river induces new modes of being that reorganize masculine modalities. Such metamorphic violence epitomizes Gaston Bachelard's articulation of aqueous becoming: "a being dedicated to water is a being in flux. He dies every minute; something of his substance is always falling away . . . The pain of water is infinite."[8] While Bachelard addresses the psychoanalytic imaginary that water worlds avail, this chapter takes seriously the endowment of infinite pains that become viscerally mapped onto the bodies of Gulliver and Stedman, which continue to make messy the boundaries of what we might consider embodied or embodiment. For the two, the amplified discomfort results from the ways both the simian intercession and the aqueous site induce fluctuating states of falling away.

The encounters patterned here are intimate in their violence, and thus I trace the erotic and potentially erotic contexts that triangulate the human-simian relation—a method that addresses alternative queernesses. The queering that I offer to Swift and Stedman reacts to eighteenth-century scientific treatises and natural histories, including those by Edward Tyson,

Carl Linnaeus, and Georges-Louis Leclerc, the Comte de Buffon, which emphasize female vulnerability to simian species. For instance, Edward Long's *A History of Jamaica* (1774) and Thomas Bewick and Ralph Beilby's *A General History of Quadrupeds* (1790) in repeated, almost plagiarized fashion, rumor the "oran-outang" to "sometimes surprise the female negroes, and carry them of into the woods, where they compel them to stay with them."[9] In Long's version the oran-outangs "carry off Negroe women into their woody retreats, in order to enjoy them."[10] Bewick, Beilby, and Long's collective descriptions of predatory orangutang behavior document how unbridled animality threatens constructions of purity, whiteness, and human supremacy. These unfounded and scandalized narratives position the simian threat to humanity through the potential for abduction and normalized sexual violence against women, especially women of color.

But this motif is spun on its head in *Gulliver's Travels* and *Narrative*. Swift and Stedman unconsciously revise this emergent ethology by revealing the vulnerabilities laid bare by *male* protagonists' encounters with the monkey. These scenes of encounter trouble depictions of the masculine subject: for Gulliver, the destabilization occurs at the hands of the Yahoo's inimical sexual threat; for Stedman, the destabilization that accompanies monkey murder is disorienting, forcing him to reflectively pause, overwhelming him with feeling, and vacating his hunger: "I felt so much on this occasion, that I could neither taste of him nor his companions, when they were dressed, though I saw that they afforded to some others a delicious repast."[11] Stedman's admission serves to highlight forms of queer relationality that emerge alongside the threats of simian interaction, which fracture modes of self-sure masculinity and thus telegraph the porous state of a masculine imperialism.

Juno Salazar Parreñas's *Decolonizing Extinction* looks to the prospect of orangutan extinction (a foregone conclusion at this point in the Anthropocene) to examine decolonial affects, specifically care, spurred by our commitment and embeddedness with nonhuman animal selves. "The work of care . . . is an effort at decolonizing extinction," Parreñas writes.[12] Whereas Parreñas accurately characterizes coloniality as mediating a binary of violence and benevolence, I want to pause to consider not the liberatory praxis that violence avails in the human-simian waters I chart below but rather how moments of intimate interspecies contact that are read as violent account for a differential anticolonial politics, namely one in which structures of relationality, identity, and intimacy are radically resituated, redefined, and rebirthed. The queer anticoloniality pronounced by the moments traced below is at once an excavation of colonial masculine hubris and an invitation for exploring how anticolonial readings and encounters among species reveal divergent modes of relation not beholden to colonial projections and violence. In other words, what violent worlds might appear when we reconfigure or revisit violence as something not strictly an anthropocentric privilege? How might an animalized anticolonial politics bring into relief our presuppositions of violence and their concomitance with eighteenth-century empire?

CONSTRUCTING THE EIGHTEENTH-CENTURY SIMIAN

The eve of the eighteenth century proves to be a fruitful moment to visualize the efflorescence of primate knowledges, encounters, and interest throughout imperial Europe. Richard Nash, for example, reports that the first chimpanzee made landfall—that is, first appeared on English home turf—in 1698.[13] Brought over from Portuguese-colonized Angola, the male chimp became a central attraction for a circus, but quickly succumbed to an oral infection. For Nash, the introduction of the chimpanzee into the English homeland represents a watershed that induced a radical epistemological shift: one that began to conceptualize "the borders of human identity."[14]

Only months later in 1699, the forefather of comparative anatomy, Edward Tyson, published his seminal *Orang-Outang,* which offers yet another cultural edifice of primatology. "Orang-outang" is of course a misnomer in that the anatomy of the "pygmy" that so much constitutes his comparative study is actually a chimpanzee. "I will not urge," Tyson notes, "any more thing here, why I call it a *Pygmie:* 'Tis necessary to give it a name; and if what I offer in the ensuing *Essay,* does not sufficiently Account for the *Denomination,* I leave it to others to give on more proper."[15] Concerns of nomenclature muddle the coupling of natural history and emergent primatology, especially pre-1758, the year in which Carl Linnaeus introduced in *Systema Naturae* his quadripartite system for organizing primates: *Homo, Simia, Lemur,* and *Vespertilio.*[16] For Nash and Laura Brown, the term "primate" only gained momentum post-Linnaeus, and the eighteenth century thus also failed to distinguish New World monkeys from hominoid apes.[17] Londa Schiebinger, to this point, notes that Eurocentric science during the seventeenth and eighteenth centuries "indiscriminately" used "orangutan" (from the Malay portmanteau meaning "wild man" or "man of the woods") to categorize all great apes of Africa and Asia.[18] Tyson evidences this.

Around the same time, some 350 miles away in Amsterdam, the Dutch welcomed a captive orangutan—truly an orangutan this time, given the colonial holdings in the Dutch East Indies (to which my conclusion will return)—to the Blauw Jaw menagerie in the city center. As Robert Crib, Helen Gilbert, and Helen Tiffin write, the Blauw Jaw, as a "clearinghouse for exotic animals," made visible the import of expropriated exotic flora and fauna—especially as menageries, zoos, and curiosities exploded across the continent—for jingoistic colonial goals.[19] Upon the orangutan's death, a social and philosophical melee erupted as to whether the specimen would be subjected to taxidermy or necropsied dissection (and thus medical theatre). The Blauw Jaw orangutan, like the Angolese chimp who died on English soil, thus embodies what Nash reasons as the qualifiable disambiguities among human and nonhuman species, and also the central nexus by which eighteenth-century natural histories and sciences honed their chops.

The fascination with various simian species quickly evolved to represent the ape and its primate kin as a nonhuman menace that exploited human susceptibility. This cultural evolution was begat by the mutual construction (and oftentimes constitution) of natural histories, pseudosciences, and literary fiction that captured the attention of Europe. Consider Voltaire's mid-century *Candide* (1759), which furthers the Enlightenment's lascivious ape rumor-milling. Candide and Cacambo, in a "strange land," stumble upon two women being pursued by two monkeys "biting at their behinds."[20] Always the chivalric hero, Candide shoots the monkeys dead: "'God be praised, my dear Cacambo, I [Candide] have rescued two poor girls from a most perilous situation.'"[21] The humorous and potentially perverse twist is that the monkeys are the women's lovers, information that only comes to light following a shocking outpouring of feminized mourning.

Stedman's diaristic natural history invariably follows suit, which again suggests a discursive crosshatching among literary, historical, and scientific narratives. Stedman's insistence that monkeys are so lascivious that they "sometimes Attack the female of the Human Species" occurs dozens of times in his journal and fans the rumored flames of unbridled simian sexuality.[22] Richard and Sally Price's careful investigation of Stedman's publication history reveals that moments like these, in the 1796 version, were expurgated by Stedman's editors because of issues of "coarseness."[23] While the Prices do not explain why the sexual monkey attack might have been redacted, I read this expurgation as one that perhaps realized the scandalizing nonsense of such a suggestion, but more likely showed great concern for a reading public that might likewise fall prey to the rumored horrors of bestiality. Stedman's editors' intent may be lost to the vagaries of publication history, but the abridgement lasts and consolidates an uneasiness about simian capabilities to potentially resist colonial powers that seek to dominate and inferiorize. In other words: the animal fights back.

The refrain that women and particularly women of color are repeatedly harassed and assaulted by simians develops out of eighteenth-century Europe's commitment to imperial gender-race-sex systems prompted by Galenic humoralism. Echoing the orthodoxy bequeathed from classical epistemologies, Galen's humoralism argued that lechery resulted primarily in women's bodies because of the physiology of the vagina, which was determined to be warmer and thus prone to rampant desirousness. The gender essentialism offered here—that any and all individuals with vaginas are women—is a direct result of a colonial pseudoscience masquerading as biomedicine, which persists today and has rightly been critiqued by María Lugones and Susan Stryker.[24] This humoral logic becomes even more questionable considering racialist implications that paired women of color with insatiable lusts (e.g., the Khoikhoi and other racialized and global Indigenous peoples).[25] Bewick and Long reiterate this anti-Black rhetoric by implying that the female "negroes" abducted by oran-outangs implicitly consent to bestial relations. Amplifying fears of both the uncontrollable lascivious simian as well as the hypersexualized, racialized woman, Bewick and Long typify a twinned racist and animalizing tendency.

But as the century progressed, and because of a desire to differentiate white women from women of color, eighteenth-century authors and natural theorists dismissed the depiction of white women as sexually forward. These depictions were ultimately replaced by stereotypes and socially restrictive mores of purity and sexual repressiveness, which were then ostensibly jeopardized by simian interaction. Allegedly hypersexual in nature, the male ape seems by all accounts to have been unable to control himself around females of any species (not only reifying the sanctity and violence of heteronormativity), thus configuring, in Schiebinger's words, "the wildest fantasies of violent interspecies rape."[26] Hypersexualization becomes a taxonomic characterization that blurs species, race, and gender lines and participates in racist constructions that justify violence, dehumanization, and enslavement. Put simply, the taxonomy of hypersexualization results in material consequences for those rendered as exceeding humanity or insufficiently human.

But, in a strange twist, the natural histories disclose female apes as paradigms of chastity, modesty, and female wholesomeness. Jacob Bontius depicted the young female ape as inspiring admiration because she hid her "'secret parts' with great modesty from unknown men," perhaps best illustrated by Nicolaes Tulp's heavily-circulated depiction of the female orangutan in his *Observationes Medicae* (1641).[27] The primate coyly gazes downwards, her lips likewise turned as if to reflect a coquettish smile, while her two hands rest over her genitals in an effort that seems to conceal them. Tulp's fictive image thus sets into motion an artistic tradition that participated in gendering the simian and, ironically, disordering systems of taxonomy that set out for standardization. For example, Tulp's orangutan was replicated (read: plagiarized) in 1748 by J. V. Schley to commemorate the oblation of an(other) Angolese chimpanzee bestowed upon Frederic, Prince of Orange. George Edwards's copper-plated print of the St. Jago/green monkey likewise illustrates these identical artistic poses alongside the simian. The print details a monkey of indeterminate sex but with an arm drawn across chest and leg akimbo. While the sex of the monkey is hidden by the leg, the accompanying description of this particular monkey aligns it within the same modest and maternal narratives of other natural historians—so much so that it is difficult not to read Edwards as contributing to these species-overlapping constructions of gender and their primatological referents, especially in his work as a fellow of the Royal Society. As Ingrid Tague has shown, Gérard Jean Baptiste Scotin II's "Madame Chimpanzee," popularized by the *Gentleman's Magazine* (September 1738) strikes a nearly identical pose.[28] Madame Chimpanzee likewise covers her nipples and her distended belly eclipses her genitals. The recirculation of these poses and artistic renderings consolidate gender-species systems.

Like Tulp's orangutan, Edwards's depiction seemingly corroborates the fact that the green monkey conceals her—the pronoun used by Edwards—genitals in gestures of inevitable modesty and shame. Edwards writes, "I once had an opportunity of seeing, in the house of the late Duke of Richmond, at Whitehall, an old she Monkey, who had been brought to England with young; and she brought forth a single cub, of which she was very tender. It was pleasant to see her hold it in her arms, and suck it: her actions and manner nearly resembled a woman's nursing her child."[29] While I will return to this admiration of suckling, which rears its head in

George Edwards's St. Jago/green monkey from *Gleanings of Natural History* (1758). (Biodiversity Heritage Library)

Brobdingnag, Edwards waxes poetic about the pleasant sight of this effusion of maternal affection and care. Such an affective rhapsody reinforces the dichotomous positioning of female primates as paradigms for chastity (and desirable constructed notions of womanhood) while doubling-down on the inimical threat that male apes pose in their ostensibly lewd virility. As these natural histories in their narrative leanings indicate, the simian somehow subscribes to these sexual heteronorms and behaviors, which reveal colonial epistemologies and their constructions of gender and sexuality across, within, and despite species lines.

SWIFT, SEXUAL VIOLENCE, AND SATIRE

While disclosures of male primate sexual violence litter eighteenth-century natural histories, literatures, and scandalizing print media, "to my knowledge," Schiebinger writes, "there was not one account in this period of a female ape taking a man or even of intercourse between a female ape and a male ape."[30] For naturalist tracts this may be accurate, but fictionally—and I am suggesting that all of this fearful lore was and is, in fact, fictive[31]—there is an exception: the fourth voyage of Jonathan Swift's *Gulliver's Travels*, wherein Gulliver is nearly raped by a female Yahoo while bathing in a river. My focus here is not to debunk Schiebinger's careful work or even to suggest that female primates, fictional or not, can be rapists too. My goal, instead, is to closely examine this strange and unforgettable moment as one that configures the river as a site of sexual violence where the female Yahoo undermines Gulliver's secure sense of self. Water's queerness enables an epistemological vantage point that can upheave and revise projected histories of animalized gender essentialism and sexuality and, in doing so, reimagine literary primal scenes in which interspecies intimacies are fecund plots for dispossessing masculine hubris and colonial expansion.

Because I directly address sexual violence, it behooves me to contextualize and define what I mean. I do not deploy rape lightly or with the intent to scandalize. Rape is not a metaphor or a metonym. Rarely is Gulliver's riverine interaction with the female Yahoo read as attempted rape, and instead, these moments are repeated indications—so the logic goes—of the novel's satiric leanings. I take up the failures of such a justification below. In recent years, eighteenth-century studies has been invigorated by what Erin Spampinato and Doreen Theirauf have termed "Theorizing the New Rape Studies."[32] Both Frances Ferguson's "Rape and the Rise of the Novel" and Melissa Sanchez's *Erotic Subjects* are essential to this framework and speak to how discourses of rape predate on conventions of "credulity," personhood, and theft of property.[33]

Because I teach classes on censorship in literature as well as eighteenth-century culture, I am all too familiar with the pedagogical implications of "new rape studies." In the classroom, I approach these moments by first, in advance, making my students aware that we will tackle issues of sexual violence that are difficult to stomach. This operates as, but is different than, a trigger warning. I do not downplay the lived realities that make these moments especially unsavory or unpalatable for my students—especially at a campus that experiences higher than statistically average encounters with sexual violence. I reason that to ignore, expurgate, or omit such readings would imply that sexual violence is not real, lived, or encountered habitually. Reading sexual violence should be uncomfortable, not because we need more discomfort in our lives, but because, in my classrooms, the best way to acknowledge this discomfort is by naming it, addressing it, and ensuring we know what it looks like. This goal intends to unseat any apologist standpoints and denounce rape's normalization.

The introduction of the nonhuman animals, I'll admit, makes these conversations about sexual violence murkier. And yet eighteenth-century natural histories certainly do not shy away from these murky encounters, especially in the narrative pattern by which women of color are repeatedly subject to primate sexual assault. I thus use "attempted rape" and "sexual assault" to identify Gulliver's encounters with the female Yahoo, despite the fact that Gulliver does not name it as such. His repeated bodily violation, commenced in Brobdingnag with the elephantine court monkey, reaches a horrific sexual pinnacle when he unsuccessfully responds to the Yahoo mating ritual (despite his awareness of said ritual) and thus becomes brutalized precisely because of his lack of consent—an issue I explore at greater length in my conclusion, "Sea Monsters." Interspecies violation and attempted rape thus become repeatedly insinuated in the broader matrix of *Travels*, and their repetition demand critical inquiry, not expurgation.

By looking to moments of sexual violence between Gulliver and his simian interlocutors, I am not interested in espousing sexual violence as somehow intrinsically queer. Such a jejune reading would only replicate social violences. Instead, the nontraditional queer reading I fashion based on my discussion of Gulliver's sexual assault corresponds with Declan Kavanagh and Ula Klein's acknowledgment that Swift's works have largely escaped queer attention, despite the staggering queer potentiality that his oeuvre embodies. The two observe, "Swift's invective serves to remind us of the inherent queer potential of the satiric mode: its ability to twist and bend tacitly accepted ideologies out of shape."[34] By generic conventions, satire ostensibly justifies or lessens the very real moments of pain, danger, and violence that I trace below. My queer reading of Swift's simian-human entanglement seeks to model how these intimacies upend structures of heteronormativity, while attending to the material conditions of sexual violence and interspecies intimacies.

Satire does not justify sexual violence; it certainly doesn't make sexual violence any less real or material. Michael F. Suarez notes that Swift's satire in particular is centrally about "what it means to be a person."[35] Swiftian Menippean satire, Suarez continues, intends "to educate our capacity for critical reflection on the human condition and, hence, to enlarge our capacity for humanity."[36] With this in mind (and it is important to note that Suarez does not broach the potential-Yahoo-attempted-rape moment) the satire of Gulliver's interaction with the lustful female Yahoo is entirely unclear. The fact that this moment has been mostly eclipsed in reflections on Swiftian satire suggests to me that if, as Suarez contends, satire attempts to apprehend the humanness/personness of humanity, then the interaction with the Yahoo befuddles that even further. Laura Brown is one of very few who has explicitly responded to this moment and envisions it (following H. W. Hanson) as an extension of the "ape-rape" mythos. "Male and female sexual roles are reversed in Swift's version of the anecdote," Brown writes, "and as a consequence African and European identities are superimposed so that Gulliver occupies the position of both male and female, African and European at once." As influential as Brown's readings are, my concern is that this one demands we see substitutive and elided racial and gendered admixtures. I do not. There remains an implicit presumption that sexual violation (at least in this continued mythos) is predicated on being an African woman. Beilby, Bewick, and Long assuredly attend to this, so there are historical justifications for such a reading. However, this presumption, at best, articulates a desperately necessary focal point for eighteenth-century studies and literature to take up the intersectional issues of race, gender, and sexuality. At its worst, Gulliver is cast into both blackface and two genders with which he does not identify. My reading thus accounts for how Gulliver's encounter with the female Yahoo queerly imagines a violent interspecies intimacy and yet does not remove either the Yahoo or Gulliver from their genders or alleged races.[37]

My symptomatic readings of the Brobingnagian monkey and the Yahoo do not disregard the satirical veil of Gulliver's adventures, but I am not convinced that Swift offers a parodic perspective on sexual violence just for *shits and giggles,* a deliberate pun I use to recognize that Gulliver's introduction to Houyhnhnmland is welcomed by fecal throwing and (humorous) humiliation by the Yahoos, and also apropos given Haraway's invitation of becoming-with, which induces "unexpected collaborations and combinations, in *hot compost piles.*"[38] Instead, the satire apparent within Gulliver's interaction with the female Yahoo is one that unsettles, in John Bullitt's conception, the endeavor "to arouse moral action"; "expose men's vices in shameful and ludicrous ways"; and feature the pain that accompanies "man's natural and innate desire for superiority."[39] Swift's satirical valence assuredly destabilizes the seemingly finite borders between humanity and animality. It is a satirical question that, with a blank stare, asks for the audience's reconsideration of what constitutes humanity and the human, especially in instinctive moments of lust, passion, and misrecognition. Laura Baudot soundly notes: "Writing about Swift's satire is difficult. It is difficult to build an argument flexible enough to accommodate the splenetic restlessness of Swift's satire—a restlessness that refuses to settle too comfortably into any one intellectual or moral position."[40] In echoing Baudot's concerns for approaching Swift's tangled satire, I do not write off these incidents as satire for the sake of satire, that is to say, bereft of any metareflective qualities. I read and emphasize these encounters as "real"—and really threatening to Gulliver in ways that demonstrate his vulnerability and therefore speak to his particular model of masculinity: the presumption of infallible awareness and the privilege of a (presupposed) impenetrable body.

SWIFTIAN SIMIANS: PART ONE

While Gulliver's immodest encounter in the fourth voyage may reveal one thing about anthropoid simians in Swift's novel, it is important to remember that there are two monkey anecdotes located in *Travels*. The oft-forgotten one occurs during Gulliver's second voyage to Brobdingnag—the inversion of Lilliput, the Brobdingnagians are giants—where he is nearly nurtured to death by a pet monkey. Despite his menial size and his own pet-like capacities in Brobdingnag, Gulliver refers to his congress with the monkey as "the greatest Danger I ever underwent in that Kingdom."[41] Gulliver's experience as a pet,[42] one that comes with being shown about like some side attraction, resonates with the first chimpanzee from Angola that arrived in England in 1698. Gulliver writes: "My Master's Design was to show me in all the Towns by the way, and to step out of the Road for fifty or an hundred Miles, to any Village or Person of Quality's House where he might expect Custom . . . She [his Brobdingnagian nurse] often took me out of my Box at my own Desire, to give me Air, and to show me the Country, but always held me fast by a Leading-string."[43] Gulliver's admission that he was "shown in eighteen large Towns besides many Villages and private Families" narrativizes a potential "it-narrative," a genre of popularity for eighteenth-century fiction, in which an ordinary object or thing anthropomorphically is given voice.[44] But this it-narrative gives say to Gulliver, the pet—a perspective we can imagine to be like the Angolan chimpanzee's—who is, in Brobdingnag, mistaken for a monkey by a monkey ("I have good reason to believe that he took me for a young one of his own Species") and is later understood in Houyhnhnmland to be a refined Yahoo, or primate species member.[45] This invocation of "species" becomes even more troubled given that, as Harriet Ritvo reminds us, the term is bound up in heteroreproductivity: a species is identified by the ability to generatively and successfully reproduce fertile offspring.[46] Gulliver stymies this in both Brobdingnag and Houyhnhnmland. He balks at the insinuation of his own fellow simian qualities and fails the reproductive litmus test that might characterize species compatibility. Species becomes then, by Swift's handling, irremediably bungled.

Yet Gulliver's horror in Brobdingnag is not that he has become a pet that is gifted from Brobdingnagian bumpkin to Brobdingnagian royalty.[47] He accepts this fate—his enslavement—tout à fait: "She asked whether I would be content to live at Court. I bowed down to the board of the Table, and humbly answered that I was my Master's Slave, but if I were at my own Disposal, I should be proud to devote my life to her Majesty's Service."[48] Gulliver's greatest terror realized stems from being accosted by the Court's pet monkey. Lorbrulgrud, the Brobdingnagian seat of power, is replete with animals, and Gulliver narrates his interaction with rats, the cat, the gardener's spaniel, flies, frogs, and a linnet. The monkey poses the greatest threat because of its verisimilitude. The monkey's voyeurism—that it can see and behold him—frightens Gulliver. He repines, "I saw this frolicsome Animal, frisking and leaping up and down till at last he came to my Box, which he seemed to view with great Pleasure and Curiosity, peeping in at the Door and every Window."[49] The monkey's curiosity, spurred by scopophilic pleasures, is the cause of Gulliver's dismay. Gulliver recognizes the monkey as being able to experience "great Pleasure and Curiosity," and this recognition of nonhuman pleasure comes back to bite him in the ass, almost literally, in his fourth voyage. Gulliver observes a simian desire, one that pairs curiosity with eroticism, and this monkey craves touching Gulliver. The monkey's fascination with Gulliver demands a tactile interaction; it is not enough to just behold Gulliver in his box, he must hold him. And this spurs Gulliver's fear for his own safety and a fear of being treated the way he has subjected animal others.

The fear of hybridity is primal for Gulliver, as it was for eighteenth-century naturalists, whose scientifically motivated colonial expansion sought out interspecies miscegenation. Jean-Jacques Rousseau, for instance, set out to confirm (and failed to corroborate) the myth that "women of Africa and Asia 'mixed' voluntarily or through force with male apes, and that the products of these unions had entered into both species."[50] Ann Cline Kelly locates this fascination as both a scientific one and also one that titillated a larger reading public: "Hybrid individuals who defy species categorization were of interest not only to the Royal Society and but [sic] also to the general public, whose love of the 'strange and wonderful' encouraged the popular press to headline unnatural linkages and amalgams that simultaneously proved the rule of the Chain of Being and contested it."[51] Swift, while not in direct conversation with Rousseau (whose fame would come later in the century), satirically plays with the larger cultural concern of hybridity. By inverting the genders in his own fiction—women of Africa and Asia are not the recipients of primate attempted rape, while a white, male colonizer is—Swift demonstrates the porosity of Gulliver's masculinity in a topsy-turvy world. Gulliver's self-governance is jeopardized by the Brobdingnagian monkey and the female Yahoo because they exert themselves upon him in a way that forces him to concede.

Swift assures the reader that any such attempt to crossbreed, while failed, is still deeply troubling. In other words, in *Gulliver's Travels*, the procreative moment—that is, the congress between simian and human—is foreclosed, and with it, following Ritvo, the potentiality for species compatibility. After the monkey absconds with him, Gulliver describes that "he took me up in his right forefoot and held me as a Nurse does a Child she is going to suckle."[52] Gulliver's Brobdingnagian keeper interrupts this queerly maternal feeding, and Gulliver does not suckle from the male monkey.[53] Instead, the monkey, in fleeing those attempting to capture it, "holding me like a Baby in one of his forepaws," begins to force-feed Gulliver.[54] The maternally male monkey maintains the necessary foresight and awareness to realize that his ersatz baby, Gulliver, will not breastfeed.[55] The monkey then resorts to satiating his forged infant's hunger by hand, to the concerns of the Brobdingnagian court.

After the people pelt the monkey with stones, Gulliver falls and, with the help of his nurse, vomits. Gulliver deliberately and forcefully rejects the monkey's attempt to hybridize: "I was almost choked with the filthy stuff the Monkey had crammed down my Throat; but, my dear little Nurse picked it out of my Mouth with a small Needle, and then I feel a Vomitting, which gave me great relief."[56] The monkey seeks to suture his body to Gulliver's—to mix bodily fluids with generative, nurturing possibility. But Gulliver refuses. He staunches the monkey's infantilizing gestures (though he does not refuse infantilization by the other Brobdingnagians) as a means of solidifying a pure sense of humanness and recuperating his lost masculine autonomy. The monkey's force-feeding must be rejected, but the phallic needle is welcomed. He recognizes the monkey as perverse and nonhuman and thus must vomit any trace of the monkey. Like Crusoe before him, emetic behavior works to disassociate while at the same time concretizing one's binarized understandings of self and alien.[57] Gulliver's emesis foretells the monkey's demise: "The Monkey was killed, and an Order made that no such Animal shall be kept about the Palace."[58] These two moments occur within the same paragraph. Gulliver here models what close interactions with monkeys must foretell: expulsion and violent jettisoning. The death of the monkey also ensures that no other hybrids can occur in Brobdingnag, and Gulliver becomes, once and for all, top dog/monkey.

The monkey, though, does not die there in Brobdingnag; the crisis instigated by this comically threatening scene lives on. Upon recovering from the trauma, Gulliver convenes with the King of Brobdingnag, who asks him how he might have handled this situation in England. Gulliver replies:

> I told his Majesty, that in Europe we had no Monkeys, except such as were brought from Curiosities from other Places, and so small, that I could deal with a dozen of them together, if they presumed to attack me. And as for that monstrous Animal with whom I was so lately engaged (it was indeed as large as an Elephant), if my Fears had suffered me to think so far as to make use of my Hanger (looking fiercely and clapping my Hand upon the Hilt as I spoke) when he poked his paw into my Chamber, perhaps I should have given him such a Wound, as would have made him glad to withdraw it with more haste than he put it in.[59]

Gulliver explains his failure to protect himself as a result of his "Fears" of the monkey. But in imagining what he would have done, what implicitly underscores Gulliver's words is his own penetrability. The monkey is monstrous not because of its size—everything is giant in Brobdingnag, Gulliver accepts this—but in his seemingly defenseless state, the maternally male monkey attempts to penetrate Gulliver, and he implicitly recognizes this violation as a potential assault: "he poked his paw into my Chamber." In what assuredly feels as a self-aggrandizing gesture meant to recuperate his threatened masculinity, Gulliver imagines giving the monkey "such a wound" as to prevent the simian's hasty, violating insertion. In Brobdingnag, like in Houyhnhmnland, the monkeys penetrate; whereas in England, Gulliver's native place, the monkeys embody the penetrated: "I could deal with a dozen of them together, if they presumed to attack me." The satiric humor here, in characteristically Swiftian style, is the reader's awareness that Gulliver's presumptive "if" *has* already occurred. The Brobdingnagian monkey has already attacked him, and the Yahoo in Houyhnhnmland will ape this behavior. Gulliver's macho-babble projects a superior image of himself, which reinforces the situational irony of the moment. Yet, Gulliver recognizes the penetrating abilities of simians while also attempting to reconfigure his own, tarnished masculine patina.

SWIFTIAN SIMIANS, AGAIN

Inasmuch that Gulliver deplores the Brobdingnag monkey, he must too vehemently disdain the Yahoos: "Upon the whole, I never beheld in all my Travels so disagreeable an animal, nor one against which I naturally conceived so strong an Antipathy."[60] While Gulliver complains repeatedly about the officious nature of the Yahoos—"the more I came near them, the more hateful they grew"—the apparent danger for Gulliver, like with the Brobdingnag monkey, is a series of displacements and misrecognition. In bathing in the river, Gulliver enflames the desire of a female Yahoo, which gives way to a disastrous misrecognition that ultimately befuddles desire and understandings of self, other, and species. Gulliver fears the displacement of self that accompanies the threatening interaction, which dislocates his erstwhile masculinity.

The muddied relationality between Gulliver and the Yahoo finds a home in the river, corresponding with Margaret Cohen's revelations of riverine waters that "give this tension [the dichotomy between home and abroad] elemental form as it derives its distinctive muddy aspect from the home-bound earth found in riverbanks and riverbed, mixed with the river's water that flows to the open oceans."[61] The river, for Cohen as for geologists and environmental scientists, is an aqueous arterial waterway that blends and borrows the sea's aqueous and semiotic nature. I read the muddiness of the river's silt and sediment to foster the entangled violent tensions that occur near or in the river, by making these interactions opaque. As with Charles Darwin's vision of the bank, painted with cornucopian beauty—"from so simple a beginning endless forms most beautiful and most wonderful have been, and are being evolved"—the wonder of these entanglements also lies in their different forms of touch and interaction, which are ostensibly muddied by both entanglement and surrounding.[62]

Gulliver cries upon witnessing the Yahoo up close, "My Horror and Astonishment are not to be described, when I observed, in this abominable Animal, a perfect human Figure; the Face of it indeed was flat and broad, the Nose depressed, the Lips large, and the mouth wide."[63] Gulliver holds the Yahoos' figuration with "Horror and Astonishment" only because under the veil of deeply seated hate exists "a perfect human Figure." Gulliver's disdain arises from the Yahoos' uncanny resemblance to himself, "to which I owned my Resemblance in every part," and those with whom he is familiar, especially in Houyhnhnmland, where there are no proto- or pseudohumans.[64] Gulliver's masculine identity is predicated on his exceptionalism throughout his adventures: in Lilliput he is the largest, in Brobdingnag he is the smallest, in Luggnag he is the only mortal, in Houyhnhnmland he is the only anthropoid, and so on. In resembling the Yahoos, Gulliver's exceptionalism, which informs and invigorates his masculinity, is thwarted.

The queering of Gulliver's masculinity accompanies his admission that the Yahoo is both "a perfect human Figure" and an "abominable Animal," a metacognitive reflexivity that undercuts his exceptionalism and projects a self-hatred. Like the maternal monkey that with disastrous results coddles Gulliver, his sojourn in Houyhnhnmland forces a radical reconceptualization of a self that is no longer independent, singular, and indomitable. This moment, Brown contends, canonically represents "the complex and reciprocal relationship between the attack on human superiority and the development of racialist thinking . . . and the most widely read version of the miscegenation story."[65] The toxic self-hatred that reorients the masculine colonizer's understanding of self and other surfaces again in Stedman's *Narrative*.

As with the Brobdingnagian monkey, Gulliver proves yet again unable to staunch the Yahoo's attempts at hybridizing, and the river is the stage for this failed mating ritual. Enjoying a particularly warm day with the accompaniment of his protector, the Sorrel Nag, Gulliver strips and bathes in a river. Sadly for Gulliver, the trope of simian voyeurism carries itself from Brobdingnag to Hoynhnhnmland:

> It happened that a young Female Yahoo standing behind a Bank, saw the whole proceeding, and enflamed by Desire, as the Nag and I conjectured, came running with all speed, and leaped into the Water within five Yards of the Place where I bathed. I was never in my life so terribly frighted . . . She embraced me after a most fulsome manner; I roared as loud as I could, and the Nag came galloping towards me, whereupon she quit my Grasp, with the utmost Reluctancy, and leaped upon the opposite Bank, where she stood gazing and howling all the time I was putting on my Clothes.[66]

Simian voyeurism is a conduit by which Gulliver's body becomes brutalized—a conceit that the novel recycles. With his seeming panopticism, Gulliver and the Sorrel Nag are attentive to the "whole proceeding," and yet, in another failure, Gulliver is unable to properly prepare for the impending attack. In a hyperbolic repetition originally attributed to the Brobdingnagian monkey—"I was never in my life so terribly frighted"—Gulliver characterizes the lascivious Yahoo's embrace as "fulsome." Etymologically rich, *fulsome*, in this context, can describe both the moral reprehensibility of the action (which Gulliver intends) or the "corpulent, oversized, and overfed" quality of the embrace.[67] Thereby the Yahoo's potentially doubled fulsome embrace emphasizes the excessive and entangled nature of graphic touch. For Gulliver, this is an attempted bestial rape, which ultimately fails, but not without effect. Gulliver's rejection of the Yahoo's fulsomeness paints the embrace as one that is not only unwelcomed and uncomfortable but also brutal and forceful.

The intensity of the touch is so disorientating that it causes Gulliver to fumble his retelling. Whereas the female Yahoo is originally the aggressor, when the Nag comes to save the day, Gulliver unwittingly implies that he has reciprocated the aggressive touching. "She quit my Grasp," of course, intends to suggest that the female Yahoo finally releases Gulliver, and yet his literal phrasing reveals the opposite. The prepositional phrase "with the utmost reluctancy" maintains an ambiguous subject, and given that it immediately follows the uncertainty of who was touching whom, it literally reads one of two ways: Gulliver was unwilling to release the Yahoo, or the Yahoo was unwilling to be released. In both situations, consent is uncertain, and since both Gulliver and the female Yahoo "roar" and "howl," respectively, it is unclear whether these animalizing onomatopoeia are gestures of pleasure or pain.

Donna Haraway's invocation of interspecies entanglement identifies expressions of tactility, which are framed by Gulliver and the female Yahoo as an integral component of "becoming-with." Haraway writes: "Touch ramifies and shapes accountability. Touch does not make one small; it peppers its partners with the attachment sites for world making. Touch, regard, looking back, becoming with—all these make us responsible in unpredictable ways for which worlds take shape. In touch and regard, partners willy nilly are in the miscegenous mud that infuses our bodies with all that brought that contact into being. Touch and regard have consequences."[68] While Haraway's mission proposes a positive, sustained dimension to touch and subsequent world-building, this is not the case for Gulliver and the Yahoo. The haptic fulsomeness staged in the river gives birth to bastardized consequences that develop from Haraway's conception of touch. Gulliver's general repulsion of the Yahoo touch suggests that in Houyhnhnmland certain forms of touch are licit and others are illicit. Michael Franklin has made a similar observation by noticing that the Houyhnhnm Master deigns to allow Gulliver to kiss his hoof.[69] Gulliver can, then, seemingly touch all he wants, but beware those who attempt to touch him. The privilege of touch is thus fundamental to his construction and presentation of masculinity. For Gulliver, to be untouchable is to ensure a static, incorruptible sense of self coincident with an impenetrable masculinity. The Yahoo's transgressive embrace proves to test the boundaries of this masculine façade.

The riverine moment, however, highlights other failures on Gulliver's part. Before the Yahoo's violating caresses, Gulliver, almost as foreshadowing, preempts the scene with the Houyhnhnm Master's ethnographic observation of Yahoo sexual behavior: "His Honour had further observed, that a Female Yahoo would often stand behind a Bank or a Bush, to gaze on the young Males passing by, and then appear, and hide, using many antic Gestures and Grimaces, at which time it was observed, that she had a most *offensive Smell;* and when any of the Males advanced, would slowly retire, looking often back, and with a counterfeit show of Fear, run off into some convenient Place where she knew the Male would follow her."[70] Not only does Gulliver's prefatory inclusion foretell his attempted sexual assault at the hands of the female Yahoo, but it also locates the "bank" as the site for Yahoo breeding rituals.[71] The bank, of course, abuts the river, and yet in Swift's novel the river goes mostly unexplained and underdeveloped because it is an ancillary setting detail. As the present analysis reveals, it's not.

Invaluably, it is on the "entangled" (river)bank that Charles Darwin famously closes *On the Origin of Species* (1859): "It is interesting to contemplate an entangled bank, clothed with many plants of many kinds, with birds singing on the bushes, with various insects flitting about, and with worms crawling through the damp earth, and to reflect that these elaborately constructed forms, so different from each other, and dependent on each other in so complex a manner, have all been produced by laws acting around us."[72] Darwin's bank teems with layered life that epitomizes struggle, engagement, and dependence "in so complex a manner"—perhaps *fulsome* would work equally well, as a synonym for *complex*. And while my use of Darwin may appear anachronistic, the description of the riverbank, which homes "flitting" and "crawling" entanglements, is precisely what Swift orients. In Houyhnhnmland, we experience a Darwinian prehistory. The only difference is that Swift's riverbank is transmuted in violence in Gulliver's recognition that he and the Yahoo are "so different from each other." In Houyhnhmland, the messiness of the river fosters the messiness of Gulliver's interaction with the Yahoo, an incident that displaces desire, touch, and stable understandings of the masculine body.

Even more, this short but visceral moment between Gulliver and the female Yahoo offers the violating encounter as one in which Gulliver's rationality and literacy collectively fail. Gulliver is told firsthand that the female Yahoo awaits her mate alongside the riverbank, emitting a pungent odor, and then waits for her mate to follow her for copulation. Gulliver fails to realize that this is the Yahoo's intent. The disastrous misrecognition hinges on the admission of conjecturing, an acknowledgment that realizes a failed inference or logic. Attributing the attack to the Yahoo's "enflamed Desire," Gulliver models the lewd uncontrollability of the female Yahoo while underscoring his own erotic zeal. He is so taken with himself that he is hubristically assured of his sexual effervescence and allure. Such a hubris is ironic and humorous given that the female Yahoo begins the mating ritual dance with the assumption that Gulliver is in fact a Yahoo.

The female Yahoo charges at Gulliver based on this faulty presumption, but Gulliver equally fails to recognize the female Yahoo's phenomenologically communicative attempts, which include body language as well as sensory expressions. Gulliver, who prides himself on his polyglot abilities and his affinity for Houyhnhnm rationalism, fails in reading the signs of a species to which he is most akin: "For now I could no longer deny, that I was a real Yahoo, in every Limb and Feature, since the Females had a natural Propensity to me as one of their own Species."[73] The moment of attempted sexual violation brings Gulliver to a closer realization of self—I can no longer deny that I am not a Yahoo[74]—but also characterizes the riverbank as the locale for this epiphany. Franklin acknowledges that in the fourth voyage both the Houyhnhnms and Gulliver become tangled in "misrecognition and misreading," but "it is only civilized Gulliver who resorts to violence."[75] The disorientation spurred by misreading demonstrates that, for Gulliver, his only option for recuperation manifests through violence. In the river, where Gulliver intends to clean himself, he purges himself of self-denial and comes to exhibit a cracked, self-righteous masculine patina. This is brought about, almost as emollient, by the Yahoo's attempted violation, which Gulliver is just barely able to shake. Such depictions of the river reveal a strange irony: Gulliver only enters the river to cleanse himself, which suggests that the riverine waters, originally meant to purify, inevitably malign too. The mediation of these antinomies is part and parcel of water's queerness and its violent displacements.

MONKEYING STEDMAN

In tandem, the river and the monkey return, enmeshed in reverberating violence, in John Gabriel Stedman's *The Narrative of a Five Years Expedition against the Revolted Negroes of Surinam* (1796). The moment in which Stedman maims and murders a monkey is perhaps the most striking one—Stedman himself refers to it as a "Catastrophe"—despite the fact that the narrative abounds with similar moments of human and nonhuman slaughter, violence, and torture.[76] What endures about *this* particular moment is the explicit and intentional drowning of the monkey in the river, where Stedman intends to eliminate the monkey's gaze—something Gulliver fails to do. Through monkey murder, Stedman reifies anthropocentric, especially (Dutch) colonial, violence as something with which to reckon. Emily Senior sums up the text's negotiation of violence: "While much of the *Narrative* describes violence against slaves, this passage portrays Stedman reenacting colonial violence upon the monkey—the next best thing, it appears, to an African."[77] Senior's larger claim is one that exposes the porosity of skin, racialized enslaved skin in particular, and while I am wary of Senior's analogous monkey-African collapse, the violent, disorienting mediation of touch between human and nonhuman skin is apposite here. To remedy the disorientation begat by simian interaction, Stedman must annihilate the monkey to naturalize a hierarchy conditioned by anthroparchy. Yet Stedman's reflective reaction to his violent actions destabilize this hierarchy and reveal the exchange between monkey and man as once again demonstrating how violent touch generates experiences of pain that are immersive yet iniquitous.

The fact that this interaction occurs in yet another river suggests that this site is one in which exchange is inevitable and power relations become, to quote Haraway, "miscegenous."[78] The river complicates Stedman's colonial exploration in that it, one, remains a primary conduit to spread the disease of colonialism, and two, is crowded with exotic flora and fauna, to which Stedman is painstakingly attentive, rendering his *Narrative* one that blends ethological, botanical, and natural sciences in the metaphoric colonial vat.

In their trenchant introduction to Stedman's *Narrative*, written some two hundred years after the journal's publication, Richard Price and Sally Price situate Stedman, as both author and narrator, in a glowing, nearly deified light. The Prices regard Stedman as possessing "empathy for all creatures," even at an early age, and cast him as a victim forced to bear witness to the atrocities in Suriname.[79] This phrase may better characterize Stedman's relationship with Joanna, his Suriname wife, who he is unable to manumit, but in my reading the narrative is not characterized by overwhelming empathy—a loose, almost broken, myopic, and self-serving buzzword that has received its appropriate criticisms.[80] He is there, after all, to violently curtail a revolt of marooned enslaved peoples; his diaristic entries do not excuse his complicities. Curiously enough, the Prices use the exact moment on which I want to focus—the killing of the monkey—to highlight Stedman's affinity for empathy. In summarizing the effect of the monkey murder on Stedman, they write, "He recounted how, in the rain forest, after shooting but not killing a monkey, he was forced to put the animal out of its misery with his bare hands."[81] Stedman, it would seem, is troublingly affected by his own actions and seemingly forced to execute his crime out of some gesture of mercy.

While I disagree with the Prices' characterization of Stedman's actions in this moment as somehow beneficent and warranted, their introductory materials make clear the importance of touch for Stedman and his nonhuman interlocutors. As Haraway reminds us, the attachment made possible by touch forges world-making possibilities that are inscribed in our communication with nonhumans and generate an unequivocal becoming-with. But Stedman's tactile interaction with the monkey does not feel merciful; rather, Stedman's touch is violent—one that is intent on killing—and intends to eliminate the monkey's looking-back, or a type of animalized recognition that preys on Stedman's emotionality.[82] The monkey haunts Stedman, even in its death, which further destabilizes the human-nonhuman power hierarchy and underscores the constitution of their interaction.

Debbie Lee argues that Blake's engravings of the monkeys symbolize a larger abolitionist sentiment on both Stedman's and Blake's parts that suggests that Stedman's narrative description of the monkeys and Blake's decision to engrave them "outweighs its otherwise trivial place" in the

Detail from *The Mecoo and Kishee Kishee Monkeys*, William Blake. (National Gallery of Art)

narrative.[83] Lee's suggestion regarding Stedman's abolitionist politics aside, I find that the monkeys that hang, as illustrated by Blake, so jovially over the river have more than symbolic value: Stedman's interaction with the monkey exposes a serious threat to his colonizing mission, and this is magnified by the violent entanglement that occurs in the river.[84]

In August of his first year in Suriname, Stedman and the Surinamese hunting crew set out to hunt monkeys, a particular delicacy. Stedman, mindful of his reading public, offers a caveat to his European readers: "however uncommon and Strange it may appear [that is, eating monkeys] to the reader I had nevertheless found to be extremely good, while this may be owing in part to my being in Want of other fresh provisions."[85] It is here, along the river, and poised between the search for food and colonial exploration, that the Stedman-monkey encounter unfurls. The haunting anecdote is worth quoting at length:

> Seeing me on the side of the river in the canoe, the creature made a halt from skipping after his companions, and being perched on a branch that hung over the water, examined me with attention, and the strongest marks of curiosity: no doubt, taking me for a giant of his own species; while he chattered prodigiously, and kept dancing and shaking the bough on which he rested with incredible strength and agility. At this time I laid my piece on my shoulder, and brought him down from the tree into the stream;—but may I never again be a witness to such a scene! The miserable animal was not dead, but mortally wounded. I seized him by the tail, and taking it in both my hands to end his torment, swung him round, and hit his head against the side of the canoe; but the poor creature still continued alive, and looked at me in the most affecting manner that can be conceived, I knew no other means to end this murder, than to hold him under water till he was drowned, while my heart felt sick on his account: for his dying little eyes still continued to follow me with seeming reproach, till their light forsook them, and the wretched animal expired.[86]

The monkey's observation of Stedman cannot be overlooked, nor can Stedman's realization, like Gulliver's, that the monkey must take the narrator to be "a giant of his own species." Recognition, or rather misrecognition, unfolds between the monkey and Stedman. While we may question the reliability of Stedman's narration, what remains is an implicit projection in that Stedman believes the monkey to assume that he is, in fact, a relative species. Perhaps in monkey-face, Stedman's narration uncovers his own uneasiness with simian similitude. Because Stedman is both our narrator and protagonist (like Gulliver), his painstaking retelling of this moment heightens this disorienting encounter.

The monkey appears to find safety in Stedman's physical similarity, but that safety is immediately broken alongside the corresponding gaze. The passage's movement suggests that the locked eye-contact incites Stedman's attempt to shoot and kill the monkey: it is unsettling and uncomfortable, and must be stopped. Gulliver's own experiences as voyeured subject anticipate the destabilizing effect of being watched, especially by the simian, that appear here. Whereas the monkey "chattered prodigiously" as perhaps an attempt to communicate, Stedman eschews any form of communication by immediately reaching for his weapon: "At this time I laid my piece on my shoulder." The monkey intends to use verbal communication; Stedman intends to weaponize violence. The breakdown of communication and the posturing of violence following miscommunication are both mainstays of colonial histories and the contact zone.[87] Unable to kill the monkey with a single shot (Stedman's subsequent interaction with an anaconda, which I discuss elsewhere, proves he is a poor shot altogether) the monkey falls into the stream, where Stedman is forced to "witness" his own actions following his failed aim. Blake's engraving of the "Monkee-Monkee" (squirrel monkey) provides one possible, though unintentional, visualization of the deathly descent. Stedman is witness to his own actions, perhaps an endeavor to indemnify himself of the further violence that he will enact.

We see then two juxtaposed moments of failure in these beginning lines: the monkey's failed attempt to communicate echoed by Stedman's failed attempt to murder. Together these failures make possible the traumatic touch that follows when Stedman and his hunting party attempt to retrieve the monkey from the river. Stedman announces: "The miserable animal was not dead, but mortally wounded." In this pronouncement, Stedman seemingly removes the monkey from its animality—"the miserable animal"—by relocating the monkey's status as something that has become "mortally wounded." Of course, Stedman means to suggest that the shot kills the monkey. But it doesn't. Why else would he need to drown it? The etymology of "mortal," as a noun, refers first and foremost to "a person" or, more suggestively, "one who is destined to die."[88] The *Oxford English Dictionary*'s insistence on a person, rather than an entity, object, or animal, is especially aligned with Stedman's narration, positioning the monkey as potential nonanimal (freed from the alleged shackles of animality) but also "one who is destined to die." The adverbial form of the word, as used by Stedman, strengthens such a reading. As early as Chaucer, "mortally" referred to an attempt "to bring about the death of an adversary" and characterized an "inextricable connect[ion] with human mortality." In this way, Stedman's depiction of the monkey as "mortally wounded" elevates the monkey to an adversary that must die, but more importantly, to an adversary unbound by the inferiority of animality. It is almost as if the monkey's misrecognition of Stedman is contagious and forces Stedman to also misrecognize. Through misrecognition and consequent failures of identification, the liminal borders by which to apprehend the human-simian divide become even more opaque.

Following the initial injury, Stedman realizes that he has incompletely killed the monkey, and violently erotic resonances blossom. What follows may appear as some form of eighteenth-century mercy killing (if we believe the Prices), but I find Stedman's action to induce exacerbative pain rather than palliative care. Seizing the monkey's tail by two hands, Stedman bashes the monkey's head against the canoe. The erotic touch that transpires here becomes colored by pain. In tracing the appearance of the monkey through early modernity, Gordon Williams reads the monkey as a "figure of lust," undoubtedly in mode with the natural histories traced above, and the monkey tail as a symbol for the penis.[89] Such an invocation allows for the violent interaction to also map out erotic possibility for Stedman ("I seized him by the tail"), which reveals a grammatical form of simian congress that Gulliver actively foreclosed. By grasping the monkey's tail with both hands, Stedman reaches for this phallus and intends to eradicate its symbolism and existence entirely. The monkey's tail is the means to destroying the monkey altogether. Stedman's queer grasp of the phallus works to position the monkey as one vulnerable to harm and emasculation, while at the same time reasserting Stedman's masculinity as one of strength and impregnability.

Stedman may successfully emasculate the monkey, but the monkey's gaze reflects "the most affecting manner that can be conceived." Even more, the monkey's tail, "it," is grasped to "end his torment." Both the "it" and "torment" are ambiguous here. First, while we may reasonably infer the "it" as the monkey, the immediately preceding grammatical object refers to the monkey's tail. Stedman must fully grasp the monkey's priapic tail as a means of vacating its penetrative capabilities, which reveal the penetrating gaze that the simian can induce. Stedman performs a symbolic castration. Almost ironically, however, this castration is then extended to Stedman in that the (mis)recognition between the two creates an unsettling interrelational bond. By castrating the monkey, he commits a self-castration foreshadowed by the ocular misrecognitions that foil literacy. (Pardon this Freudianism). And it is this castration that triggers an aqueous death. The "torment" highlighted here is, arguably, not only the monkey's physical anguish and pain but also the torment the monkey can impart. We witness the multivalent capacities of violent touch and also the iniquitous, intersubjective markings that are performed. Stedman's symbolic castration of the monkey voids the simian penchant for penetration. Removing his hands from the tail, Stedman struggles to strangle the monkey underwater, which he himself qualifies as "murder"—a violent category that often precludes animals. The river then becomes the site not only for Stedman's graphic emasculation but also an arena for violation, as was the case with Gulliver, murder, and the ruptures of speciation.

The monkey's gaze, which opens Stedman's anecdote, follows Stedman, even underwater, and becomes overlapped with queer, mythic associations. The gaze is amphibious in this way and even permeates the river's fluidity in that "his dying little eyes still continued to follow me with seeming reproach." Stedman admits that this scene causes him heartsickness, and I read this sickness as one configured by misrecognition and amplified by needless violence. The reflective nature of the monkey's and Stedman's gaze through the river resonates with the myth of Narcissus—another death by the riverbank—which similarly positions the river as a consuming reflection that portends catastrophe. Stedman's account of the monkey mirrors the Ovidian mythos. As Steven Bruhm opines, Ovid's capitulation of Narcissus is endowed with a "queerly disruptive paradigm" that derives from an originary same-sex desire (with Echo, who embodies the anguish of the beloved). Ovid transposes this narrative with a decidedly heteronormative slant, albeit with the effect that such a mythic transposition is, Bruhm notes, "dazzling and confusing in the way it both conflates and separates desiring subjects, desiring objects, objects and subjects of desire."[90] The amphibious gaze staged between the monkey and Stedman replicates the Narcissus-Echo transposition and furthers the queer layering by incorporating this interspecies, affectively-charged tête-à-tête. The lack of sound noted by Stedman and uttered by the monkey points to the unspeakable nature of such a violation; Echo, in other words, is nowhere to be found to commemorate the loss.

Stedman, strangely though, does not mention the turbulent waves or ripples that must accompany such violence performed in water. What he does emphasize—almost unbelievably—is a clear ability to see the monkey's eyes despite the intermediary water layer. It is as if, without the turbulent ripples, this monkey murder is without struggle. But the lack of riverine tempestuousness is of equal importance. The river's transparent and reflective qualities further intensify the intimate violence: through the vehicle of the river, the narrator interpretively sees both the monkey's expiring face, that which is below the water, but also his own face laid over the monkey's, as the river reflects back his own image. Stedman writes: "his dying little eyes still continued to follow me with seeming reproach, till their light forsook them." In an extension of this uncanny moment, Gulliver experiences this same crushing reality when faced with the Yahoo: "When I happened to behold the reflection of my own form in a lake or fountain, I turned my face in horror and detestation of myself, and could better endure the sight of a common yahoo than of my own person."[91] For Jean Baudrillard, every act of aqueous reflection is one deeply imbricated in both absorption and seduction. The mirror of water, Baudrillard writes, "is always a matter of self-seduction . . . all seduction in this sense is narcissistic."[92] Like Gulliver, who attempts to refuse his own simian similitude, Stedman's simian similitude, or perhaps the monkey's anthropoid similitude, is recognized and by the same token refused. The river absorbs both Stedman's image—his face looks back—and also his brutal actions. The monkey is the impetus for this absorption, and whether or not Stedman can acknowledge the looking-between, it unsettles him. In extending Baudrillard, both the monkey and the river participate in this self-seduction: Stedman is drawn to both. Such a realization furthers the triangulated relationship—colonizer, monkey, river—and the invocation of narcissism. The monkey, then, must die to give Stedman proper breathing room, and in so doing Stedman elevates his own brand of humanness, an ironic inhumaneness, and violating masculinity.

As a potential example of what the Prices read as "empathy for all creatures," Stedman upon returning to camp refuses to eat the monkey that he has murdered: "Never Poor Devil felt more than I on this occasion, nor could I taste of him or his Companion when they were dress'd."[93] Stedman feels too much—the monkey has somehow inscribed itself on the narrator's interiority—and this vacates his hunger by inducing durational ramifications. His refusal of the meal, though, is moot. The monkey has been and remains consumed, and by this I mean symbolically inscribed, inwardly resonant within the narrator. He need not eat to dominate. As Heather Keenleyside reasons in a reading of Locke's *Second Treatise,* the process of eating (especially as a distinction of personhood) is appropriative: it demonstrates the slippery nature by which what is consumed participates in the construction of possession and person.[94] In a sort of Leviathan-adjacent model, eating mechanizes the body into a "collection of goods" that is constituted by the ingestion of those goods.[95] Stedman's refusal to eat the monkey disavows this appropriation. In an unconsumed state, the monkey continues to unsettle this narrative of domination. Stedman cannot shake the monkey, because the animal becomes affectively and psychically engrained. The simian's parasitism lives on in Stedman and his journal.

INTERMEZZO

Reading Swift on the Planet of the Apes

Planet of the Apes, my students are surprised to realize, maintains a satirical prehistory. Penned first in French in 1963, Pierre Boulle's *Le Planète des Singes* was quickly translated into English by Xan Fielding in the same year. Its popularity shot-put it to the silver screen in 1968, directed by Franklin J. Shaffner and starring Charlton Heston.[1] Fielding's original translation of Boulle's "social fantasy" attracted curious attention from print news media at the time, especially the novel's evident derivation from Swift's *Gulliver's Travels.* The *Atlantic Monthly,* for example, acknowledges that "this novel is respectfully descended from Swift on one side, and Verne on the other." The *Louisville Times* reminds readers that *"Planet of the Apes* is tomorrow's *Gulliver's Travels."* These critical reviews acknowledge the genealogical connection that Boulle's science fiction bears in a lineage sired by Swift (nursed by Verne too). This intermezzo highlights these fecund, transhistorical connections and examines how eighteenth-century satire gives birth to a media phenomenon that still thrives, some three hundred years later. What has gone underexplored, however, is that the literary connection between Boulle and Swift hinges on moments of aqueous encounter and interspecies violations. *Planet of the Apes* is Houyhnhnmland 2.0.

Boulle, unwittingly or perhaps wittingly, locates bodies of water as sites of sexual violence, intrigue, and eroticism. *Planet of the Apes* thus reframes Swift's riverine moments so as to demand our recognition of water as central to interspecies intimacies. The narrator, Ulysse Mérou, observes upon arriving on Soror (the name of the actual planet of the apes): "It was a waterfall. On coming to it, all three of us were moved by the beauty of the site. A stream of water, clear as our mountain torrents, . . . Perhaps this liquid was not water at all and might be extremely dangerous. . . . 'It can't be anything but water,' he [Professor Antelle] muttered. He bent down again to plunge his hand into the lake, when we saw him suddenly stiffen. He gave an exclamation of surprise and pointed toward something he had just discerned in the sand. . . . There . . . was the print of a human foot."[2] The surprise for the eighteenth-century reader is not singularly the repurposing of Swift, but another eighteenth-century interlocutor: Defoe's *Robinson Crusoe*. Crusoe's out-of-body experience and consequent anxious bloodlust instigated by the "cannibal" footprint here too become the vehicle for recognizing otherness—an inescapable irony given that like Crusoe and Gulliver in all four of his voyages, Mérou and his crew are the trespassers. Littoral zones stage and heighten these moments of surprising recognition precisely because of the liminal placement between terrestrial surety and oceanic uncertainty.

While entranced by the iconography of the footstep, Mérou, unencumbered by the inquisitive logic of his companions, spies an Eve reincarnate. Such a characterization comes to engender Nova's role in the novel as Mérou's sexual partner and mother of his child, Sirius, and is abandoned by the filmic version, which opens with four space explorers, one a white woman, who barely makes it beyond the opening credits. Charlton Heston's character, Taylor, informs the other two upon her accidental death that she was to be their "new Eve, of sorts."[3] With the new Eve dead on arrival, the cosmonauts seek further replacements, thus remanding the female body exclusively to its reproductive value. Mérou recounts his original vision of Nova: "I shall never forget the impression her appearance made on me. I held my breath at the marvelous beauty of this creature from Soror, who revealed herself to us dripping with spray, illuminated by the blood-red beams of Betelgeuse. It was a woman—a young girl, rather, unless it was a goddess."[4] The deification of Nova is second only to the erotic—almost pornographic, almost pederastic, perhaps *Humbertian* would be the most suitable adjective—description of the young girl, a signal reiteration of Swift's violating female Yahoo, who "could not be above eleven Years old."[5] Despite or perhaps because of her youthfulness, Mérou reveals, "It was plain to see that the woman, who stood motionless on the ledge like a statue on a pedestal, possessed the most perfect body that could be conceived on Earth."[6] Gulliver, on the other hand, reports the female "Black as Sloe" Yahoo "not . . . altogether as hideous as the rest of the Kind," precisely because of her youth.[7] For Gulliver, clearly a youthful body trumps facial attractiveness, but Boulle's rendition demands that we gravitate towards the "white race" in the form of the Yahoo-like young woman.[8] There are no obstacles, in other words, to the interspecies intimacies that, in Boulle's text, literally give birth to a child savant (Sirius begins speaking at three months old)—one that, unlike Gulliver's violation by and unactualized congress with the black Yahoo, can uphold white supremacy. The racialist thinking of both novels is not to be underestimated and undoubtedly comprises the embryonic tissue that further ingratiates Boulle to Swift (and Swift to Boulle).

In Soror, with the transformation of the female Yahoo into a china doll beauty,[9] the watersports the two engage in likewise become transformed. Mérou reports, "I decided to make an experiment. As she approached me, cleaving the water with a peculiar swimming action resembling a dog's and with her hair streaming out behind her like the tail of a comet, I looked her straight in the eye and, before she could turn her head aside, gave her a smile filled with all the friendliness and affection I could muster. The result was surprising. She stopped swimming, stood up in the water, which reached to her waist, and raised her hands in front of her as a gesture of defense."[10] Nova's canine and comet-like characterization is a reminder of her nonhumanity—a curious detail that seems to undermine Mérou's attention to her pristine, anthropocentric beauty only pages before. As with Swift, what Boulle illustrates here is a volatile interspecies contact zone where body language mutually fails and devolves into illegibility. The failures of communication between species are legion and may very well reframe Haraway's *When Species Meet*. Jane Goodall, Dian Fossey, and Biruté Galdikas—the trifecta of female primatologists, whose lifework has been dedicated to chimpanzees, gorillas, and orangutans, respectively—have all keenly documented the ways in which human facial expressions and body languages are distinctly incommensurate with those of other great apes. Bared teeth, which often accompany smiles in humans, are noticeably threatening in chimpanzee cultures; they also can be gestures of subordination. Prolonged eye contact in gorillas is yet another territorial offense. Boulle highlights these disparities, just as Swift discloses how Gulliver's presumed awareness of the Yahoo fails miserably in the river. While Mérou intends to express "friendliness and expression," Nova assumes it to be cause for alarm.

The moment that immediately follows activates a sort of Swiftian echo chamber that visualizes the fungible hierarchies in which humans and primates are enfolded in Soror. Alongside the threat of the smile, Hector, the crew's pet chimpanzee (absent from the film), appears to join in the fun and games. "I was amazed," Mérou notes, "to see the bestial expression, compounded of fright and menace, that came over the young girl's face when she caught sight of the monkey. . . . As he passed close by, without noticing her, she sprang out. Her body twanged like a bow. She seized him by the throat and closed her hands around his neck, holding the poor creature firmly between her thighs. Her attack was so swift that we did not even have time to intervene."[11] Nova kills Hector here; a learned reactionary behavior that reasons the threat that chimpanzees pose to Nova and her human ilk in Soror. Indeed, only chapters later, Nova will be subjected to chimpanzee medical experiments that reimagine an inversion of (continued) human trials on great apes. She is poked and prodded while pregnant—something Mérou only finds out after Nova's first trimester—which is described as her "illness."[12] Where Swift forecloses the interspecies primal scene, Boulle reimagines it. Unlike Gulliver who fails to staunch the violating simian touch of the Yahoo, Nova, in killing the chimpanzee, differentiates herself from the simian in an endeavor that at once imposes human supremacy and also less-than-human supremacy given that Mérou does not understand Nova to be identically human. "Her attack was so swift," becomes both allusion and pun that demonstrate a revision of Swift's and *Planet of the Apes*'s admitted linkages.

Shaffner's film version, which only loosely adopts Boulle's urtext, nonetheless incorporates the cascading waterfall and male rear nudity in ways that repopulate Swift's illustration of Gulliver's bathing. Taylor (Heston), Landon (Robert Gunner), and Dodge (Jeff Burton) strip nude to relish the pool's water, despite having, immediately prior, traversed the larger body of water that homed their crash landing.[13] Unlike in the original novel, the crashed space travelers are not inundated with the Edenic female nakedness embodied by Nova. Instead, their clothes and equipment are burgled, which makes the moment feel much more like an elementary school prank played near the local watering hole. In other words, the film version of *The Planet of the Apes* sanitizes, both literally and figuratively, the moment that had so much captivated Swift's and Boulle's imaginations. It instead becomes a site of US colonial intervention evidenced by, first, the planting of a miniature American flag as soon as they make landfall and, second, Taylor's surveyance after finding the subordinated human interlopers. "They look more or less human," Taylor observes of the individuals devouring raw corn cobs and coconuts, "I think they're mute."[14] "Vegetarians," Dodge notes.[15] "If this is the best they've got around here, in six months we'll be running this planet," Taylor responds.[16] The peep show performed by the pool with cascading waterfall, then, erases the forms of bodily vulnerability that attract *Gulliver's Travels* and Boulle's *Planet of the Apes*, revealing instead how, in their refreshed state, Taylor, Landon, and Dodge become renewed in their intention to make quick work of colonizing the vegetarian, disabled class.

CHAPTER 3

Aqueous Punishment

As with chapters 1 and 2, which differ in both their specific aqueous sites and the ways they negotiate multimodal expressions of queerness, this chapter shifts to address how histories of water torture are situated throughout the long eighteenth century and become revived in Gothic fictions. The Gothic novel upholds and dispenses with its own conceptions of justice and recompense, which repeatedly manifest through aqueous means. I highlight two narratives that offer liquid locales as sites of graphic violation: William Beckford's *Vathek* (1786) and Matthew Gregory Lewis's *The Monk* (1796). As these novels reveal, bodies of water become harnessed as sites of exquisite torture and pain that reinforce biopolitical control over wayward, transgressive bodies that endeavor to trespass against heteronormative sexual economies. And while torture, violence, and exquisite pain may be fundamental to the plots and terrains of each novel, my attention to water's queerness is repeatedly found in the fluid fringe—that is, auxiliary moments that appear to us only through careful diving. Aqueous punishment is a means to dispossess transgressive, Gothic bodies of their hubris and remand them to a queered, desexualized state in which heterosexual inclusion is forbidden. The queerness of water, as this chapter would have it, is a reminder that violent waters can work both with and against queered bodies and relations, and ultimately induce world-shattering tortures. In the shattered cuts, alternative, non-innocent or utopic queer worlds seep in.

Vathek, William Beckford's magnum opus, was marked by scandal that plagued both Beckford's personal history and the publication of the novel, which Beckford—English by birth and nationality—wrote in French and had translated into English, in a pattern that Oscar Wilde, similarly plagued, would emulate a century later. "*Vathek*," Kenneth Graham avers, "is one of the most imaginative of the oriental tales originating in western Europe in the eighteenth century. It has held sway over imaginations since its unauthorized publication in 1786 . . . Its creative audacity and dark vision continue to charm and trouble its readers."[1] As I have discussed elsewhere, the fallout from the 1784 Powderham Scandal, an incident in which twenty-one-year-old Beckford was found in bed with his fourteen-year-old male cousin, Viscount "Kitty" Courtenay, forced Beckford, who William Boyd has called "England's Wealthiest Son," into self-enforced exile on the continent.[2] The social stigma and revulsion regarding Beckford's same-sex, pedophilic attraction (Graham writes, "he was intensely, emotionally, and indiscreetly attracted to boys") became the impetus both for his short "Arabian Tale" and for *Vathek*, as well as for three additional "Episodes," which, while imagined as integral to *Vathek* as a novel, did not surface until the early twentieth century due to editorial malfeasance.[3]

Set in fictionalized Samarah, the Caliph Vathek reigns over the Arabian world and possesses occult powers by way of an enviable evil eye: "His figure was pleasing and majestic; but when he was angry, one of his eyes became so terrible, that no person could bear to behold it; and the wretch upon whom it was fixed instantly fell backward, and sometimes expired."[4] "Being much addicted to women and the pleasure of the table," Vathek, coddled by his equally vainglorious mother, Carathis, is a gourmand with a proclivity for the pleasures of the flesh.[5] The short orientalist narrative features Vathek's desirous, power-hungry subplot as an internal framework. The external framework reveals a pseudo–*My Fair Lady* challenge between Mahomet—Muhammad, father of Islam, by another spelling—and a shape-shifting "genie" (jinni) that seeks to test Vathek's hubris and potential for atonement. Mahomet is assured that Vathek, if given the opportunity, will repent for his hubristic affronts and the genie agrees to the wager insomuch that he can administer the test. Vathek's gluttony and search for absolute omniscience foretell his failure and consequent purgatory in Eblis, *Vathek*'s hell. The narrator describes Vathek as someone who "wished to know every thing; even sciences that did not exist."[6] En route to hell, Carathis, Vathek, and his paramour, Nouronihar, raze cities, enact genocides, sadistically punish, and scoff at exculpation. The account ends in the bowels of Eblis, where all three—mother, son, and lover—meet other unrepentant sinners and are literally branded with burning hearts for eternity.

The Gothic diptych on which I will focus emerges from water's subtle inclusion in *Vathek*. Whereas the giant oceanic maw that predates on Crusoe is palpable in chapter 1, the microscopic attention to water in Beckford's novel provides alternative sea/see-scapes by which to visualize water's manifold queerness. I focus on the occult gulph where male youths are sacrificed and devoured and the sybaritic baths where the head eunuch is brutally tortured as geographies of aqueous punishment. Like the other authors this book unites, Beckford subtly reveals water's violating potential and its queer waves that make evident different scales (gulphs and baths are bodies of water too) of a critical water studies approach.

The ridiculous and violating nature of aqueous interactions similarly migrates to M. G. Lewis's novel, where the exaltation of heterosexual bonds is synonymous with the punishment of the desexualized priest's body. *The Monk*, published shortly after *Vathek* and invariably in conversation, is replete with violence, sexual assault, blasphemy, apostasy, unbridled passions of the flesh, genderbending and crossdressing, infanticide, misogyny, bodily mutilation, and parricide, to name just a few. Its plot and reading effects are difficult to place into words, and this is precisely what brings about the Gothic pleasures of Lewis's genius.

The Monk is set in Inquisition-era Madrid and opens with the titular monk, Ambrosio, whose unknown origin story only stimulates the city's obsession with his oratory prowess and good looks. In a series of erotic, humorous, and ghastly tribulations, Ambrosio succumbs to the Devil's temptation through Rosario/Matilda, a genderbending supplicant that joins the monastery explicitly for the passions of Ambrosio's embrace. The two consummate their affections, and the Devil-in-disguise fosters Ambrosio's penchant for sinfulness, which includes the forfeiture of his priestly vows and, in a harrowing moment suffused with demonic magic, matricide, and the rape of his (spoiler alert) sister, Antonia. This represents only one pornographic thread animated by Lewis.

The secondary plot follows Don Raymond and his preternatural journal around the continent to consolidate his ardor for Agnes, who he rapes and who, in desperation following her assault, joins a convent. Lorenzo (Agnes's brother), Raymond, and Raymond's devout errand-boy, Theodore, plot to free Agnes from the convent so that Raymond can make amends. This is foiled by the sisters, who, led by a masochistic abbess, imprison, starve, and torture Agnes when her pregnancy is disclosed by a wayward epistle. As should be clear, Lewis does not shy away from his exacting criticisms of Catholicism and its gross hypocrisies. Agnes's freedom is procured only by the razing of the church and the literal evisceration of the nuns. Her stillborn baby withers in her arms and she is married to her rapist in a convenient and disgusting marriage plot.

The novel concludes with Ambrosio's wrongs brought to light. Matilda sells her soul to be free of the Inquisition and she encourages Ambrosio to the do the same. He twice rejects the offer and, in an ironic twist of fate, at the moment he is to be exonerated, he signs the Devil's contract (a queer marriage that I unpack at length below) and is subjected to torturous demise. Max Fincher neatly sums: *"The Monk* contains just about every conceivable possibility of anti-heteronormative sexual interests: incest, sado-masochism, auto-eroticism, necrophilia, voyeurism, and same-sex desire. Meanwhile, an ambiguously gendered Cagliostro-figure destroys the reputation of a symbol of a tyrannical and repressive institution that regulates its members' sexuality. What more could one ask for?"[7] While these abound, my focus here is less invested in adumbrating the sins and vices of the characters (a Herculean task) and instead zeroes in on two peculiar fringe moments in which the violation of bodies occurs in streams or rivers—yet another Gothic diptych. I magnify moments that, while ostensibly disconnected, I read as intimately in conversation with one another. The first is the incantatory Danish ballad, "The Water-King," which warns readers of the occult otherness of Denmark but configures the flaw of gullibility as that which leads to an aqueous death. In "The Water-King," the gleefully ignorant and enamored maiden's drowning death punishes her smitten naivete. Water then performs a rude awakening, one from which she truly never awakens. The second is the final moment of the novel, which carries the punished and tortured Ambrosio away in a deluged stream. Ambrosio's punishment by the Devil is preordained by early chapters and yet also enables water and other torturous methods to perform an echoed rude awakening like that of the ignorant maiden, revealing yet another queer echo. Put simply, I pair these two moments because the ballad operates as an aural semaphore that foretells the downfall of Ambrosio. In these fluid fringe moments, we witness how water participates in defining Gothic violation and justice.

GOTHIC DESEXUALITY

I emphasize the desexualized male body as a particular embodiment that has heretofore gone underresearched and undervalued within sexuality studies. The term "desexuality" is not itself novel and has received considerable attention from those who approach bourgeoning and necessary conversations regarding asexuality. I draw from these discourses because they produce a helpful lexicon to approach my understanding of desexuality in the Gothic novel; though I submit that desexuality is not identical to asexuality and vice versa. Kristina Gupta, Eunjung Kim, and Ela Przybylo, for example, each reason that legacies of desexualization legitimate and proceed from the social disenfranchisement of asexuality within Western cultures. Gupta's overview of compulsory sexuality acknowledges how desexualization can be deployed to sociosexually exclude bodies and identities whose reproductive value is nonnormative (such as racial and ethnic minorities; the elderly; the disabled, which Kim more pointedly addresses; and people of size) and thus viewed as undesirable to the maintenance of the state's deeply held white supremacist, ableist, and heteronormative value system.[8] In concert, Przybylo recognizes the irony in which desexualization and hypersexualization run directly parallel because they represent nonnormative performances of sexuality that are seen as either insufficient or excessive, respectively.[9] Both desexualization and hypersexualization seek to brand populations that are undesirable and thus necessitate the state's management. We witnessed projections of this within the animalized natural history presented by chapter 2.

The recent asexual turn proves a generative way to approach allegiances to compulsory sexuality that underline and normalize the state's biopolitical control of bodies deemed *out* of control. Desexuality, as I chart it below, refers to a specific coterie of characters whose vocations and social standings require desexual comportments in that they must be extricated from the heteronormative sexual spheres in which they seek to participate. This is where my use of desexuality differs from the majority of asexual studies scholars. Pryzbylo, for instance, attends to how notions of queerness may be disentangled from the sexual—towards the nonsexual and the asexual—to foster textures of eros that are not strictly subsumed by sex (a Freudian holdover). In the examples I address below, the sexual persists: the desexualized subject desires to remain within the heteronormative sexual economy. Sex remains paramount. Both Bababalouk (not the Babadook, whose own queer cult iconography may be more familiar to readers), who is Vathek's trustworthy and sycophantic head eunuch, and Ambrosio—Lewis's monk—are inscribed in culturally sanctified and accepted desexualized roles. For Bababalouk, desexuality is enforced on him through his eunuchry, a social standing bestowed on him through castration, and for Ambrosio, desexuality is requisite through his acceptance of the priesthood, which necessitates a vow of celibacy and inspires his queer figuration.[10] The sex these two seek to engage is not what we might understand to be nonnormative through the lens of heteronormativity: Bababalouk attempts to forfeit his eunuchry in favor of sex with the princess Nouronihar and the harem, and Ambrosio engages in a variety of consensual and nonconsensual heteronormative sex acts with the Devil-in-disguise and his sister, respectively. These moments are not queer sex. However, because the two must maintain predetermined performances of desexuality, any intrusion or participation in sex acts—at all—anticipates a queer leaning (a desexualized body turned desirous) and, as a result, their torturous encounters with watery environs. Desexuality registers queer affects in that it signals a body whose desires are seen as transgressive, excessive, and obsolete within heteronormative systems.

Aqueous punishment manifests as one carceral exercise enacted on the body of the desexualized dissident to curtail transgressive sexual participations. It thus prefigures a Foucauldian *supplice* in which biopolitical maintenance and policing is enacted through bodies of water. Contemporarily used in French to mean "torture" or "torment," Foucault traces the etymology of supplice to signify "corporal punishment, painful to a more or less horrible degree" that is "an inexplicable phenomenon that the . . . imagination creates out of the barbarous and cruel."[11] For Foucault, the supplice participates in creating a spectacle of the punishment and criminal while marking the body in violent ways; it is, as a result, synonymous with the phenomenological pains that accompany torture. Aqueous punishment is, without question, a genre of supplice.

Neither novelist nor narrator assess the moments I locate as torture. But this lack of explicit acknowledgment, as I suggested in chapter 2, of Gulliver's refusal to name his own sexual violence, does not nullify the material effects of the fictionalized punishment. By not speaking torture's names, these narratives perpetuate long histories of obfuscating torturous behavior, which become institutionalized, as I show here, within literary genres. Torture becomes a proprietary means of upholding narrative comeuppance and thus insinuates the reader into this fallacy of justice.[12] The Gothic novel, in its various iterations of dissenting bodies, verboten passions, and manifold sexual appetites, would seem to be the most appropriate genre by which to test a disciplinary framework of internalized justice wrought by torturous ends. My focus on torture thus returns to concerns prompted by Steven Bruhm, who observes that the Gothic novel's rendering of the body in pain bespeaks an epistemological problem—one that extends from discourses of sentimentalism earlier in the century—that betrays "the history of pain written on the body in the judicial, medical, and military theatres of Europe."[13] The Gothic novel dramatically writes and rewrites these graphic violations and their consequent cicatrices, echoing Foucault's aperçu that torture is "the theatre of hell."[14]

Aqueous punishment is a multimodal exercise of sublime power that punishes the desexualized body through troubled waters. I offer a comparative empires approach that considers, more capaciously, how desexualized bodies inform, frame, and are reshaped by the inner workings of empire, epitomized by *Vathek*'s Abbasid Caliphate in the Levant and the Spanish Inquisition in *The Monk*. Aqueous punishment becomes a means for empire to putatively govern, and thereby discipline, bodies that necessitate intervention, namely, those desexualized ones whose social function is predicated not on their inclusion but their maintenance of the sovereign's repro-normative desires. I do not, however, seek to equalize these empires or their effects; rather, I seek to acknowledge the consolidations of empire in both Gothic novels, which make evident genres of colonial infrastructure in which aqueous punishment finds a home. *Vathek* and *The Monk*'s deployment of aqueous punishment illustrates the disciplining of these transgressive bodies, but also the failures of empire to effectively condition a desexualized social function. In other words, the necessitation of aqueous punishment is de facto a subversive critique of the imperial sovereign's ability to govern, discipline, and condition bodies it deems necessary for its preservation. The Gothic novel, in turn, unveils revelations of the interior machinations of empire; and this chapter, unlike the previous two, looks inside empire rather than to an exploration outside of an imperial home. Aqueous punishment narratively highlights how desexualized bodies transcend the restraints of empire, and yet seeks to remand them to the sovereign's control by enacting torturous pain. Therein lies an ill-gotten Gothic justice that stems directly from empire's failures and its liquidations.

PUNISH AND TORTURE

In *On Crimes and Punishment* (1764)—published in the same year as what is widely accepted as the first Gothic novel, *The Castle of Otranto*—Cesare Beccaria writes, "Punishments and the method of inflicting them must be chosen such that, in keeping with the proportionality, they will make the most efficacious and lasting impression on the minds of men with the least torment to the body of the condemned."[15] Beccaria, an eighteenth-century Italian jurist, is generally considered the forefather to Jeremy Bentham's utilitarianism, and heralded as the philosopher most responsible for suspending European capital punishment. Originally penned in Italian, translated into French (1765) and soon after into English (1767), *On Crimes and Punishment* has a great deal to say about the inutility of the death penalty and the means by which the state doles out punishment with impunity.[16] Beccaria's primary critique takes to task "a cruelty condoned by custom in most nations": torture.[17] Torture is wielded by the tyrannical state under the auspices of truth. And this practice is of particular importance to eighteenth-century England, which refused to abolish torture. Julie A. Carlson notes: "Britain is anomalous in the history of European torture for never legalizing recourse as a sanctioned element of criminal adjudication . . . justification of torture was never on the books and thus England did not participate in the wave of torture abolition."[18] As a result, England's punitive exceptionalism emerges as nationalistic pride that separated England from the continent, and serves as a two-sided coin: one, (an ironic) moral superiority by way of violent corrective and two, characterization of a particular imperial aesthetic.

This culture of torture may explain why torturous violence saturates so many eighteenth-century narratives, especially in the Gothic, which Gerard Cohen-Vrignaud suggests was integral in making visible and possible torture abolition. In *Radical Orientalism*, Cohen-Vrignaud contends that in their connection, Gothic literatures and Romantic Orientalism showcase "scenes of corporeal vulnerability" that ultimately informed and gave way to "legal containment of capricious violence" like that of torture and "promoted penal advances such as rarefying the death penalty, guaranteeing judicial moderation, and tempering police repression."[19] The deployment of torture within *Vathek* and *The Monk*, as Gothic exemplars, bespeaks not only the emergence of a liberal ideology that set out to dismantle the state's abuses of torture without consequence, but as Cohen-Vrignaud reveals, also enabled an "enduring affection for despotic depravity"—a signal tie to Foucault's discussion of the spectacle of the scaffold.[20]

The goal of torture is, on the surface, a pursuit of justice and knowledge, but more importantly, a tactic for disciplining bodies whose appetites, representations, or behaviors necessitate intervention. Legally sanctioned exercises of torture, James Simpson reasons, require a great deal of mental acrobatics, for the law "as we all like to believe, is designed to underwrite civil society. We all know that torture undoes our humanity; even the torturers know it."[21] Records from the Old Bailey—London's Criminal Court abutting Newgate Prison—as well as Rictor Norton's extensive queer historical digging in *Mother Clap's Molly House*, reveal forms of punishment (pillory, transportation, imprisonment, and death) deployed by the state to discipline nonnormative desires. Norton's querying of queerness here exemplifies attention to buggery, sodomy, and other forms of what we might consider same-sex congress. Punishment and its kin, torture, operate under the auspices of social correctives that physically reformat and retool wayward desires. Even the *London Journal*, for example, advocated for painfully disfiguring the bodies of those accused of sodomitical passions and actions. Printed on 14 May 1726, the following was advanced: "'Tis humbly propos'd that the following Method may not only destroy the Practice [sodomy, molly subculture, sex between men] but blot out the names of the monstrous Wretches from under Heaven, viz., when any are Detected, Prosecuted and Convicted, that after Sentence Pronounc'd, the Common Hangman tie him Hand and Foot before the Judge's Face in open Court, that a Skillful Surgeon be provided immediately to take out his Testicles, and that then the Hangman sear up his Scrotum with a hot Iron, as in Cases of burning in the Hand."[22] This vicious proposal, which festers with carnivalesque tortures, intends to rectify sodomy through metaphoric and biomedical violence: the process of neutering the sodomite and branding his scrotum is only one means of rending him necropolitical detritus. The sodomite must also have his name blotted out for perpetuity. His name and genitals are effaced; he must be excised from the repro-normative communities that he has ostensibly offended.

As Foucault observes in *Discipline and Punish*, "At the end of the eighteenth century, torture was to be denounced as a survival of the barbarities of another age: the mark of savagery that was denounced as 'Gothic.'"[23] Foucault's use of "Gothic" here is more synonymous with barbaric or reminiscent of days past characterized by incivility. But Foucault's acknowledgment of "Gothic" likewise accommodates a genre that this chapter takes up. The two Gothic novels surveyed here illuminate what forms of unwieldy punishment—and thereby acts of "capricious" and "corporeal" cruelty—are enacted by immersion in water. As modeled by the baths and the stream, water plays an integral role in the arbitration of punishment, what I will characterize as water torture.

Stephen Eisenman defines water torture as the practice in which victims are placed in supine positions, their faces covered with towels or clothing, and then doused with gallons of water nearing the point of lost consciousness.[24] Circulating since at least the late Medieval period and practiced, by Eisenman's estimation, on literally every continent except for Antarctica, waterboarding is elsewhere called "the water cure" or "slow drowning." The purpose of such a method "is not the extraction of truthful testimony—the victim will say anything to stop the ordeal—but the eliciting of confession: confession of error, apostasy, or moral responsibility."[25] This is the point that Beckford and Lewis implicitly make when they deploy aqueous punishment. For these characters, there are no confessions to be had—and the veracity of confessions under torture have consistently been questioned throughout history.[26] Rather, these textual Gothic moments employ water to rectify a character's transgression of immorality, as modeled by their desexualized-*cum*-sexualized awakenings. By doing so, the administration of aqueous punishment implicitly realizes an awakened sexuality that must be forfeited—violently—and in doing so return the individual to a desexualized state, which often accompanies death.

VILLAINY AND VATHEK

Beckford's formative years and career expressed magnetism towards the Orient, in which he firmly places *Vathek* and thus aligns with what Srinivas Aravamudan has described as "Enlightenment Orientalism."[27] While in exile for his illicit appetites (a thread interwoven into Vathek's character), Beckford spent extensive time researching Islam, Zoroastrianism, and cultures of the Levant, so his vision in *Vathek* is loosely adapted from these, rather than entirely fictionalized. John Beynon notes that Beckford was enraptured by the *Arabian Nights* during his tutelage years, and Lewis Melville suggests that "the Oriental tales had taken full possession of this impressionable reader [Beckford] . . . They had fired his youthful mind and held his imagination captive; their influence over him never waned all the days of his life."[28] According to Graham, "orientalism unleashed the *agent-provocateur* in the youthful Beckford, uncomfortably and ambivalently situated at the centre yet on the periphery of his culture."[29] Beckford's Orient provided "the vehicle for [his] own protest against the oppressions of his earth-bound compatriots [and became] a metaphor for the untrammelled imagination: there everything is possible."[30] Such embellishments of the eighteenth-century Orient correspond with Aravamudan's definition, extending Edward Said, of enlightenment orientalist narratives, which "projected Europe onto the Orient and vice versa in order to make larger inductions about sexuality, religion, and politics; and they expressed a strong desire to understand civilizational differences both relativistically and universally."[31]

Beckford assuredly participates in what Aravamudan describes. But *Vathek*'s orientalist orientation, which would position the Orient as uncivilized and thus barbaric, is not enough to justify the traces of fantastical violence that spring up throughout the narrative. In agreement with Aravamudan, I find the co-constitution of the occidental and oriental narrative apparent in this Gothic tale, and thus the disclosure of aqueous punishment reveals not just a "barbarism of the East," but rather a cross-cultural deployment of imperial disciplinary techniques meant to harness desiring bodies for biopolitical control.

THE CANNIBALISTIC CHASM

The moments of water torture represent fluid fringe moments in that they are not fundamental to the overall movement of *Vathek*. They are instead furtively incorporated as risible anecdotes that arise from perversion, fanciful disbelief, and grotesque violence. Beckford's first insinuation of aqueous punishment positions a magical, embodied chasm, forged by water, as the site of pederastic, cannibal appetites, an emblem of what Cohen-Vrignaud calls "Oriental immoderation," which exclusively seeks the conjoined passions of violence and pleasure.[32]

Before Vathek ventures across the Arabian Peninsula in quest of omniscience, he is tested by a "perfidious Giaour" (the genie in disguise) who demands payment before escorting the Caliph to his just desserts. The Giaour preternaturally transforms himself into an elastic ball and awaits Vathek in "an immense gulph in the valley whose opposite side was closed in by a steep acclivity."[33] The narrator notes that the gulph looks as if "a continual fall of water had excavated [it]."[34] The aqueous excavation noted here positions the gulph as a location where water is participatory and embodied: the gulph is a literal manifestation of the flagitious genie with an appetite to w(h)et. The excavation of water coincides with the excavation of pedophilic desires. The Giaour demands not money but flesh as payment for Vathek's progression: "Impatient Caliph!—Know that I am parched with thirst, and cannot open this door, till my thirst be thoroughly appeased; I require the blood of fifty. Take them from among the most beautiful sons of thy vizirs and great men; or neither can my thirst nor your curiosity be satisfied."[35]

The water-excavated gulph then becomes a cannibalistic mouth by which Vathek must feed the mighty Giaour the most beautiful of young boys.

The *Oxford English Dictionary* predates the arcane use of "gulph" to the mid-sixteenth century, where it meant "to rush along like a gulf or a whirlpool" or "to eddy or swirl." By the early nineteenth century, when Beckford was just finalizing an authorized edition of his novel, the word came to mean, "to swallow like a gulf; to engulf." As is clear to readers of *Vathek*, the Giaour-*cum*-gulph showcases the consumption of bodies by other bodies—a recasting of the consuming oceanic waves tracked by Crusoe's narrative. Put simply, the embodied gulph does, in fact, engulf in a way that mirrors consumption, which is enacted through aqueous means. This etymology then reasons, yet again, the way that bodies of water are mobilized and how they potentially violate, and personify extensions of, the body. The remittance of cherubic, young boys as pederastic sacrifice suggests that the gulph illustrates how *Vathek*'s waters are encoded in narrativizing bodies in pain.

But the aqueous punishment demonstrated by the gulph anticipates desexualized punishment that is more fully realized by Bababalouk later. The cannibalized prepubescent youths are likewise subjects of punishment because of their desexualized state. Whereas Bababalouk's desexuality follows his enforced castration; the young boys' desexuality stems from the fact that they have not yet reached sexual maturity. As Jeffrey Masten and Thomas A. King have each shown, the early modern fascination with boys was often one of pederastic inclinations and thus a potentially queer engagement.[36] Both Masten and King locate the boy as a crucial sexual component in the elastic pederastic economy, somewhere between not-yet-man and never-becoming-woman. The eighteenth-century boy, in this same fashion, epitomized the desexualized body, given that the male youth was always in a state of coming into sexual maturity, and yet was valued and sought after as an absence of said maturity. Eighteenth-century periodicals echo this. Anja Müller argues that periodicals "map out a desexualized space as the legitimate realm for the child."[37] Whereas Müller finds desexualization as a result of the degendering of children, my reading of "desexualized" here focuses on male youth, who are often disregarded by gendered analyses or are merely the focal object of desire for discussions of pederasty. Desexualization does not, like with Bababalouk the eunuch, imply the boy's extrication from the sexual social sphere. Quite the opposite, the desexualization apparent in *Vathek* places the boy within an immersive sexual ecology and yet realizes the boy's body as one that approaches the sexual maturity, awareness, and abilities that normative sexual bodies achieve following pubescence. This is precisely what appeals to the pederastic gulph that Beckford depicts.

Vathek submits to the Giaour's terms and so begins a comical pageant by which the fifty young boys are selected: "It was not long before a troop of these poor children made their appearance, all equipped by their fond mothers with such ornament, as might give the greatest relief to their beauty, or most advantageously display the graces of their age. But, whilst this brilliant assemblage attracted the eyes and hearts of everyone besides, the Caliph scrutinized each, in his turn, with a malignant avidity that passed for attention, and selected from their number the fifty whom he judged the Giaour would prefer."[38] This moment assuredly resonates with a similarly villainous display of bodies, which are equally eroticized, in the Marquis de Sade's *120 Days of Sodom* (1785), and it's just kismet that both works were not published in their entirety until the beginning of the twentieth century—*Vathek*'s Episodes lost to translational censorship and Sade's furtively concealed in the Bastille. In both texts, beautiful boys are assailed by ruses which subject the youths' health, beauty, and ultimately lives to lascivious violence.

After having selected the fifty for gastro-payment, Vathek offers "to celebrate a festival on the plain, for the entertainment of the young favourites."[39] The group gathers at the newly forged gulph, and a soundtrack of water is the only thing heard in this entrapment: "No sounds were heard save the murmurs of the four fountains; and the reeds and voices of shepherds calling to each other from different eminences."[40] The gulph then becomes mired in both the aural and visual imagery of water. Contextually then, the queerness of water evidenced here induces phenomenological worlds in which the aural and visual resonances prepare the reader for the sacrifice of young boys. To see and hear water in the Gothic novel is to anticipate modes of queer violence that result, in *Vathek*, from pederastic cannibalism.

The gulf that has literally become embodied by the Giaour hungers for the young boys, further situating the novel's punishment of—here it assumes the role of consuming—desexualized bodies.[41] Having divested the young boys so that their naked beauty can be admired for "the suppleness and grace of their delicate limbs," Vathek announces: "'Relentless Giaour! Can nothing content thee but the massacre of these lovely victims? Ah! wert thou to behold their beauty, it must certainly move thy compassion.'"[42] The voracious animated gulph responds: "'Perdition on thy compassion, babbler! Give them me; instantly give them, or, my portal shall be closed against thee for ever!'"⁴³ One reading may suggest that Vathek attempts to renegotiate with the Giaour, somehow realizing the sacrificial acts (times fifty) that he is about to commit. But such a gesture of compassion, even momentarily, is uncharacteristic of the Caliph. Rather, Vathek's address to the Giaour only further whets the occult gulph's appetite, while dangling the promise of beautiful sacrifice over the ajar maw. The Giaour demands beautiful, young boys, and so Vathek's ostensible pleading, "'behold their beauty, it must certainly move thy compassion,'" is less about mercy and more about exciting the Giaour's appetites for young sacrificial lambs. The carrot-on-the-string act works and ends in a fantastical moment of occult cannibalism. By the novel's purview, all desexualized male characters are casualties in the search for knowledge and self-edification.

This episode of male youth consumed plays with the novel's theme of sadism and further situates the imbrication of water and punishment. Indeed, even Beckford's complementary Episodes play up the notion that aqueous scenes heighten both sybaritic eroticism and grotesque violence.⁴⁴ Within the original novel, Vathek, too, participates in the striptease to which the young boys are subjected. The boys are lured by Vathek's promise of jewels and jewelry: "The Caliph . . . undressed himself by degrees; and, raising his arm as high as he was able, made each of the prizes glitter in the air; but, whilst he deliver it, with one hand, to the child, who sprung forward to receive it; he, with the other, pushed the poor innocent into the gulph; where the Giaour, with sullen muttering, incessantly repeated: 'more! more!'"⁴⁵ The humorous erotics of this engagement cannot be underestimated: Vathek continues to feed boy after boy into the gluttonous Giaour's mouth, all the while that same mouth cries for more. Once all the boys are consumed, to Vathek's dismay the gulph closes itself: "to his utter amazement, the chasm closed, and the ground became as entire as the rest of the plain."⁴⁶ With no more boys to consume, the embodied gulph suspiciously seals itself and in doing so severs itself from aqueous affinity. What was once excavated by water and surrounded by an aqueous soundtrack is now only "as entire as the rest of the plain." It would appear as though, with no more punishments to wield or desexualized youths to consume, the resonances and phenomenology of water disappear altogether.

But this eldritch fiasco is not without consequence. The realization of Vathek's horrendous and egregious sacrifice spurs an uprising by the parents who witness this "festivity" and extends the notion of the gulph as an arena for both punishment and, now, justice. Despite his plausible bald-faced lie—"Your children while at play, fell from the precipice, and I should have experienced their fate, had I not suddenly started back"—the parents are incredulous.[47] "'Our Caliph,' said they, and the report soon circulated, 'our Caliph has played us this trick, to gratify his accursed Giaour. Let us punish him for perfidy! Let us avenge ourselves! Let us avenge the blood of the innocent! Let us throw this cruel prince into the gulph that is near, and let his name be mentioned no more.'"[48] In the fervor of pseudorevolt, the parents of the lost boys attribute two important capacities to the gulph. First, the gulph is a place of erasure where, once one is condemned, one's name can be "mentioned no more." The gulph becomes the site in which identity and self are blotted out. Second, the parents render the gulph as the site of retribution and punishment. The aggrieved look to the gulph, which has since fastened itself, to punish Vathek. The death of their children calls for the punishment of Vathek, who must be put to this identical end. These twofold implications suggest that the gulph lives on as a site of painful memory but also a geography where Vathek can justifiably be put to this same pain and potentially an identical desexualization. This fails.

As the peoples' revolt against Vathek grows, the Caliph looks to his vizier, Morakanabad (whose two sons have been sacrificed) and Bababalouk, the head of the eunuchs, for aide: "'Bababalouk,' continued he, 'put yourself at the head of your eunuchs: disperse the mob, and, if possible, bring this unhappy prince to his palace.'"[49] Bababalouk "having been spared the cares as well as honour of paternity, obeyed the mandate" and thus becomes the vehicle by which Vathek is able to avoid the encroaching skirmish and potential retributive punishment.[50] Bababalouk's desexuality, pronounced here by the narrator, enables him to assist Vathek with his villainous escape. As with the sacrifice of the fifty youths, desexualized characters become conduits for Vathek's success and progression. The novel's heteronormative expansion and supremacy, led by Vathek and his paramour, Nouronihar, is thus paved on the backs of desexualized bodies.

SADISTIC BATHING

Further along his journey to gain omniscience, Vathek and his entire caravan, seraglio included, pause to bask in the hospitality of Fakreddin, Nouronihar's father, wherein the aqueous site of the baths becomes another locale for sadistic punishment. As with Gulliver's encounter with the female Yahoo, the oasis and baths—sites of sated thirst and hygienic comforts—become maligned with alternative modes of queer violation. Such a literary constellation announces: beware the illusory effects of seemingly purifying or restorative waters. At this oasis, Bababalouk continues his requisite eunuch responsibilities, which demand he safeguard the harem: "The circumspect guardian, having gone up to the thin veil of carnation-colour silk that hung before the door-way, distinguished, by means of the softened splendor that shown through it, an oval bath of dark porphyry surrounded by curtains, festooned in large folds. . . . Bababalouk perceived his young pupils, indulgingly expanding their arms, as if to embrace the perfumed water, and refresh themselves after their fatigues."[51] The sybaritic baths are as lavish and erogenous as their description, and despite his eunuchry, "the looks of tender languor; their confidential whispers; and the enchanting smiles with which they were imparted; the exquisite fragrance of the rose: all combined to inspire a voluptuousness, which even Bababalouk himself was scarce able to withstand."[52] The sensory profusion of the baths troubles the desexualized state into which Bababalouk has been forced.

While Bababalouk's biography is not disclosed in *Vathek*, the sensuous arousal he evidences provides a more nuanced way of reading the eunuch body, which has long been theorized as and predicated on lack. That is, castration renders the body "disabled" and thus incapable of arousal, desire, or pleasure; herein lies the zeitgeist of asexuality projected upon bodies that lie outside of hetero-reproductive systems. Graham characterizes eunuchs as "men who have been emasculated (usually before puberty) by either of two methods: by cutting away the penis and testicles, or, more commonly, by incising the scrotum with a red-hot blade and removing the testicles but leaving the penis. Eunuchs were the most valuable slaves, acting often as intermediaries in the harem between the master and his wives or concubines."[53] From a biomedical perspective, Richard Wassersug and Thomas Johnson posit that depending on the timing of the castration—pre-, during, or post-puberty—it is very likely, especially for the latter two cases, that the eunuch would be capable of physical or phantom erections and ejaculation.[54] My point here, and as I have discussed elsewhere, is not to read erections where they are not, but rather to acknowledge the plural potential of eunuchs to experience eroticism or sensuality that would have otherwise seemed implausible because of obdurate notions of eunuchry that position them as defective or disabled.[55]

The bathing rituals that Bababalouk is meant to oversee become chaotic, and the chaos that abounds from the feminocentric space is predicated on the sadistic trickery that Nouronihar uses to foil the transgressive eunuch. That Bababalouk falls prey to Nouronihar's sadism gives way to the second half of *Vathek*'s aqueous punishment diptych.[56] The sadism modeled in the bath mirrors the spectacle performed by Vathek in the gulph, and while the gulph becomes a means to an end, Bababalouk's water torture serves no purpose. It is, however, this act of sadism that seemingly binds Nouronihar's fate to Vathek's and preordains their descent to hell, coupled. The heteronormative dyad, yet again, becomes sanctified by the violence against and torture of desexualized bodies. Desexuality is thus a requisite sacrifice for the maintenance of Gothic heteronormative villainy.

Nouronihar's sadism unfolds with acrobatic flair: "The young Nouronihar, daughter of the emir, who was as sprightly as an antelope, and full of wanton gaiety, beckoned one of her slaves to let down the great swing which was suspended to the ceiling by cords of silk: and whilst this was doing, winked to her companions in the bath: who, chagrined to be forced from so soothing a state of indolence, began to twist and entangle their hair to plague and detain Bababalouk; and teased him besides with a thousand vagaries."[57] The feminized space of the bath is a place of "indolence" for Nouronihar and the rest of her harem. Ironically, the Latinate etymon, *indolentia,* means "freedom from pain." But the indolent pleasures of the baths are only experienced by Nouronihar and the harem; for Bababalouk they become an ironic inducement of pain. Freedom from pain is only available to nondesexualized bodies, that is, bodies whose sexualities corroborate the desires of heteroreproductivity. The unwanted order and intrusion that Bababalouk effects ultimately spurs the all-women group to "plague and detain" him. Women's bodies in the baths become the means of bringing about entrapment and torture, which in a potential gesture of protofeminism reworks the trope of executioner or torturer, by convention an exclusively masculinized role. Bababalouk plays into this erotic trickery and concedes to Nouronihar's advances: "Caught by these flattering accents, Bababalouk gallantly replied: 'Delight of the apple of my eye! I accept the invitation of your honied lips; and, to say truth, my senses are dazzled with the radiance that beams from your charms.'"[58] Not only has Nouronihar thoroughly ensnared the eunuch, who she finds "eminently disgusting," but the seeds she has planted blossom into a confession of fleshly caresses and congress that are without question forbidden him.[59] Nouronihar's torture brings about Bababalouk's uncensored confession, namely the espousal of sexual desires. Such a confession, which contrasts his desexualized station, ultimately necessitates his experience of violation—inciting more punishment, more torture, despite a confession that intends to stop the pain altogether.

The baths thus evolve into an arena for queer female engagement that pairs eroticism with the administration of pain. As Katharine Binhammer sums in historicizing female same-sex desire at the end of the eighteenth century: "Thinking about female same-sex desire as a 'singular propensity' connects friendship and sex, not by centering on the images' content but by charting their form and function within a larger sexual discourse. Romantic friends and female same-sex flagellators coexist on sensibility's continuum on either side of moderate domestic conjugal pleasures. Pain is what brings them together on this continuum, and sex is what pulls them apart."[60] While Binhammer's discussion of pain is more ensconced in psychic and empathic experiences between historical figures, I find the emphasis on "pain is what brings them together" apropos. The harem employs this torturous moment as one that secures their feminocentric, potentially Sapphic, space by inducing pain in the eunuch. In this way, female same-sex communities can be constructed both by the recipience and wielding of experiences of pain, rather than exclusively the former. Such a claim seeks not to vilify women but rather to more capaciously theorize how violence and gender coalesce. With the bait set, "The rest of the women, having aptly conceived her design, sprang naked from the bath, and plied the swing, with such unmerciful jerks, that it swept through the whole compass of a very loft dome, and took from the poor victim all power of respiration."[61] The naked women pounce in collusion and subject Bababalouk to suffocation. The risible attack continues: "The sultanas and their slaves, stimulated by these pleasantries, persevered at the swing, with such remitted assiduity, that at length, the cord which had secured it, snapt suddenly asunder; and Bababalouk fell, floundering like a turtle, to the bottom of the bath. . . . The deplorable animal, in water to the chin, overwhelmed with darkness, and unable to extricate himself from the wrappers that embarrassed him, was still doomed to hear, for his further consolation, the fresh bursts of merriment his disaster occasioned."[62] The breathless moment described here positions Bababalouk as a victim in what looks painfully similar to waterboarding. We witness yet another topsy-turvy juxtaposition of violating power in which both the "sultanas and their slaves"—that is, the harem community that eunuchs are tasked with overseeing—participate in torturing the eunuch, which induces "fresh bursts of merriment." The eunuch is the waterboarded butt of the joke and becomes a means to foster feminocentric bonding. Resonant with

John Gabriel Stedman's encounter with the maimed monkey, Bababalouk becomes animalized, which ostensibly downplays his humanity. His literal fall, in which he "flounder[s] like a turtle," precipitates the negation of his humanity, and he remains a "deplorable animal," still immersed in water by the time the torture halts.

The wounds Bababalouk sustains in the baths are salted by Nouronihar's goad, which alludes to yet another Ovidian mythos of violation and transformation. Adding insult to injury, Nouronihar taunts: "'Oh gentle white dove, as though soar'st through the air, vouchsafe one kind glance on the mate of thy love: melodious Philomel, I am they rose; warble some couple to ravish my heart!'"[63] Graham glosses the allusion to Philomel in two words: "the nightingale."[64] Yet, to remember the Ovidian origins of such a gloss is to remember the truly sinister justification for Philomela's transformation into a bird of song. Ovid recounts that King Tereus's wife, Procne, desires her sister, Philomela, to join the newly minted connubial estate. Tereus sets out to shuttle his sister-in-law to his new wife, and when he beholds Philomela, he is awestruck by her beauty. Consumed with incestuous thoughts, he resigns himself to "erode her attendants [sic] care, and her nurse's loyalty, even seduce the girl herself with rich gifts, to the extent of his kingdom, or rape her and defend the rape in savage war."[65] When Philomela refuses to cuckold her sister, Tereus uses her own hair for bondage, cuts her tongue out, and mutilates her body. Procne soon happens upon this slaughter and through prayer to the gods is transformed, with her sister, into a bird: "One of them, a nightingale, Procne, makes for the woods. The other, a swallow, Philomela, flies to the eaves of the palace, and even now her throat has not lost the stain of that murder, and the soft down bears witness to the blood."[66] Nouronihar's invocation of Philomel antagonizes the tortured Bababalouk and retools the Ovidian mythos by positioning Nouronihar as the tyrannical Tereus.

Bababalouk's pleas to Vathek similarly go unanswered and further situate Nouronihar and Vathek as a perfect match given their affinity for torture. Bababalouk, finally extricated from his sadistic bath, approaches the Caliph: "But, instead of sympathizing with the miserable sufferer, he [Vathek] laughed immoderately at the device of the swing and the figure of Bababalouk, mounted upon it."[67] The spectacle triggers laughter from Vathek, and this comes as no surprise given Vathek's own penchant for torturous pleasures. When Bababalouk criticizes Nouronihar as "too wicked to spare even majesty itself,"[68] Vathek is immediately intrigued: "These words made, for the present, but a slight impression on the Caliph: but they, not long after, recurred to his mind."[69] The incident ends here. The aqueous punishment brandished here castigates Bababalouk for his seeming transgression—that is, his attraction to Nouronihar—by violently marking his body and remanding it to a desexualized state. The bath situates yet another aqueous means by which desexualized bodies are dispossessed by traumatic violence. Such violence serves to keep desexualized interlopers at bay from heteronormative economies and, as a result, to mold heteronormative coupling and attraction.

INCANTATORY DEATH

Samuel Taylor Coleridge's 1797 critical evaluation of *The Monk* is generally lambasting. Coleridge couches his criticism in Lewis's perversity: "The sufferings which he [Lewis] describes are so frightful and intolerable, that we break with abruptness from the delusion, and indignantly suspect the man of a species of brutality, who could find a pleasure in wantonly imagining them."[70] He applauds the rich imaginative powers that *The Monk* conjures but abjures that imaginative prowess as brutal and unwieldy in its perverse effects. Describing *The Monk*'s poetry "interspersed through the volumes" as "in general, far above mediocrity" remains the closest the Romantic poet comes to praise.[71] The insufficiently studied poetic vignettes found throughout the novel motivate my focus here.

Like Nouronihar, whose violent actions and words ring with poetic allusion, the invocation of "The Water-King" makes a similar gesture. To liberate Agnes from the convent, Raymond employs Theodore to locate Agnes's whereabouts within the cloister. The nuns swear that Agnes has died, in childbirth no less, but neither Don Raymond nor Theodore believe this falsified public pronouncement. Theodore secures the nuns' trust with his amiable charms: "the Nuns admired the delicacy of his features, the beauty of his hair, and the sweetness and grace which accompanied all his actions. They lamented to each other in whispers, that so charming a Youth should be exposed to the seductions of the World, and agreed, that He would be a worthy Pillar of the Catholic Church."[72] The irony of these lines is twofold: first, Theodore's willful deceit hardly qualifies as a sweet or graceful action, and second, to suggest that such deceit would prepare Theodore to become a "worthy Pillar" of the "order of the Capuchins," the monastery counterpart to the convent, would be shockingly cynical.[73]

The novel's explicit disgust with Catholicism resonates with A. W. Barnes's, George Haggerty's, Diane Long Hoeveler's, and Goran Sanivukovic's assessments of the Gothic's penchant for criticizing the religion's hypocritical and ironic refutation of, yet capacity for, vice or nonnormative sexual pleasures.[74] For Hoeveler, the Gothic "functioned as a form of fictional mystification, characterized by extreme religious ambivalence and an alternating demonization of and flirtation with the Catholic clergy, their practices and their properties."[75] In *The Monk*'s recapitulation of these tropes, all atrocious acts are conducted under the aegis of Catholicism. It comes as no shock, then, when the nuns are regaled by Theodore's recounting of "The Water-King," where atrocity and anguish are commonplace.

The Monk's version of "The Water-King" derives from the account titled "Der Wasserman" in Johann Gottfried Herder's *Volkslieder* ("folk music"), which Lewis translated from German in the early 1790s. Lewis's iteration of the folk song assumes the form of twenty quatrains told in rhyming couplets. The ballad details the submarine and supernatural Water-Fiend's longing for a young maid who travels along the river's bank to church. The Water-Fiend, obsessed with this young maiden's visage, pleads with his "Mother-witch": "'Oh! Mother! Mother! now advise, / How I may yonder Maid surprise: / Oh! Mother! Mother! Now explain, / How I may yonder Maid obtain.'"[76] The Water-Fiend's mother obliges her son, and by her magical prowess and command, she constructs a suit of "armour white" alongside "a Steed, whose housings were of sand."[77] Bedizened in this new garb, the Water-Fiend morphs into the Water-King and hies to the church, where he promptly proposes to the maiden. She, seeing this male nymph in his magisterial glory, immediately accepts the proposal. They are married on the spot. The Water-King—the "Traiter-Bride-groom"—leads the maiden back to the river where, despite her pleading to stop,

> Three times while struggling with the stream,
> The lovely maid was heard to scream;
> But when the Tempest's rage was o'er,
> The lovely Maid was seen no more.[78]

The didactic moral from the ballad, Theodore sings: "Warned by this Tale, ye Damsels fair, / To whom you give your love beware! / Believe not every handsome Knight, / And dance not with the Water-Spright!"[79] Theodore's final couplet teaches two sobering yet enmeshed lessons to the nuns: one, beware the powerful, deathly associations of embodied water, and two, young women must refrain from their innate head-over-shoulders attractions, lest they meet their end.

The drowning death of the lovely maid gives voice and song to the experience of water, which the novel frames as deeply painful. Ignorant to the horrors of the ballad, "the Nuns were delighted with the sweetness of his voice, and masterly manner of touching the Instrument," and they too become complicit in the retelling of the maiden's demise, as with the anguish experienced by Agnes within the bowels of the convent.[80] Like the fifty young boys in *Vathek*, the young maiden is subject to the cannibalizing death—she is consumed whole by the water, which is both the Water-King's realm and integral to his physicality—that accompanies her interaction with the Water-King. She screams "stop" seven times in succession in hopes of halting her imminent death:

> 'Stop! Stop! my Love! The waters blue
> E'en now my shrinking foot bedew!'
> 'Oh! lay aside your fears, sweet Heart!
> We now have reached the deepest part.'
>
> 'Stop! Stop! my Love! For now I see
> The waters rise above my knee.'
> 'Oh! lay aside your fears, sweet Heart!
> We now have reached the deepest part.'
>
> 'Stop! Stop! for God's sake, stop! For Oh!
> The waters o'er my bosom flow!'—
> Scarce was the word pronounced, when Knight
> And Courser vanished from her sight.[81]

The call and response modeled by the maid and the Water-King amplifies a process of bodies violated in and by water. The encroaching stream starts from the maid's feet and quickly engulfs her, from foot to head. The repetition of "stop" reveals the frightening violation of this assault. "Stop" functions as both an interjection to heed but also as a call for help. Both go unanswered, goaded only by the Water-King who sadistically assures the maiden that they have reached "the deepest part." Of course the deepest part is never met by the maiden, and the calls for help cease altogether: this is shown by the em dash that follows the maid's exclamation that the water has surpassed her bosom.

The stream homes this sexual violation—her insistence on "stop" followed by the recalcitrance of her perpetrator—and extends Elaine Scarry's synthesis that the body in pain results in the erasure of language. For Scarry, the moment of pain "causes a reversion to the pre-language of cries and groans" and becomes "the destruction of language"; to witness this is "almost to have been permitted to be present at the birth of language itself."[82] The young maid's voice literally becomes mute as, we are to infer, water stifles her ability to communicate and drowns her. Water becomes the supplice by which silence and violation are forged. Her death includes not only the cessation of her cries but also the blinding of her vision: her "Courser" vanishes from sight and the ballad mutes her perspective altogether. The muffling of the young maiden's voice is in fact inscribed in the *OED*'s etymological trace of "stop," which from the mid-sixteenth century signified "the block of the mouth." The young maiden's emphatic repetition of "stop" then becomes a perverse self-fulfilling prophecy—she calls for him to stop and yet her dictum performs the silencing of her voice. We see then an ironic, sadistic, and watery inversion of J. L. Austin's "performative utterance" (and an echo of Ovid's Philomela) that coincides with marital vows—a point we see recast again at *The Monk*'s end. But what is even more unnerving is the lesson that this account means to teach. It is not *beware the depths of water*, or *learn how to swim*. Rather, the lesson for the audience (both readers and the nuns simultaneously) is to distrust the beautiful charmer, especially by way of the Water-King, because he will assuredly lead you to your death, and a painful one where no one will heed (or hear) your cries.

CONTRACTS AND COMEUPPANCE

As preposterous as this perverse didacticism may seem, "The Water-King" functions as a microcosm for the entire novel. "The Water-King" is a surrogate for Ambrosio, the beautiful charmer incarnate, who lures Antonia to her virginal death and kills her (and their mother for interceding) following the rape.[83] But Ambrosio and the Water-King meet different ends. Unlike the Water-King/Fiend who can escape to his watery palace with impunity, Ambrosio is tried and in refusing to admit his guilt, sentenced to torture before death: "Returned to his dungeon, the sufferings of Ambrosio's body were far more supportable than those of his mind. His dislocated limbs, the nails torn from his hands and feet, and his fingers mashed and broken by the pressure of screws, were far surpassed in anguish by the agitation of his soul, and vehemence of his terrors."[84] Scarry neatly sums such a graphic description: "Torture aspires to the totality of pain."[85] Darius Rejali differentiates modes of torture as employing a "clean" technique versus a "scarring" one. The Inquisition subjects Ambrosio to torture that is both clean and scarring. For Michael Richardson, after Rejali, "clean tortures leave the body unmarked; scarring ones do not."[86] Ambrosio's suffering body recalls both the spectacle of torture and the psychological damage that accompanies. But this grotesque disfigurement is only the start for Ambrosio: Lucifer himself doles out the exacerbated torture he experiences, resonating again with Foucault's claim about the torturous performances that steal the limelight in hell.

In *The Monk*'s theatre of hell, Lucifer's torturous offer becomes the means by which a queer sadistic marriage is performed between Ambrosio—unrepentant priest—and the Devil. Before the Inquisition can acquit Ambrosio of his crimes, Lucifer appeals to the tortured monk with his usual Faustian bargain: "'I am condemned to die;' He [Ambrosio] said with a faint voice, his blood running cold, while He gazed upon his dreadful Visitor. 'Save me! Bear me from hence.'"[87] But first Lucifer must have his remittance: Ambrosio to give of himself body and soul. When Ambrosio becomes hesitant to bequeath his soul in exchange for emancipation, Lucifer makes clear his desire for Ambrosio—all of him: "'I must have your soul; must have it mine, and mine for ever.'"[88] Overwhelmed by this passionate demand, dejected Ambrosio sends Lucifer away only to, shortly after, realize the error of his choice: "The Bell announced mid-night: It was the signal for being led to the Stake! As He [Ambrosio] listened to the first stroke, the blood ceased to circulate in the Abbott's veins: He heard death and torture murmured in each succeeding sound."[89] Ambrosio, in turn, beckons Lucifer's return. Already a broken man, Ambrosio must pick his poison: either he must sell his soul and lie with the Devil for eternity, or he must come to terms with the Inquisition's demand for justice, which will inflict additional torture and potential death. It is as if Ambrosio's aversion to the torture he has already experienced—let us recall the mangled hands and dislocated limbs—secures his choice to ultimately sell his soul.

The irony of this is that the monk's aversion to torture only breeds more torture. In the final moments of the novel, Ambrosio signs the Devil's parchment, and like the Water-King ballad, a pseudo–marriage ceremony is performed:

> "Take it!" said the God-abandoned; "Now then save me! Snatch me from hence!"
> "Hold! Do you freely and absolutely renounce your Creator and his son!"
> "I do! I do!"
> "Do you make over your soul to me for ever?"
> "For ever!"
> "Without reserve or subterfuge? Without future appeal to the divine mercy?" . . .
> "I am yours for ever and irrevocably!" cried the Monk wild with terror: "I abandon claim to salvation! I own no power but yours! Hark! Hark! They come! Oh! save me ! Bear me away!"[90]

In these lines, connubial vows unfold between Lucifer and Ambrosio—a queer marriage performed—which Coleridge eerily replicates (despite his loathing of *The Monk*), as I discuss elsewhere, in *Christabel*, the first part of which was penned only months after the publication of *The Monk*.[91] As is still common, what seals Ambrosio's bond to the Devil, in unhappy matrimony, is his emphatic, "I do! I do!," which is soon followed by his pronouncement: "I am yours for ever and irrevocably!" The macabre ceremony aside, in this exchange Ambrosio—morphed into the Water-King himself by luring young women to their demise—has suddenly become the young maiden that seeks emancipation from a treacherous fiend, endowed with total trust. Ambrosio's repetition of "Hark!" functions identically to the young maiden's invocation of "Stop!": both exclamations go unanswered. "Hark" and "Stop" stand in for the scream that is seemingly missing in these moments. These exclamations go ignored by the torturer. Thus, not only is voice debased through torture, but any invocation of voice falls on actively unlistening ears. Yet, as with all Faustian bargains, the newly husbanded Lucifer, in his infinite ability to inflict pain, gets the last laugh. The narrator reveals, "Though rescued from the Inquisition, Ambrosio as yet was insensible of the blessings of liberty."[92] And for good reason.

Upon prostituting his soul, Ambrosio's comeuppance is realized at the hands of the Devil, who "darting his talons into the Monk's shaven crown, He sprang with him from the rock."[93] The literal fall reads as the apogee of pain and intensified torture for Ambrosio, who "Headlong fell through the airy waste; The sharp point of a rock received him; and He rolled from precipice to precipice, till bruised and mangled He rested on the river's banks."[94] As in my discussion of the entangled riverbank in chapter 2, *The Monk*'s riverbank—where the novel leaves Ambrosio—likewise becomes immersed in doleful gestures of bodily manipulation. Within Darwin's, Swift's, and Stedman's narratives, the river flits with creatures. But in a horrific, perhaps characteristically Gothic twist, these life-forms feast on Ambrosio. On Lewis's riverbank, "myriads of insects were called forth by the warmth; They drank the blood which trickled from Ambrosio's wounds."[95] Here he is subject to "tortures the most exquisite and insupportable": eagles consume his flesh and enucleate him, and thirst torments him.[96] Ambrosio's own animality—his lewd and crude behavior—is ostensibly reflected in the fauna that now participate in his bodily deterioration, yet another signal tie to Beckford's gleeful torture of Bababalouk. As final punishment, Ambrosio become detritus and prey to the animalized bodies that feed upon the tormented and tortured monk. It is a comeuppance, of course, for his own predatory maneuverings.

This riverbank, however, proves to amplify the pain rather than remediate it. Despite proximity to the river, Ambrosio is unable to drink. The absence, yet reminder of, water performs the feat of a torturous thirst, corresponding with the myth of Tantalus, whose hellish punishment was insatiable hunger and thirst. The excess of water does something similar in *Crusoe,* as discussed in chapter 1: shipwrecked Robinson Crusoe, surrounded by the ocean, cannot slake his thirst. Ambrosio, in hellacious fashion, endures this thirst for seven days, which repositions a biblical numerology but more importantly coincides with the exact number of times the drowned maiden utters "stop." In this way, Ambrosio's fate reconstitutes the Water-Fiend and the forlorn maid: "On the Seventh a violent storm arose: The winds in fury rent up rocks and forests: The sky was now black with clouds, now sheeted with fire: The rain fell in torrents; It swelled the stream; The waves overflowed their banks; They reached the spot where Ambrosio lay, and when they abated carried with them into the river the Corse [sic] of the despairing Monk."[97] The novel's final lines illustrate a deluge of water that transports his body down the river to finality and erasure. What looks like a cathartic cleansing of his body from the novel is only an extension of the pain Ambrosio must endure en route to his death. Water, both in its scarce and plentiful forms, participates in Ambrosio's aqueous punishment.

Whereas "The Water-King" ends with the "courser" vanishing from the maiden's sight, the novel concludes with Ambrosio's "corse" disappearing down the flooded stream. The homophonic similarity encodes the dangers and disappearance of bodies in water. Like the maid, Ambrosio meets his demise in bodies of water that silence voices and deliver them into oblivion.

But it is Ambrosio's violent and dependent relationship with Lucifer that further queers this punishing episode. Following Lucifer's agreement with Ambrosio, who realizes the technicality that has ensnared him, Ambrosio's very final line is: "Have you forgotten our contract?"[98] What Ambrosio experiences after this is assuredly an egregious act of domestic violence. I see the queer marriage contract between the two as yet another justification for the torture that Ambrosio experiences. Ambrosio is hardly a desexualized character—he enjoys the pleasures of the flesh as much as Vathek—but his role as abbot mandates his desexualization. His watery end appears as justice served given that he is finally castigated for violating his priestly vows. But it is also the queer engagement with Lucifer that magnifies the torturous ending. Ambrosio invokes the contract, as a sign of fidelity and mutualism, in his final words, and the Devil ignores this reminder, thus eroding the sanctity of such a document. It is one thing to break one's desexualized identity by engaging in heteronormative sex acts. It is entirely another to give oneself to the Devil, who notably neither consents to nor respects the norms associated with the betrothal. Aqueous punishment disciplines the overly sexualized character who should be—but is not—desexualized by their archetypal role. While Ambrosio's comeuppance is expected and justified, the wielding of punishment in this final moment solidifies the sanctity and security of the heteronormative bond. The novel's final disavowal of Ambrosio not only employs Lucifer as the arbitrator of torture, but insists upon aqueous punishment as a means of correcting sexual and potentially queer transgression.

By the end of the eighteenth century, Foucault contends, penal reform was heavily underway. The social process that brought about these penal reforms intended "not to punish less, but to punish better; to punish with an attenuated severity perhaps, but in order to punish with more universality and necessity; to insert the power to punish more deeply into the social body."[99] But, of course, any attempt to "punish more deeply" becomes an endeavor to mark bodies more emphatically and legibly. The moments I have traced here illustrate that the supplice of aqueous punishment does just that: it is the pressure point by which torturous and painful relationality are mapped onto the Gothic novel. Both *Vathek* and *The Monk* speak to the personalized and socialized praxis of inflicting pain upon and humiliating the transgressive recipient, and these affective resonances participate in the clarified marking of bodies. Like other torturous means, aqueous punishment intends to mark the body so intensely that the mark has both personal and social ramifications. The state's attempt to biopolitically mark the body performs double duty. First, it makes the social wrong visible to the public, which intensifies social damage—look what that individual has done to merit such punishment! In Foucault's words, "It is intended, either by the scar it leaves on the body, or by the spectacle that accompanies it, to brand the victim with infamy."[100] Second, this branding instills a self-corrective by which the state participates in cognizing one's own internalized policing—look what I have done to merit such punishment!

Yet in *Vathek* and *The Monk,* readers are less privy to the personalized affective ripples that accompany aqueous punishment. Rather, aqueous punishment indexes the physical cicatrices that catalyze additional pain. Bababalouk's waterboarding experience punitively corrects his sensuous longing for Nouronihar. Because he is a eunuch, Bababalouk's expression of attraction for the woman predestined to be the Caliph's own problematizes his socially accepted role as a myrmidon whose desexualized castration remains his skeleton key to mediating public and private spheres. His outpouring of affection for Nouronihar forfeits this desexualization, and his aqueous punishment painfully reminds Bababalouk of his constrained positionality, facilitating his return to a desexualized state. Ambrosio's sexual rampage undoes his vow of chastity, and thus, he too must be punished by way of water. As both demonstrate, the procedural by which aqueous punishment is effected underscores a heteronormative model that remands both desexualized and queer desires in order to exalt and sanctify heteronormative ones. Aqueous punishment thus performs an embodied, social corrective. Water's deployment in these moments insists that it has reparatory potentialities: it disciplines the body, it assists in categorizing social insiders from intruders, and it punishes with impunity. The novels, in short, wash their hands of the desexualized interlopers.

INTERMEZZO

Off with Her Head

The statue of *The Little Mermaid* ("Den lille Havfrue" in Danish) is only a stone's throw from Copenhagen's city center. The most recent renovation of her sits afoot the aquamarine waters of the Øresund, which divides Denmark from Sweden and connects the Baltic and North Seas. She is thusly positioned in flux, at the observational hub of one of the busiest waterways in the world. The bare-chested bronze mermaid rests on a tawny boulder. Her face is somber, perhaps woeful, contemplative at the very least. Her hair is neatly pulled behind her. Her legs are folded beneath and reveal vestiges of her previous mermaid form: she has not yet fully relinquished her flukes, which characterize her human-nonhuman hybridity. Her sculpted form catches her transformation in situ.

Commissioned in 1909 and unveiled in 1913, Edvard Eriksen's four-foot sculpture of the little mermaid commemorates the short story by the same name penned by Hans Christian Andersen in 1837. The tale has found renewed, fanciful attraction and royalty status in Walt Disney's animated film *The Little Mermaid*, released in 1989, and in Disney's acquisition of the distribution rights for Hayao Miyazaki's even looser adaptation, *Ponyo*, in 2008.[1] The happily-ever-after afforded by Disney's rose-colored-glass song-and-dance is nowhere to be found in the original text. In Andersen's story, the little mermaid's love for the prince proves unrequited and to return to an oceanic way of life and the sorority of her five sisters, she must decide between murdering the prince or sacrificing herself. "Before the sun rises," the sisters reveal to the little mermaid, "you must plunge it [a magical knife constructed of their bargained hair] into the heart of the prince; when the warm blood falls upon your feet, they will grow together again, and form into a fish's tale, and you will be once more a mermaid, and return to us to live out your three hundred years before you die and change into the salt of the sea foam."[2] The blood of the mortal prince thus serves as the betokened life blood—the obligatory remittance—of the youngest princess's renewed return as a mermaid.

But the little mermaid rejects the offer and dives into the ocean, a pseudoreunion with an aqueous home that is only shortly lived: "She cast one more lingering, half-fainting glance at the prince, and threw herself from the ship into the sea, and though her body was dissolving into foam . . . [she] did not feel as if she were dying."[3] For not killing the prince (this is after failing to gain his love, which would have granted her an immortal soul), the "daughters of the air" rescue the little mermaid and transform her into one of their ilk: "You, poor little mermaid, have tried with your whole heart to do as we are doing; you have suffered and endured and raised yourself to the spirit-world by your good deeds; and now, by striving for three hundred years in the same way, you may obtain a mortal soul."[4] A strange, almost-Faustian bargain, the daughters of the air grant the little mermaid a second chance wherein she may advance her selfless good deeds. Yet, in so doing, she must also accept the self-flagellation that accompanies her suffering.

Despite her long-held iconography and affection from tourists, in a frightening shift of fate, the bronze statue that sits along the Langelinie Promenade is also made to bear similar sufferings. She has twice been decapitated (in 1964 and 1998) and thrice more maimed: in 1984 her right arm was sawn off; in 1990 a failed decapitation ploy left her throat slit; and in 2003 explosives were attached to her body that left her knees and wrists damaged. These violations only partially account for the fact that the little mermaid has become a semaphore for social activism. Her body has been so repeatedly vandalized that it would seem she is the repudiated cynosure against which to rebel. She has been doused in paint to protest environmental degradation. Dildos have been affixed to her to disavow her story's misogynistic trappings in honor of International Women's Day. Vandals have sprayed her with red paint in recognition of Danish whaling exploits in the Faroe Islands. In truth, since 2017, graffiti artists have employed her body as a canvas by which to advertise protestations of, one, the precarity of Somalian refugees in Denmark and, two, the disintegration of democracy in Hong Kong. Most recently her body has been vandalized to lend support to the Black Lives Matter movement.

The little mermaid's body, as this evidences, too easily and too often frames violence or defilement under the auspices of social justice. The statue seems to evince her iconoclastic complicity with the poaching of endangered mammals, a virulent Danish jingoism, patriarchal instantiation, white supremacy, and the erosion of democracy. The destruction enacted against the statue, which sits abreast a militarized channel, thus serves to broadcast ostensibly activist-oriented protestations that center misogynistic violence acted against and written upon the hybrid female body. As in Andersen's original tale, the statue's body is meant to bear the violent brunt of social exclusion in hopes of instituting social harmony.

The material reality of Eriksen's statue accounts for how torturous violation and degradation of the female body—emblematized by the little mermaid—extend forms of aqueous punishment. This intermezzo, then, serves to couple "Aqueous Punishment" with "Sacrif-Ice," where Frankenstein's creature engenders another hybridized embodiment, which becomes further entangled in the lore of affection and its concomitant aqueous violence. While the statue is not waterboarded or drowned in swelling streams, the vandalism her body is forced to own accounts for a different trajectory by which to imagine aqueous punishment: namely, that the little mermaid must be punished because of her iconography and likewise because, I contend, of her hybrid human-nonhuman form. The violence enacted against her announces the little mermaid's exclusion from what constitutes the human, especially in its disabled adjacencies—a point to which I will return in my conclusion. The stunning reality is that Andersen's source material also details the forms of bodily violation that mermaid embodiment demands. In other words, both Andersen's little mermaid and the vandalized bronze state inspired by literary fiction recognize that mermaid embodiment accompanies repeated and striking violence that reeks of palpable misogynies, even sometimes ironic ones, as documented by the paint- and dildo-bombing to celebrate International Women's Day. The little mermaid's statuary is offered as the sacrifice by which socially just causes file the weapons of exposure and dissent. She is, put simply, a beloved tourist trap that is simultaneously abhorred.

Those familiar with Disney's rendition will remember that Ariel, besotted with Prince Eric, beseeches the evil sea witch, Ursula, to exchange her voice for a pair of human legs. These characters likewise appear in Andersen's short story (by different names), but the exchanging of goods is more vividly maligned in the fairy tale and becomes a means by which the little mermaid is subjected to torture. The sea witch foretells the little mermaid's fate:

I will prepare a draught for you, with which you must swim to land tomorrow before sunrise, and sit down on the shore and drink it. Your tail will then disappear, and shrink up into what mankind calls legs, and you will feel great pain, as if a sword were passing through you. But all who see you will say that you are the prettiest little human being they ever saw. You will still have the same floating gracefulness of movement, and no dancer will ever tread so lightly; but at every step you take it will feel as if you were treading upon sharp knives, and that the blood must flow. If you will bear all of this, I will help you.[5]

The little mermaid unabashedly accepts the pain and anguish that protrusive weapons thrust upon her "at every step" induce. The induction of bipedal form is paved by bloody footsteps. The sprightly elegance of her footwork results from the stabbing anguish she feels in her feet with every step; aesthetic elegance and pain walk together step by step. Yet her beauty syntactically results only from the metaphoric sword and the pain it registers: "Then the little mermaid drank the magic draught, and it seemed as if a two-edged sword went through her delicate body: she fell into a swoon, and lay like one dead. When the sun arose and shone over the sea, she recovered, and felt a sharp pain; but just before her stood the handsome young prince."[6] As promised, the draught produces legs at a cost, which pushes her deeper towards the mortality she seeks to test in pursuit of a mortal love. What follows the little mermaid's pain is an exclamation not of her own beauty but the beauty of the prince, whose "coal-black eyes" admire her "pretty," "white legs."[7] Her pain then exists as an exchangeable affective commodity by which her own and others' beauty is fully realized. Her body, like in its bronzed statuesque form, must shoulder and stomach (neck, arm, and knee as well) repeated and enduring viscera of pain for aesthetic beauty to manifest—social activism too.

The sea witch, however, demands payment for the draught by way of the princess's voice, which further maims her, thus dissecting her from realms of humanity and wholeness that become ironically desirable: "'There it is for you,' said the sea witch. Then she cut off the mermaid's tongue, so that she became dumb and would never again speak or sing."[8] Whereas Disney's Ariel has her voice magically captured by Ursula, the economy of exchange offered by the sea witch in Andersen's version is one that is contingent upon the exacerbated dissection of the little mermaid's body: "'But if you take away my voice,' said the little mermaid, 'what is left for me?'"⁹ The sea witch responds, "'Your beautiful form, your graceful walk, and your expressive eyes; surely with these you can enchain a man's heart.'"¹⁰ Infatuated with the promise and passion of heteronormativity, the little mermaid's pursuit of enchaining the prince's heart remains contingent on forms of her own enchantment, which sever her tongue and further disable her body in hopes that such a metamorphosed state becomes even more desirable. The little mermaid's alternatively abled form is the means to both aesthetic beauty and erotic appeal, which recuperates the notion that her disabled form derogates and positions her outside the realms of humanity and the normativity of heterodesirability.

The didacticism of these layerings cannot be understated; indeed, Andersen closes with a lesson for children that tethers the little mermaid's fate to those of her audience. As the transformed little mermaid becomes onboarded as a newly minted daughter of the air, one of her sisters details their end goal:

> "After three hundred years, thus shall we float into the kingdom of heaven," said she. "And we may even get there sooner," whispered one of her companions. "Unseen we can enter the houses of men, where there are children, and for every day on which we find a good child, who is the joy of parents and deserves their love, our time of probation is shortened. The child does not know, when we fly through the room, that we smile with joy at his good conduct, for we can count one year less of our three hundred years. But when we see a naughty or a wicked child, we shed tears of sorrow, and for every tear a day is added to our time of trial!" ¹¹

The story promptly ends there. Andersen positions his fairy tale as a reminder—in almost Santa Claus–like fashion—for children to behave and, more strangely, "deserve" the love of their parents, which has the effect of powerfully rewriting the narrative of unconditional love culturally spoon-fed. But what underpins this conclusion is the fact that ill-behaved children (which are legion) unconsciously rewind the clock of the purgatorial ether with which the daughters of the air are forced to reckon. The wickedness and naughtiness of others thus induces lachrymose outpourings from the sisters, and it is their emotional attunement to these gestures that inevitably demands further probationary time served. The lesson to learn is "be good." However, what subtends this lesson is again the forms of trauma that the little mermaid must bear.

Her hybridity is punished in both its elemental forms (aqueous and aerial), and we are instead left with a reminder of the emotional burden and physical violence that these feminized hybrid embodiments must abide—even in their invisibility as ether. The various genres of physical and emotional violence likewise become invisibilized yet indelibly marked on the little mermaid's body. Such enactments of violence telegraph beautiful becomings of radical alterity. Vandalizing her body, garroting her, and ultimately decapitating her bronze form further remind us of the uncomfortable ethos of aesthetic violence perpetrated against the female body as a somehow didactic dog-whistle. If the first intermezzo embraced the inevitable mermaid metamorphosis, then Andersen's "The Little Mermaid" and its resulting statue operate as two models that highlight the hazards of mermaid becoming. We must unlearn the mode of mermaid becoming hawked by "The Little Mermaid," to better assume other, revived mermaid trajectories of resilience, self-love, and—as I show in my conclusion—the queer care that rising waters might home.

CHAPTER 4

Sacrif-Ice

Framing *Frankenstein* (1818) with Arctic bookends, as Mary Shelley does, is no coincidence. The character Robert Walton's Arctic expedition (by way of Russia) situates the novel and makes possible the Gothic narrative that Dr. Frankenstein sets out to retell as he exhaustedly knocks on death's door. Deliberate as it may seem, the Arctic framework was not in the original draft, and thus was added sometime in late 1816 or early 1817.[1] The addition of the hoary outer framework serves to structure the narrative and remind readers that ice is interwoven in the very fabric of the novel (the glaciers above Chamonix are central to creature and maker's convenient reunion), offering icy encounters *around, within,* and *throughout*—queer prepositions that anticipate water's queer crystallizations and their consequent violences. If torture is the theatre of hell, as I suggested in chapter 3, this chapter interrogates what happens when hell freezes over.

Frankenstein situates a narrative deep freeze that taps into cultures of polar exploration bridging the eighteenth and nineteenth centuries, which have been adeptly traced by Jessica Richard, Siobhan Carroll, Jen Hill, Adriana Craciun, and Hester Blum, to name just a partial list.[2] This chapter pivots on this icy literary and cultural attention, rather than rehearsing it, to more specifically zero in on the genres of violent relationality that are both opened and foreclosed by glacial extremity. Following models offered in chapters 2 and 3, I locate the ice world—a term I employ to characterize the human exploration of and affective reaction to the Arctic and the glacial writ large—as yet another violent stage. The novel's repeated invocation of the ice world reiterates a history of Arctic exploration, begat by colonial expansion, while revealing these locations as quagmires where communities are foreclosed and death beckons through sacrificial means. Sacrifice is the hinge upon which I read the violent, queer relationality installed upon ice worlds.

The word sacrifice appears seven times in *Frankenstein*. I attend to both the implicit and explicit use of *sacrifice*, which connotes sacrosanct violence while also inscribing "ice," a convenient (and false) phoneme for this chapter, in its very articulation. *Ice*'s etymology is of course radically different than *sacrifice*'s. But the novel performs sacrifice *only* upon ice worlds, and thus, while the phonemes may be false, the recognition of their mutually informative nature, by the novel's constitution at least, is not. The Arctic bookends and the glaciers above Chamonix become thoroughly saturated in painful, violent disassociations. Ice operates as an elemental signal directing readerly attention to violent appeals that ingratiate, repulse, and knit together Walton, Frankenstein, and the creature.[3] In the previous chapter I posited that the Gothic novel's watery sites participate in biopolitical registers that expunge the desexualized body from heteronormative sexual economies, relocating it to the socially ordained periphery. This chapter continues that biopolitical inquiry by exploring how sacrificial appeals and executions that materialize on *Frankenstein*'s ice worlds become yet another means to imagine the dissolution of queer bonds that are rendered monstrous, perverse, and excessive. Fluidity may have heretofore characterized the queerness of water, but in this chapter, the crystallization of water into ice similarly crystallizes moments of violence, community upheavals, and dislocations of masculinity's relational pull through irremediable isolation. Therein lies sacrifice's queer drift.

In the protobiopolitical treatise *Violence and the Sacred* (1977) and a later series of corresponding lectures, *Sacrifice* (2011), René Girard identifies how the enactment of sacrifice is the making and doing of the sacred. "The function of sacrifice," Girard writes, "is to quell violence within the community and to prevent conflicts from erupting."[4] For Girard, communities exercise sacrifice to corral eruptions of excessive violence into a singular substitution and, as a result, ritualistically scapegoat a tokenized individual to establish momentary peace. This, in turn, requires additional sacrifices for maintenance. A community's dedication to the sacrifice, Girard contends, "hop[es] in this way to protect themselves from their own violence by diverting it onto expendable victims, human or animal, whose deaths will not cause violence to rebound because no one will bother to avenge them."[5]

However, in *Frankenstein,* both violence and sacrifice rebound, immuring the trifecta of male protagonists in a repeated praxis of failed sacrifices and, thus, failed queer affiliations. The queer potential of sacrifice lies in the way in which the sacrificial victim—the individual who is sacrificed, or is intended to be—is encoded in a violent interrelationality that maintains unmistakable irony: the sacrifice enacted (through appeal or dedication) seeks to connect, protect, and unify communities (where the prospect of queer connection may manifest), and yet the novel's representations of sacrifice only disconnect and disunify the sacrificial dyad (where the prospect of queer connection fails).

My discussion pends on the creature's condemnation of his maker, where sacrifice's import assumes center stage, at the novel's close:

> Fear not that I shall be the instrument of future mischief. My work is nearly complete. Neither yours nor any man's death is needed to consummate the series of my being, and accomplish that which must be done; but it requires my own. Do not think that I shall be slow to perform this *sacrifice*. I shall quit your vessel on the ice-raft which brought me thither, and shall seek the most northern extremity of the globe; I shall collect my funeral pile, and consume to ashes this miserable frame, that its remains may afford no light to any curious and unhallowed wretch, who would create such another as I have been. I shall die.[6]

Saturated with melancholic tones and suicidal ideation, the novel's—and the creature's—penultimate paragraph displays how sacrifice is wielded, while also demonstrating the importance of the geographic terrain that is to become the funereal plot. The creature's idea of self-sacrifice arises from his reading of Goethe's *The Sorrows of Young Werther,* one of the primary texts provided by the DeLaceys that foster his literacy. He reveals, "the disquisitions upon death and suicide were calculated to fill me with wonder."[7] The Arctic becomes aligned with these same doleful tropes: the performance of sacrifice—real or imagined—and the invocation of death within "the most northern extremity." Francis Spufford similarly recognizes these fraught tropes: "If the pack-ice is primarily conceived as the climactic setting to the battle between Frankenstein and the monster—if Walton is really only an extra in the main drama of the book—he [Walton] learns at least, from the scenes that he witnesses, what the meaning of the place he has sought out actually is."[8] Walton comes to realize how ice worlds are entangled with violence, death, and self-sacrifice. As Spufford acknowledges, the Arctic "proves to be an enemy to the human body," and Shelley's use of the polar North is an endorsement of this location as one imbricated in "abnegation, expiation, death."[9]

In *For All Waters*, Lowell Duckert coins "cryocompositionism" as "a reminder of how we slowly compose with and are composed by the icy world" and how ice "alter[s] our imaginations as well, sponsor[s] new shapes of intimacy across ice's translucent sluices."[10] This chapter imagines *Frankenstein* as a novel that queers cryocompositionism's icy intimacies. Dr. Frankenstein's and the creature's hot-potato-like juggling of sacrifice illustrates the queer interrelationality that undergirds their violent intimacy: they each deify the other to the divine plane in hopes of affiliation and fellowship. Such communal belonging for the two is, of course, impossible and suggests that in *Frankenstein,* ice worlds are sites where queer affiliation is frozen to the point of erasure: kinship is impossible (Frankenstein and creature), queer intimacy fails (Frankenstein and Walton), and the violated body (Frankenstein and creature) reaches its psychic and physical demise. The crystallizations of queerness that surface and are broken by the novel are not strictly homoerotic in nature; the queernesses that I see unfolding among the trifecta include forms of queer attachment and intimacy that cannot be bound by the limited imaginary of colonial heteronormativity.

Frankenstein's myriad sacrifices thus account for what Jack Halberstam has termed "the queer art of failure." "Failing is something queers do," Halberstam writes, "and have always done exceptionally well; for queers failure can be a style, to cite Quentin Crisp, or a way of life, to cite Foucault, and it can stand in contrast to the grim scenarios of success that depend upon 'trying and trying again.'"[11] Whereas Halberstam articulates the queer art of failure to address exceptional forms of queer being—"Queerness offers the promise of failure as a way of life"[12]—I, not fully convinced by this recuperation, tell a different story. I read the novel's repeated attempts at sacrifice as queer failures in that the plural invocations of sacrifice make impossible the communal reallocation that they ostensibly set out to reinstate. The queer violence of *Frankenstein*'s sacrificial appeals rests upon the fact that these invocations of sacrifice fail to accomplish the proposed social repossession. Dr. Frankenstein can never be reconciled with Walton—the former's convalescence and death inhibits this—just as the creature cannot be reconciled with Frankenstein. Ice worlds and the sacrifices pronounced upon them inhibit queer interrelationality and, in so doing, inaugurate an immersive loneliness: Walton, Frankenstein, and the creature all accept their diassociated singularity by novel's end. The creature's woeful resignation serves as a chyron that might connect the three: "I am alone."[13]

The genres of crystallized and failed queer intimacy inform the anticolonial thread that I have so far woven. I want to imagine Frankenstein's glacial worlds as locales of potential anticolonial intimacy that could be delinked from Enlightenment-era strictures of heteronormativity, and which of course fail. Such an imagination is a commitment to reframing, unlearning, and resisting (neo)colonial structures, which require an adherence to gendered and sexual norms. María Lugones, for example, reminds us that the infrastructures of heteronormativity as we know it, and the way they influence notions of gender, are inherited from coloniality's global vise-grip. "Categorical, dichotomous, [and] hierarchical logics," Lugones writes, "are central to modern, colonial, capitalist thinking about race, gender, and sexuality."[14] Our notions of gender and sexuality—of ardent attempts to queer these frameworks and free ourselves from these staid constructions—are reliant on colonial epistemologies bequeathed to us by the eighteenth century. M. Jacqui Alexander's "erotic autonomy" likewise reclaims forms of bodily, intimate, and erotic autonomy that have heretofore been denied Black and Caribbean women in particular.[15] Erotic autonomy enables Alexander to name this erasure and to "path" (a denominalization advanced by Sara Ahmed) with fellow decolonial and anticolonial feminist and queer intellectuals who endeavor to upset and dispel colonial strongholds.[16] These critiques of heteronormativity's Enlightenment and stifling roots by feminists of color motivate my investment in an anticolonial politics and model a necessary citational praxis.

Anticoloniality, in other words, allows me to envision two intertwined potentials that arise parasitically, a concept I traced in the introduction, within a literary canon. First, by reading Dr. Frankenstein as an arbiter of colonial (dis)order, and the creature as an embodiment of colonialism's attempt to unsuccessfully self-replicate, icy stages reveal how the failures of sacrifice, articulated many times over by the masculine trio, accompany the failures of colonial expropriation and enlargement. *Ice worlds forestall colonialism's global aspirations.* Second, anticoloniality makes possible opportunities for queer attachments that, put plainly, are an impossibility. Sacrifice becomes a means by which queer intimacies and longings are simultaneously dedicated and foreclosed. *Frankenstein* is not the decolonial novel; it instead manifests as a vehicle for imagining the cold failures of colonial expansion and, ironically with it, the conjoined and frozen failures of queer bonds that might be sanctified through sacrificial appeal.

FRANKENSTEIN'S QUEER RIPPLES

While queer and trans readings of Shelley's novel are legion,[17] often taking to task the anti-repro-normativity in which Frankenstein animates the creature (that is, sans the maternal body), the queer potentiality I imagine here identifies how violence, sadism, and irony are mediated by the novel's frozen sacrifices. The imbrication of water and queerness in the novel has mostly escaped the attention of scholars, though Susan Stryker's "My Words to Victor Frankenstein above the Village of Chamounix: Performing Transgender Rage" comes closest to the queer aqueous capacities that I see proliferating in *Frankenstein*. Stryker's performance piece, which melds emphatic indictment with memoir and poetry, ineluctably articulates water as a site of annihilation, just as the creature realizes glacial sheets and surrounding Arctic waters in identical ways. The now-foundational essay centers trans rage as a means to rail against biomedicine's erasure and gaslighting of trans livelihood and struggle. The reparative thesis that Stryker offers—one that reclaims epithetic slurs such as monster and the pronoun "it"—bespeaks a sympathetic attunement with Shelley's creature so as to realize that "we transsexuals are something more, and something other, than the creatures our makers intended us to be."[18] The monstrous body is repeatedly aligned with the trans body, and Stryker recovers this connection to dismantle transphobic rhetoric, dysphemism, and derogation. Rage, Stryker posits, courses through her body and other trans bodies that have been nonconsensually subjected to the colonization enacted by biomedicine, which Stryker describes as being "bred by the necessity of existing in external circumstances that work against my survival."[19] In rage lies a refusal to acquiesce to erasure, and in that refusal lives a trans affective and affirming state that animates trans livelihood for perpetuity.

Stryker's hermeneutics of rage, however, intimately engages aqueous becoming and thus motivates a queer and trans ecology that I read interwoven in *Frankenstein*. Through diaristic italics, which describe the birth of her lover's child, Stryker reveals water's queer and trans capacities:

I enter the realm of my dreams. I am underwater, swimming upwards. It is dark. I see a shimmering light above me. I break through the plane of the water's surface with my lungs bursting. I suck for air—and find only more water. My lungs are full of water. Inside and out I am surrounded by it. Why am I not dead if there is no difference between me and what I am in? There is another surface above me and I swim frantically towards it. I see a shimmering light. I break the plane of water's surface over and over and over again. This water annihilates me. I cannot be, and yet—an excruciating impossibility—I am. I will do anything not to be here.

I will swim forever.
I will die for eternity
I will learn to breathe water.
I will become the water.
If I cannot change my situation I will change myself.[20]

The speaker's voice eerily joins Rich's speaker in "Diving into the Wreck"; together they imagine water worlds of communion and dislocation subtended by various affective states, giving birth both to possible as well as failed queer horizons. The evocative, fluid imagery Stryker offers serves to, one, enliven the process of giving birth, articulating a voice of the becoming-born that Stryker's lover and the baby experience and, two, acknowledge water's complex metaphoricity to realize how annihilation, maintenance, and rebirth are always already intermeshed.[21] The prison of gender, for Stryker, is tantamount to the multiscalar prison of water that drowns, suffocates, and annihilates—a prison that requires conformity and biopolitical control for hetero-reproductive necessity. Frankenstein and the creature likewise realize the similarly immuring nature of repro-normativity, which I trace more fully below.

The glacial representations I pattern in Shelley's novel do not seamlessly overlap with Stryker's trans hydropoetics. However, the queer and trans affinities of ice worlds persist in that, like Styker does with the water worlds she pens that participate in attempts at erasure, Frankenstein imagines ice as a means of dispossessing and annihilating the creature. Like Stryker, who expresses fellowship with the created, the creature does not submit to these interventions and instead employs rage, mediated by endeavors to sacrifice, to "punch a hole in water / around which I coalesce / to allow the flow to come through me."[22] Water's queerness and its manifold permutations are thus indispensable in locating Frankenstein's queer (un)becomings: the phases of water (from flowing to frozen) transfigure affective, geographic, environmental, and relational textures that undergird interrelational violence as motivational factors for survivance and intimacy.

ICY OPENING

Frankenstein's epistolary opening both commemorates and denies the hardships faced by Arctic voyagers.[23] In the novel's first line, Walton writes, "You will rejoice to hear that no disaster has accompanied the commencement of an enterprise which you have regarded with such evil forebodings."[24] Assuring his beloved sister, Margaret, of his safety, Walton configures the Arctic as a site redolent with Burkean sublimity and a sirenic attraction:[25] "I cannot describe to you my sensations on the near prospect of my undertaking. It is impossible to communicate to you a conception of the trembling sensation, half pleasurable and half fearful, with which I am preparing to depart."[26] Walton's romanticized description of the Arctic voyage makes invisible the real and apparent dangers that await him: "I try in vain to be persuaded that the pole is the seat of frost and desolation; it ever presents itself to my imagination as the region of beauty and delight."[27] As if taken directly out of Defoe, wherein Crusoe confesses, "I would be satisfied with nothing but going to Sea,"[28] Walton parrots this incomprehensible allure: "There is something at work in my soul, which I do not understand . . . There is a love for the marvelous, a belief in the common pathways of men, even to the wild sea and unvisited regions I am about to explore."[29] Like the sea that dislocates Crusoe, so too is the Arctic over which Walton obsesses ultimately portending similarly disastrous results.

Walton's admission that this voyage has both emotionally and physically distanced him from his family underscores how the novel reconstructs the Arctic as a location bereft of familiarity and kinship. Walton pinpoints, in another Crusoe repetition, his father's warning against the voyage, which separates him from immediate family: "my father's dying injunction had forbidden my uncle to allow me to embark on a seafaring life."[30] The radical disassociation is further emphasized by Walton's woeful articulation of his loneliness, even as he boasts of the romantic lure of the sea: "I have one want which I have never yet been able to satisfy; and the absence of an object of which I feel as a most severe evil. I have no friend, Margaret."[31] Like the creature's dying confession, "I am alone," so too does Walton embody loneliness in his attempts to find friendship in the most treacherous and isolated of geographies: "I desire the company of a man who could sympathise with me; whose eyes would reply to mine. You may deem me romantic, my dear sister, but I bitterly feel the want of a friend. I have no one near me, gentle yet courageous, possessed of a cultivated as well as of a capacious mind, whose tastes are like my own."[32] Walton seeks similitude and projects that onto Frankenstein. The queer longing for friendship—the narcissistic search for a same self—coincides with the appeal the creature makes to Dr. Frankenstein for a companion that might eradicate the dark uneasiness of singularity; there are layers to the novel's queer friendship. As George Haggerty observes, "there is no greater concern in *Frankenstein* than this question of friendship."[33] Though Haggerty centers Frankenstein's friendship with Clerval (and Walton is a failed surrogate for that relationship), he notes that "friendship looms in the novel as a need that can only be ignored at one's peril."[34] Indeed, for both Walton and the creature, it is the isolation of the glacial setting that induces this unshakable loneliness and ironically furthers a connective tie among the male narrators: loneliness ironically unifies them.

The repeated and failed search for companionship, which gives way to violent and sacrificial interactions, registers one of the novel's many articulations of disaster. In *Writing Arctic Disaster,* Craciun contends that the concept of disaster—that is, the frequent "catastrophic losses" of colonial seafarers—is at the center of Arctic exploration and texts about those explorations.[35] I want to extend Craciun's argument to query what other forms of disaster, namely ones that tax sociality and relationality, accompany the "formative power that disaster has acquired in Arctic discourses."[36] The novel relays that Walton, Frankenstein, and the creature must sacrifice companionship/affiliation or have it sacrificed before them. The search for companionship, Walton admits, attends to a potential outcome of sacrifice, which intends to reallocate and unify. Girard notes that the mythos of sacrifice is predicated on a violent universality maintained within "disturbed communities, where it [the sacrifice] serves to restore peace."[37] Yet, the intended restoration of peace is fleeting; in its momentary nature, it demands mimetic recreation.[38] The possibility of peace gestures towards the possibility of queer intimacy among the three that might remedy the brokenness of disassociation. Peace for these characters is something that approximates community, companionship, and togetherness, and the intimacy of queerness accommodates those approximations. But in the novel, peace is, like Girard suggests, ephemeral if not absent altogether. The sacrifice, intended to reunite and connect (establishing peace), falters and instead induces isolationism, as with Walton, or the singularity of death, as with Frankenstein and the creature. Herein lies the partial failure of sacrifice for the three: the goal of sacrifice (momentary peace) may be impossible, but the means to sacrifice—that is, the violence—is not.

Walton, who is broken and beset by the Arctic plain, fails to forge friendship with Frankenstein, who has been transformed by the icy setting. The brokenness of the two reveals how ice fractures. "His [Frankenstein's] limbs were nearly frozen," Walton narrates in shock, "and his body dreadfully emaciated by fatigue and suffering. I never saw a man in so wretched a condition."[39] At the start of this same letter, Walton illustrates the immersive ice that has stagnated the ship's voyage: "We were nearly surrounded by ice, which closed in the ship on all sides, scarcely leaving her the sea-room in which she floated. Our situation was somewhat dangerous, especially as we were compassed round by a very thick fog. . . . About two o'clock the mist cleared away, and we held, stretched out in every direction, vast and irregular plains of ice, which seemed to have no end."[40] It is this environment that is responsible for Frankenstein's "decaying frame," and despite his embodied wear and tear, Walton is assured of their potential compatibility.[41] "He must have been a novel creature in his better days," Walton writes with meta-irony, "being even now in wreck so attractive and amiable. I said in one of my letters, dear Margaret, that I should find no friend on the wide ocean; yet I have found a man who, before his spirit had been broken by misery, I should have been happy to have possessed as the brother of my heart."[42] Here, Walton acknowledges the irreparable brokenness that Frankenstein exudes, which coincides with the jagged brokenness of the ice that at once impedes the polar exploration and simultaneously infringes upon Walton's access to an unpossessed "brother of my heart."

Frankenstein's prepossession with the Arctic exploration that might grant him violent reunion with the creature is the impediment to the queer community that Walton seeks to unify in his caretaking. Immediately prior, Frankenstein inquires after the "apparition"—the creature—seen by the crew and asks whether the breaking of the ice "had destroyed the other sledge."[43] Frankenstein places an inquisitive hopefulness in the ice, which may kill the creature, a task at which he has repeatedly failed—a signal tie to Stryker. Ice becomes, then, a means of doling out a perverse, retributive justice that might free the creator from the sight, memory, and actions of his affliction: the creature. Walton cannot confirm this is the case, and instead suggests to Margaret that it is Frankenstein who has been broken, rather than the creature that he seeks to break. The uncut umbilicus, in which the two are failed colonial clones, is replicated here through this slippery invocation of ice. But, as this letter illustrates, it is the brokenness, like the ice's, that both draws Frankenstein nearer to Walton while simultaneously keeping him at bay. For Frankenstein, the search to break is in fact an exploration of his own brokenness. Ice becomes bodily mapped onto Frankenstein and econarrativized by *Frankenstein*.

The novel's attention to the putative identicality of Frankenstein and the creature brings about the first use of "sacrifice." In this first moment, Walton attempts to win over Frankenstein as he convalesces. "To give utterance to the burning ardour of my soul," Walton confesses, "how gladly I would *sacrifice* my fortune, my existence, my every hope to the further of my enterprise. One man's life or death were but a small price to pay for the acquirement of the knowledge which I sought; for the dominion I should acquire and transmit over the elemental foes of our race."[44] Walton's search for omniscience and the omnipotence that might follow not only binds him to Frankenstein's obsessive intent to reanimate the necrotic but positions the sacrifice of the self as the necessary token.

This first use of "sacrifice" similarly conjures up religious imagery that consolidates the word's etymology and ritualism, which anticipate yet another ironic attachment. Walton's discussion of sacrifice and enterprise riles Frankenstein, who verbalizes a surprising outburst: "'Unhappy man! Do you share my madness? Have you drank also of the intoxicating draught? Hear me, let me reveal my tale, and you will dash the cup from your lips!'"[45] The cup imagery invoked here operates as an implicit criticism of Catholicism, which remains in mode with Shelley's critiques of wayward religiosity. As Jennifer Airey posits, *Frankenstein* "is a novel of religious doubt" that interweaves the atheism of Shelley's husband, the Calvinism of her father, and mixed views of anti-Catholic rhetoric of her period, which we've encountered in the previous chapter.[46] Such anti-Catholic sentiments snowball later on when Justine, a Roman Catholic, is coerced into a false confessional by her confessor and ultimately executed. With the invocation of the metaphoric cup, Frankenstein gestures towards the Eucharist—the Catholic process of transubstantiation by which the priest literally transforms the eucharistic wine and wafer into the body and blood of Christ—and ridicules the imbibing of the draught as that which induces madness. The image of the cup filled with the madness-inducing "intoxicating draught" emphasizes the Catholic reenactment of sacrifice that is inherent in the acceptance of the Eucharist—that is, Christ's willing sacrifice as savior—while also underscoring the ways in which both Walton and Frankenstein, on parallel paths, set out for self-sacrifice. The transubstantiation of the Eucharist, which undergirds this outburst, further discloses the tethered nature by which Walton, Frankenstein, and the creature reembody a substitutive, Gothic, holy trinity.

This parallelism captures the novel's conceptualization of sacrifice as something done by oneself, not enacted by the community. The irony of self sacrifice of course lies in the fact that while enacted on behalf of community (as with Christ), it remains an act of singularity. Girard contends, "society is seeking to deflect upon a relatively indifferent victim, a 'sacrificeable' victim, that violence that would otherwise be vented on its own members, the people it most desires to protect."[47] Self-sacrifice jettisons the individual from the community in order to protect that community from the individual. The connection that Frankenstein and Walton make in assuming self-sacrificial roles binds them in a queered relationality dependent upon their individualism—that is, the state of being bereft of kinship or community. It likewise positions them within liminal geographies in that their existence mediates life and death and, like the Eucharist, sacrifice and (hopefully) reanimation. Following Frankenstein's cries, Walton details, "I spoke of my desire of finding a friend—of my thirst for a more intimate sympathy with a fellow mind than had ever fallen to my lot; and expressed my conviction that a man could boast of little happiness, who did not enjoy this blessing."[48] Frankenstein responds, "'I agree with you, . . . we are unfashionable creatures, but half made up, if one wiser, better, dearer than ourselves—such a friend out to be.'"[49] While Frankenstein is oblivious to Walton's pointed offering of friendship, Walton's decided use of "thirst" to signify his craving for "a more intimate sympathy with a fellow mind," harkens back to the invocation of the madness-draught, which he ostensibly seeks to drink from to slake a thirst for connection. The sacrificial enterprise and cup then become imbued with an intent to self-sacrifice for the other (a gesture that the creature imitates at novel's end) that builds a queer, fraternal connection through modes of self-violation. The queer friendship that Haggerty might for example see spotlighted here becomes an absolute impossibility: gestures of togetherness are ironically accomplished only through the intent to self-sacrifice. The ice world ensures that friendship and intimacy are preordained to fail.

Ironically, it is only through their mimetic recklessness and self-abandonment that fraternity is forged between the two. For Walton and Frankenstein to be together, they must obviate safety and self, which bespeaks the intent of self-sacrifice. Yet, the process of self-sacrifice remains a failed endeavor: it fails to realize the preset promises—appeasement, deification, affiliation—in that it eliminates the self to a point of no return. If Halberstam theorizes the queer art of failure as a queer ontology that intends to bond queer individuals through recuperation, self-sacrifice is an exacerbation of this failure in a different direction forged by queer annihilation: there is no reconciliation or possibility of affiliation with community. I use *community* here in acknowledgment of its criticism, perhaps best espoused by Miranda Joseph, not to signify an "unequivocal good, an indicator of a high quality of life, a life of human understanding, caring, selflessness, [or] belonging," but to pinpoint the attempts to *commune*, which derives from the Middle English verbal root "common," meaning to "make common to others with oneself; to communicate or share with."[50] Self-sacrifice mires the individual in an indelible singularity that rejects everything community might provide. Self-sacrifice violates the queer commons. The implicit navigation of self-sacrifice on these Arctic sheets only paves the way for the creature's ultimate promise of self-sacrifice on this same terrain. The glacial sphere becomes the arena to ensure failure's absolute, ironic achievement.

GLACIERS ABOVE CHAMONIX

Shelley's illustration of the glaciers above Chamonix conjures up early modern conceptions (that later migrated into the eighteenth century) of ice's affinity with monstrosity and furthers the novel's articulation of failed connection on ice worlds. Eric G. Wilson suggests that Chamonix and the glacier were deliberately selected by Shelley: "1816 was the year that Percy Shelley and Mary Wollstonecraft, along with Clare Clairemont, made a pilgrimage to Chamonix, where, under the frozen abysses of Mont Blanc, they were stunned into new insights. . . . Percy and Mary grasped the import and complexity of the glacial crags. They realized that in those glowering giants was a mixture of geological necessities, supernatural creators, and demonic destroyers."[51] By positioning their first reunion on the glacier, Shelley pairs supernatural creator and demonic destroyer on the ice sheet to underscore ice worlds as a terrain for queer relationality and to further the pre-Enlightenment mythos of the Alpine glacier as a geography teeming with monsters—perhaps not mutually exclusive tenets.[52] Duckert, in concert, observes that early modern English voyagers noted ice's "incredible monstrosity" while also "ice's express potential to create": "There is a seduction, they discovered, in glacial alluviation. Authors flowed with and through these icy strips, often describing desire and disaster on the same page."[53] So too is this the case with *Frankenstein*.

Frankenstein condemns the glacier as home of his monstrous creation, which foretells their first reunion. Frankenstein reveals, "His power and threats were not omitted in my calculations: a creature who would exist in the ice caves of glaciers, and hide himself from pursuit among the ridges of inaccessible precipices, was a being possessing faculties it would be vain to cope with."[54] What emerges here, and as I show in the intermezzo that follows, is that glaciers not only conceal the monstrous, but the monstrous avail themselves of ice worlds. Ice, in this way, becomes its own monstrous formation that besets voyagers and also breeds and protects further monstrous embodiments like the creature. In the ice world, when the creature wants to be seen, he makes it so; when he does not, he is invisible. Crusoe and Frankenstein once again parrot each other. Crusoe's fearful wrath towards the cannibals, who can navigate the ocean currents better than he, is mirrored by Frankenstein's wrath towards the nonhuman creature who can navigate the glacial sphere more successfully than he can. "As I said this," Frankenstein narrates, "I suddenly beheld the figure of a man, at some distance, advancing towards me with superhuman speed. . . . I perceived, as the shape came nearer (sight tremendous and abhorred!) that it was the wretch whom I had created."[55] Frankenstein's fear-induced narration characterizes the horrors of the approaching, juggernaut-like creature, who here is doubled as ice. The creature's affinity with ice positions the glacier not only as home but also as natural—that is, of or belonging to nature—doppelganger. Even more, like the Arctic ice that introduces Frankenstein's nested narrative to Walton's framework, it is the glaciers of Chamonix that provide another nest: one wherein the creature can articulate his autobiography. Glaciers once again become narrativized. The creature's affinity with the ice world is indicative of a symbiotic relationship, one that provides safety and security. Yet, the creature's safety and security remain a direct threat, by Frankenstein's logic, to that of his creator, and thus express the coincident fears of both ice and creature.

These twinned fears exacerbate the ruptures of relationality, which prove to characterize communication between creator and created as a violent exercise. Before Frankenstein follows his creature "across the ice, . . . determined to at least listen to his tale," the two wield domestically violent vitriol at one another, which masks the potential reunion with aggressive posturing.[56] "'Devil,' I exclaimed, 'do you dare approach me? . . . Begone, vile insect! Or rather, stay, that I may trample you to dust! And oh! That I could, with the extinction of your miserable existence, restore those victims whom you have so diabolically murdered!'"[57] Less fury-filled than his maker, the creature responds stolidly: "Yet you, my creator, detest and spurn me, thy creature, to whom thou are bound by ties only dissoluble by the annihilation of one of us. You purpose to kill me. How dare you sport thus with life? Do your duty towards me, and I will do mine towards you and the rest of mankind. If you will comply with my conditions, I will leave them and you at peace; but if you refuse, I will glut the maw of death, until it be satiated with the blood of your remaining friends."[58] The creature recognizes Frankenstein's intent to murder what he has sown, sacrificing his creation and furthering the networks of sacrificial killings that intend to shock, awe, and bestow recognition. This underlines the creature's ultimatum: listen to what I have to say or I will further my bloodlust.

Though neither mentions the word *sacrifice*, this tête-à-tête emphasizes the mimetic quality of violence, which is done not only as a form of retributive justice but also to ensure that the other recognizes that violence is meant to induce collateral damage. Violence aspires to attention. The unending cyclical nature of this retributive violence expresses a fundamental aspect of Girard's conceptualization of sacrifice. "The miracle of sacrifice," Girard notes, "is the formidable 'economy' of violence that it realizes. It directs against a single victim the violence that, a moment before, menaced the entire community. . . . They [human communities] attempt to reproduce the miracle that has saved them by immolating a new victim in place of the first, in hope that the same cause will produce the same effects."[59] Frankenstein views his creature as a menace, and the creature experiences Frankenstein's rejection as menacing; in this way, the enactment of violence that mediates the boundaries of sacrifice intends to embroil both in sadistic connection. The creature and Frankenstein demonstrate their interchangeable affinities. To hurt one another is to remain connected. To be sadistic is to foster a pain that is dedicated to another, a connection that even violence cannot break but rather motivates.

SACRIFICIAL COMPANIONSHIP

The violent disintegration of the sacrificial body returns in necrotic splendor through Frankenstein's second creature, the demanded spouse of his first. Frankenstein's cruel destruction of the second creature instills an institutionalized misogyny (she isn't even allowed to breathe) under the aegis of a masculinist protectorate (Frankenstein worries she won't consent to her isolated life). It moreover consolidates a gesture of sacrifice as that which intends to forge a community but is, instead, fundamental to destroying that creaturely community Frankenstein begets.

Desperate for companionship, the creature proposes a detente: "What I ask of you is reasonable and moderate; I demand a creature of another sex, but as hideous as myself; . . . we shall be monsters, cut off from all the world; but on that account we shall be more attached to one another. Our lives will not be happy but they will be harmless, and free from the misery I now feel."[60] The creature (and the novel) aspire to compulsive heterosexuality—what Adrienne Rich theorizes as the presumption of participation in the hetero-repronormative economy by which all sexual relations are compared[61]—in which he can escape society and his "evil passions will have fled," for his spouse will provide him the necessary sympathies so that his "life will flow quietly away."[62] The subtle invocation of "flow," here pronounced by the creature, articulates how fluid imagery might be invoked in service of heteronormative belonging.

But of course, heteronormative inclusion is denied him. Frankenstein stops just short of reanimating the creature's mate and forces the creature to behold the sadistic destruction: "As I looked on him, his countenance expressed the utmost extent of malice and treachery. I thought with a sensation of madness on my promise of creating another like to him, and trembling with passion, tore to pieces the thing on which I was engaged. The wretch saw me destroy the creature on whose future existence he depended for happiness, and, with a howl of devilish despair and revenge, withdrew."[63] Employing the word "destroy" to mark his egregious act, Frankenstein's evisceration of the female creature marks a violent interrelationality wherein attention and affiliation between the creator and created is constructed upon the deconstruction of the female body. The sacrifice Frankenstein makes of the not-yet-animate female partner is akin to the creature's retaliatory murder of Elizabeth Frankenstein, which again reveals the doubleness that characterizes their intimacy. In both situations, the violation of the female body is enacted immediately before the consummation of heteronormativity—the creature's commitment to a female paramour and Frankenstein's much-delayed wedding night. Though what immediately follows is not performed on ice, the representations of sacrifice here establish a queerness, predicated on violent reciprocity, in which romantic heteronormative affections or familial attachments dissipate.

Ice may be downplayed in these moments, but water unmistakably returns to situate these queer entanglements. Frankenstein follows the creature into the cold Irish waters and pinpoints the sacrificial offerings that bind him, the creature, and the seemingly moot victims in a sort of queer mise en abyme. "I burned with rage to pursue the murderer of my peace," Frankenstein writes, "and precipitate him into the ocean.... Why had I not followed him, and closed with him in mortal strife? ... I shuddered to think who might be the next victim sacrificed to his insatiate revenge. And then I thought again of his words—'I will be with you on your wedding-night.'"[64] For Frankenstein, the ocean becomes, yet again, a site of potential erasure; water's potential to correct scientific, colonial, and paternal malfeasance surfaces in this exclamation. Frankenstein, at the same time, denotes that the creature's murders engender forms of sacrifice. But as Girard details, sacrifices are done unto or for something, often to "divinize" they to whom the sacrifice is offered.[65] Frankenstein is the person to whom the sacrificial offering is made: William, Justine, Elizabeth, and Frankenstein Sr. are the collective sacrificial bodies by which the creature can garner the attention he seeks from the deified Frankenstein. Violence, in this way, is colored by a monstrous hope subtended by response-ability (to borrow a phrase from Haraway), attention, and an ironic recuperation of loss.[66]

These collective moments reason that the queer potential of sacrifice destroys (the second creature) and strangles (Elizabeth's demise) the heteronormative love object in pursuit of a male-male bond that promises and yet fails to safeguard connection. Jacqueline Labbe—in conversation with Sandra Gilbert and Susan Gubar, Barbara Johnson, and Anne Mellor's feminist readings of the creature—pinpoints this exact moment by which to read the creature's promise to "consummate [his] crimes in death" on the evening of Frankenstein's solemnities as orgasmic potential. As Labbe explains, "however, it must happen that Victor's intended wife, Elizabeth, be disposed of, and that the death Victor fears be an actual consummation, for even as 'death' itself is a metaphor for orgasm, so too the expected person to be with Victor on his wedding-night is his wife."[67] While Labbe, like Johnson and Mellor, is invested in examining the uxorial complements (including the creature) that saturate the novel—indeed, self-sacrifice for Labbe typifies "the perfect wife"—the invocation of death as orgasmic lends itself to queer relationality.[68] By sacrificing Elizabeth on behalf of Frankenstein, the creature ostensibly endows orgasmic pleasure in the accomplishment of deathly violence; Thanatos lives alongside Eros. The violence that Frankenstein and the creature ultimately level at one another stays the development of the relationship and encodes sacrificial victims—those fatalities that rack up in the novel—as the tools by which sadistic, even orgasmic (perhaps one and the same here), coupling is established.

While the creature's enactment of sacrifice ironically bonds the two, Frankenstein deploys the sacrificial act to steel the barriers between him and community. "I left the house," Frankenstein orates, "the horrid scene of last night's contention, and walked on the beach of the sea, which I almost regarded as an insuperable barrier between me and my fellow-creatures, nay, a wish that such should prove the fact stole across me. I desired that I might pass my life on that barren rock, wearily, it is true, but uninterrupted by any sudden shock of misery. If I returned, it was to be sacrificed, or to see those whom I most loved die under the grasp of a daemon whom I had myself created."[69] The littoral space from which Frankenstein gleans consolation again prefigures how water is conjured with isolating effects. On the beach—perched between the terrestrial and the aquatic—Frankenstein finds "an insuperable barrier" that dislocates him from his "fellow-creatures." Frankenstein does not grant the creature the possibility of fellowship (the use of *daemon* remind us of this differentiation), and yet the invocation of a watery site is repeatedly purposed throughout the novel as a violence against community.

Though ambiguous, I read the "it" that "was to be sacrificed" as both the barren rock—a remembrance of the sublimity of Chamonix before confronted by the creature—and the loved ones who are foretold to die. The icy world becomes, once again, an eidetic memory of sacrifice, and like the comfort of the barren rock in Frankenstein's mind, so too are his safety and livelihood fleeting. The sacrifice is not only the peace of mind that he is to leave behind, but also a reminder of the second creature's dispatched body. Sacrifice reveals the detritus of the female body—three women are killed in the novel: Justine, the female creature, and Elizabeth—which manifests as fraternal sadism. Such sacrifices not only reek of misogyny (women and their bodies drop like flies) but also position a vindictive interrelationality between the two that requires the decimation of the heteronormative love object to foster a perverse and contingent filiation. These moments of sacrifice queerly cleave the lines of who can be loved and, separately, who can survive. In so doing, sacrifice delineates heteronormative kinship from queer.

COLD CLOSE

With the creature's promise of self-sacrifice lingering, the novel's close doubles down on the coupled nature of sacrifice heretofore navigated: first, sacrifice continues to be both apostrophized and conducted on the icy terrain and, second, sacrifice attempts to connect but instead amounts to failure. "Though it be more or less delayed," Girard reveals, "the sacrificial conclusion is inevitable."[70] In Walton's last letter, he informs his sister, "It is past; I am returning to England. I have lost my hopes of utility and glory;—I have lost my friend. . . . September 9th, the ice began to move and roarings like thunder were heard at a distance, as the islands split and cracked in every direction. We were in the most imminent peril."[71] The glacial ruptures yet again mirror the relational ruptures that have installed the brotherhood between Walton and Frankenstein. Like countless other eighteenth-century polar expeditions before his, Walton is forced to retreat, especially as mutiny brews. And like in Chamonix, the invocation of cracking ice and imminent peril provide the stage direction by which the creature reappears, making his own vow of self-sacrifice: "'That [Frankenstein] is also my victim!' he exclaimed: 'in his murder my crimes are consummated; the miserable series of my being is wound to its close! Oh, Frankenstein! Generous and self-devoted being! What does it avail that I now ask thee to pardon me? I, who irretrievably destroyed thee by destroying all thou lovedst. Alas! He is cold, he cannot answer me!'"[72] The creature eulogizes Frankenstein and acknowledges the mutually exchanged destruction that has so much characterized their relationship. The creature's use of "consummated" is of course deeply suggestive and calls back to their previous encounter on Frankenstein's wedding night, wherein sacrifice is suffused with orgasmic opportunity. The consummation of death reinforces a mournful queer eroticism. Tracked throughout the novel, consummation with heterosexual partners is an impossibility: neither can accomplish the act because of the other. Instead, it is the creature's "crimes," which include the "murder" of Frankenstein, that are consummated, thus positioning a longing wherein queerness is, yet again, consolidated through vicious revenge and violent necrosadism.

The creature, whose self-reflexivity exceeds that of his maker, closes the novel by addressing Walton, knitting the first and third frameworks together and exposing the queer triangulation of fraternity:

> Fear not that I shall be the instrument of future mischief. My work is nearly complete. Neither yours nor any man's death is needed to consummate the series of my being, and accomplish that which must be done; but it requires my own. Do not think that I shall be slow to perform this sacrifice. I shall quit your vessel on the ice-raft which brought me thither, and shall seek the most northern extremity of the globe; I shall collect my funeral pile, and consume to ashes this miserable frame, that its remains may afford no light to any curious and unhallowed wretch, who would create such another as I have been. I shall die.[73]

The creature's words carry an intent to self-immolate, a sacrifice that is done to divinize Frankenstein. He will stage this performance on the "northern extremity of the globe," a metonym for an ice world that will bear witness to his death. Upon the Arctic North, ice and fire mix with sacrificial intent. Like the body of Frankenstein, now "cold," the creature seeks the cold body of the Arctic to materialize self-sacrifice. There is reunification in absolute cold.

Ice ultimately performs an opportunity for connection otherwise prohibited. But as the creature prepares to depart, he reminds Walton and readers of the cyclical nature of the sacrifice that has somehow sustained the novel and titillated their mutual sadism: "Farewell, Frankenstein! If thou were yet alive, and yet cherished a desire of revenge against me, it would be better satiated in my life than in my destruction. . . . Blasted as thou wert, my agony was still superior to thine; for the bitter sting of remorse will not cease to rankle in my wounds until death shall close them for ever."[74] The cat-and-mouse game, in its sacrificial rites, has run its course, and this the creature laments. The creature desires self-sacrifice because the cycle has been prematurely foreclosed by Frankenstein's death, and as Walton, Frankenstein, and the creature know all too well, the pain of loneliness is far greater. "Yet even the enemy of God and man had friends and associates in his desolation," the creature states, "I am alone."[75] *Loneliness is cold.*

At the close of "See Monkeys," I imagined one way in which the process of eating participates in violent and shared attunements that can mediate the boundaries of self and other, human and non-. I extend that point here insomuch that eating and sacrifice have been jointly theorized. In "Eating Well," Jacques Derrida concedes that "sacrificial structure" comes to constitute the subject by way of "intersubjectivity in nursing, love, mourning and, in truth, in all symbolic and linguistic appropriations."[76] While Derrida thinks through "carnivorous sacrifice," those acts done unto the literal bodies of animals, the potential for sacrifice to suture intersubjectivity is apposite to Shelley's novel. With Frankenstein's death and the creature's inability to continue the sadistic ludicity that so greatly motivates their relationship, the absence of sacrifice forecloses the ability to love and mourn—to forge an intersubjective connection. Because the creature cannot sacrifice Frankenstein, his only recourse is to self-sacrifice, expressing the way the doppelganger theatre I have traced concludes with a tragic admission of loneliness and singularity.[77] The creature's endeavor to self-sacrifice holds the wish for an intersubjectivity—in death, they can be together—now impossible.

Sacrifice fails to appropriately foster the types of queer intimacy that Walton, Frankenstein, and the creature set out to establish through its invocation. Sacrifice embodies the novel's paradigmatic irony in that its failure accompanies the promise of intersubjective connection. In that these failures abound, we must also read this final sacrifice, to which the creature aspires, as one that equally fails: crystallizing an ineluctable loneliness that even sacrifice cannot mend, for there is no longer anyone to whom it can be dedicated. The cryosphere that once concealed and harbored the creature's existence renders sacrifice as the key to a belonging that is bungled, a kinship that is thwarted, and a queer failure that can only look like loneliness. In *Frankenstein*, to sacrifice is to fail, to connect is to induce pain, and to succeed is to perish. As Stryker puts it: *"I will swim forever. I will die for eternity."*[78]

INTERMEZZO

Freeze!

The glacial queer horizons that conclude *Frankenstein* are central to the media phenomenon of Mr. Freeze (or Victor Fries—Victor Frankenstein undoubtedly retitled), who perennially populates a cast of DC Comics villains and received his big screen debut in Joel Schumacher's *Batman & Robin* (1997). To "Freeze!," as I show, is not singularly an interpolating injunction, it is also an opportunity to magnify how the comic arts exploit queer attachment and longing in ice worlds, and how film iterations uphold queer camp and eco-terrorism as means to "freeze" and thus offset climate change realities. Ice's queer crystallizations follow humanity's exclusion of the villain-*cum*-nonhuman who portends modes of icy and environmental being that are at once horizons for queer belonging and dystopian tundra-territories of perceived malevolence.

Since 1959, Mr. Zero, a.k.a. Dr. Victor Fries (pronounced: *freez*), a.k.a. Mr. Freeze, has plagued Gotham City and its iconographic protector, Batman. In his DC Comics debut, in issue 121 of *Batman*, "The Ice Crimes of Mr. Zero," Mr. Zero narrates his catastrophic origin story: "I am the victim of a most unfortunate accident."[1] Mr. Zero reveals that, out of laboratory clumsiness, the freezing solution with which he had hoped to engineer an ice gun slipped from his hands and altered him forevermore: "I could scarcely breathe at ordinary temperature."[2] The structural frame of the strip's flashback, in which Mr. Zero dictates this prehistory, is circumscribed by wavy lines denoting a dream-like past; the frames that center the present are straight. Such subtle illustrations signal to readers that the fluid becoming of the past (shown by the waves) crystallizes in the frozen rigidity of the present. The comic thus exposes a cryonarratology in which the very structures of ice contour narratological form (the comic grid) and meaning.[3] In other words, these lines further announce Mr. Zero's transformation into an icy villain and visualize how *queer temporalities resist straight lines*. Mr. Zero realizes that his only chance for survival is to live permanently in cold storage as "a human icicle."[4] "The Ice Crimes of Mr. Zero" catalogs Mr. Zero's triumph as he perfects his freeze gun and corrects any laboratorial absent-mindedness. He ultimately sets out to bring permafrost to Gotham so as to make the city a wintery wonderland that he can access freely—no longer confined to a mountain lair that doubles as an icebox. Mr. Zero proposes to christen Gotham the site of the new ice age, where he will be the polar pontiff.

Batman and boy wonder, Robin, foil Mr. Zero's plans, ultimately imprisoning the ailed scientist in his mountainous laboratory bereft of family and friendship. However, when the heroes momentarily stumble, Mr. Zero transforms Batman and Robin into two giant ice blocks. Their heroic bodies of water crystallize into ice cubes. By freezing Batman and Robin, Mr. Zero forestalls their heroic justice. But Mr. Zero's intent is *not* nefarious, unlike other iterations of his character that portray him as a megalomaniacal sadist. He informs his henchmen that with these frozen "trophies," "I shall have the pleasure of their company as long as I desire."[5] Put on ice, Batman and Robin become the still-life fixtures that Mr. Zero craves in an existence punctuated by absence. His longing for company intends, as I discussed of the creature's longing in the previous chapter, to dispel loneliness and singularity. His entrance into the world, like the creature's, is marked by accident, and yet Mr. Zero is both the creator and the created, distilled into a singular icy embodiment. Mr. Zero, like Frankenstein's creature, seeks attachment, camaraderie, and intimacy, even. Unlike the creature who repeatedly fails, however, Mr. Zero momentarily achieves this chilled connection. While queer readings of Batman and Robin are commonplace—and this is to say nothing of the titillating, pornographic fan fiction—the introduction of Mr. Zero into the DC Comics universe is predicated on a queer longing where frozen ontologies become ironic vestiges of failed attachment.[6]

In "The Ice Crimes," Batman and Robin, to no surprise, break free from their frozen sarcophaguses. The rupturing of the ice blocks triggers the failure of the plumbing systems, which generate enormous clouds of steam—yet another catastrophic body of water that scalds, betrays, and undoes. The steam serves to free the heroic duo and at the same time cures Mr. Zero's respiratory struggles. In steam lies the curative yet toxic *pharmakon*. Mr. Zero smiles broadly, "Why . . . I—can breathe normally again!"[7] Batman responds with the final word, "Yes, Mr. Zero, that steam treatment must have changed you back to normal! Now we'll see if the law can straighten out your distorted mind."[8] Batman's crime fighting here endeavors to correct Mr. Zero's abnormality (the only time in the comic and film spin-offs in which this is possible) and simultaneously correct Mr. Zero's "distorted mind." But Mr. Zero's most distorted machinations only desire Batman and Robin's company. Batman then offers the so-called justice system as one that "straightens" out distorted conceptions of attachment, to rectify Mr. Zero's perverse longing for community. The carceral state, by this purview, intends to cure and thereby eliminate any frozen attachments that might auger queer community. With the curative steam comes the usurpation of Mr. Zero's lukewarm villainy alongside the erasure of any pleasurable company to which he so desperately clings and aspires.

In the late 1990s, almost forty years after his entrance into the DC Comics canon, Mr. Zero's backstory was revised. He also assumed his most recognizable moniker, Mr. Freeze—a rebranding bequeathed by the 1960s *Batman* live-action television series featuring Adam West. Paul Dini and Mark Buckingham's *Batman: Mr. Freeze* provide the titular villain a revisionist history through gray-scaled flashback. Born into wealth, the young Victor Fries is cursed with a manic predilection for freezing living things into a menagerie of assorted popsicles. His father remarks, "We raised our son to be a genius . . . not some damn deviant."[9] Victor's alleged deviance is cause for alarm to his bickering, unhappy parents, who enlist the help of a psychologist. When asked why he, as an amateur entomologist, freezes insects, Victor sheepishly replies, "I—I think they're pretty. I don't want them to be hurt. I want them to stay safe and beautiful forever."[10] His father offhandedly replies, "sick."[11] As with previous iterations, young Victor is portrayed as mentally unstable in his penchant for perseveration and stability, which come as reactions to the domestic violence and brokenness that saturate his home life. Indeed, prior to the flashback, adult Mr. Freeze sets Gotham on ice, not with the goal of inducing chaos, but quite oppositely, of instituting order. In the comic square, glacial structures upset militarized warcrafts, mountains of ice freeze the police in their tracks, and Mr. Freeze steps out onto Gotham as if the harbinger of a polar vortex. Mr. Freeze's affinity with glacial spheres—his body transformed to only inhabit icy worlds—harnesses the wintry environment to effect his plan—yet another callback to Shelley's creature.

With his icy success almost consummated, Mr. Freeze observes, "This is good. This is just. I have succeeded where the damnable Batman has failed.

I have finally brought order to this urban madhouse."[12] The tundraic effects instill two complimentary notions: first, they rectify forms of madness of which he was previously accused in a non-ice world. To be sane in permafrost, as Mr. Freeze understands himself, is to be relegated to the mentally unstable periphery of ice worlds. And vice versa. Second, Mr. Freeze births a frozen Gotham to restore a queer form of order and, by extension, beauty and safety. The pristine nature of the glacial world, which is uninhabitable for all but Mr. Freeze, pioneers new regimes of order and justice. Such a reworking keenly demonstrates the flaws of the previous legal systems (to which Mr. Zero was subjected in 1959) that intend and yet fail to "straighten out" wayward souls.

Ice then becomes a realm of safety unencumbered by the forms of toxic warmth that Mr. Freeze ascribes to humanity. Freeze endeavors to recuperate the emotional coldness he has endured, through a literal, environmental manifestation. In a particularly sorrowful scene, young Freeze looks outside on a grey, snowy day wherein clouds of snow capture his loneliness. He recounts, "Somehow I knew that I was destined to live outside humanity, a lonely observer of a world whose warmth would never touch me."[13] It's impossible not to read this resignation as one that parrots Frankenstein's creature: "Yet even the enemy of God and man had friends and associates in his desolation, I am alone."[14] The isolation the two must endure corresponds with the lack of haptic connection—a lack of physical warmth—that is forbidden them, and to which I will return in the conclusion. Loneliness thus triggers feelings of nonhumanity. Or, retooled: upon ice, the nonhuman reigns supreme.

After the 1990s reboot of Mr. Freeze, DC Comics authorized the use of his character as one of two central villains in *Batman and Robin* (1997), directed by Joel Schumacher. The film is a visual, slapstick feast rife with electric colors, rubber fetishwear, and body paint aglow. The campiest of the rebooted trilogy, Mr. Freeze (Arnold Schwarzenegger) is a chrome-domed, slow-speaking, and slow-walking (the costume allegedly added forty pounds of material) antagonist that shoots his frozen load of puns within the first five minutes. "Chill out," Freeze quips.[15] He continues: "My condition has left me cold to your pleas of mercy"; "Cool party"; "I'm here to break the ice."[16] And in his initial appearance, Freeze announces, "the Iceman cometh"—a red herring, under the guise of literary allusion, sacrificed for wordplay. Schwarzenegger joins the star-studded cast, which features

George Clooney (as Batman), Chris O'Donnell (as Robin), Alicia Silverstone (as Batgirl), and Uma Thurman (as Poison Ivy).

Batman and Robin resituates an origin story for Mr. Freeze, wherein his quest for domination is predicated exclusively on reunion with his cryogenically frozen wife, Nora. The film thus proceeds after Dini and Buckingham's lead, which paired Victor with Nora as a means of further justifying Mr. Freeze's transformation and consequent descent into madness. College-aged poindexter Freeze becomes smitten with figure-skating Nora (his only source of attachment), who upon their marriage quickly succumbs to a rare form of cancer. Rejected from Wayne Technologies (Batman's Fortune 500 industry), S.T.A.R. Labs (of Superman fame), and LexCorp (led by Superman's nemesis Lex Luthor), Freeze sells his soul to work for GothCorp to further pursue his cryogenic research, with the exclusive hopes of finding a cure. He discloses, "So began my distinguished career as one of the nameless drones grinding out miracles for the glory of Ferris Boyle [CEO of GothCorp], and yet it was worth it because it was all for Nora."[17] Freeze clandestinely conceals Nora in a cryogenic chamber and then is subsequently fired by GothCorp, which assumes Nora's body as collateral. Freeze morphs into his supervillain form to emancipate Nora from Boyle's grips and sets out for revenge against those who have wronged their permanently lost love. He reveals to Batman, "Victor Fries died with his wife. I am a ghost of cold rage and vengeance. Call me Mr. Freeze. Call me death."[18] Alongside this pronouncement, the gutter of the comic squares is broken by Freeze, who jumps out of the frame. His invocation of "call me death" thus accentuates Freeze's movement from beyond the order of the grid—beyond the order of what can be structurally and formally contained. Freeze erupts from the comic square in a refusal to be captured; the nonhuman icy villain will not acquiesce to enclosure. As with Frankenstein's creature, whose heteronormative pairing is denied him, Freeze's narration of personal tragedy reiterates textures of loss and brokenness that inhibit heteronormative, coupled fulfillment.

While *Batman and Robin* reimagines Nora as an ethereal beauty kept alive only by some giant aquarium, it more prominently features Thurman's Poison Ivy as the glamorous and amorous counterpart to Schwarzenegger's Freeze. She is a self-pronounced human-animal-plant hybrid resurrected by the ophidian and botanical venoms and toxins, respectively, to which she has dedicated her life's work. Poison Ivy literally pulls the plug on Nora to eliminate any competition, and by reducing a love triangle to a single love line, Poison Ivy and Freeze commence their plan for prelapsarian bliss constituted exclusively by those who embody nonhuman affiliations. Indeed, as Freeze woos Poison Ivy, he repeats verbatim from *Batman: Mr. Freeze:* "Somehow I knew that I was destined to live outside humanity, a lonely observer of a world whose warmth would never touch me."[19] He further prophesizes that he "will blanket the city in endless winter: first, Gotham, and then the earth."[20] Freeze and Poison Ivy are Adam and Eve 2.0, or as Freeze puts it, "Adam and Evil."[21]

Batman and Robin unwittingly positions the short-lived romance of Freeze and Poison Ivy as yet another closeted climate fiction narrative in which climate realities are sutured into the very fabric yet reside below the surface. The closet climate fiction of *Batman and Robin* is one in which the villains' endeavors to forestall the degradation of the environment and limit human expansion to preserve nonhuman flora and fauna is rendered a pernicious ecoterrorism. Adam and Evil at the reins of a newly minted ice age seek to rectify the gross mismanagement of the planet and ultimately remedy the Anthropocene. At film's end, the frozen effects that Freeze has set over Gotham are defrosted by Batman as he harnesses a heat ray from satellites, a larger-than-life telescope, and the sun. The heroism of filmic Batman is predicated exclusively on his ability to manipulate and further effect global warming, wherein Gotham City becomes ground zero. Both Wayne Technologies, by Poison Ivy's accusation, and Batman thus participate in exacerbating the effects of anthropogenic climate change. The kicker is that, by the film's logic, we should applaud these warming effects. In Batman's heroism and the audience's hooraying lie magnificent complicities with climate change and environmental ruin.

Batman and Robin thus reflects competing representations of geoengineering, which purportedly serve to remedy the types of large-scale planetary collapse brought about by climate change. As (ostensible) advocates for the goodness that Batman represents in his ongoing Manichean battle with Gotham villains, viewers become aligned with the affective heat that Batman's heat ray emanates in waylaying Freeze and Poison Ivy's ne'er-do-well plan. As Nicole Starosielski's attention to media heat reveals, "we must see it as a relational, lively force."[22] The heat that Batman's geoengineering proffers works doubly in its capacity to, one, institute worlds of warmth that can defrost the frozen effects of Freeze and, two, ingratiate audiences to the types of desirable warmth and heat that we imagine constituting affective bonds. If Freeze is characterized by his dispossession from human society because of his affinity for the cold, then Batman represents humanity's warmth—a material and affective register that further crystallizes Freeze's exclusion (as well as that of all those who might stand with him). Ironically, of course, the warming effects of Batman's geoengineering risk destroying the planet as we know it.

Opposite these warm complicities, the queer understory of Freeze's ice sheets and Poison Ivy's bioengineered plants imagines a climate future that is not entangled with reproductive futurism. That is, in the new ice age (prophesied by Mr. Zero in 1959), only the nonhuman will persist, and any remnant of the Anthropocene will be put on ice. Poison Ivy, who observes that in her transformation her skin has been transmuted by chlorophyll, her beauty is a result of venomous and toxic admixtures, and her kiss is (cue Bell Biv Devoe) *poison,* confronts Bruce Wayne about the environmental sacrifices offered up on the altar of technological advancement. She condemns the supremacy of the "warm-blooded," and in her affection for Freeze—of whom she quips, "that's not a man; that's a god"—the two, Adam and Evil, envisage an earth unmolested by warm-blooded attachments.[23] In the ice that runs through Freeze's body and the chlorophyll that courses through Poison Ivy's, viewers embrace visions of monstrous embodiment that reject and yet rise in their nonhumanity. Adam and Evil thus poison the heteroreproductive narrative in both their superhuman embodiments and their refusal to participate in shaping future worlds exclusively for the human. To hell with humanity, the two reason, and with warmth too.

CONCLUSION

Sea Monsters

Two families constitute the taxonomic order Sirenia: Dugongidae and Trichechidae. The latter family, Trichechidae, includes various species of manatee, with which North Americans, especially Floridians, may be familiar. In 2017, after thirty years of conservation efforts, the West Indian manatee was successfully downgraded from critically endangered to threatened.[1] Only hundreds existed in the 1970s; today populations number around three thousand. This downgrading signals the protective measures that have sought to repopulate the manatees' dwindling numbers. Still, under Florida law it is illegal to "molest, harass, collide with, injure or harm"—in other words *to touch*—manatees, due to their protected nature.[2] This logic suggests that tactile interaction is, by premise, an egregious violation. A legal and phenomenological loophole, however, realizes that touch is permissible only if the manatee touches *first*, which reinforces a notion that animal-to-human contact is innocent, consensual, and non-injurious. Gulliver might have a great deal to say about such notions, as I discussed in chapter 2. The West Indian manatee elucidates a politics of touch that ensnares issues of consent, legality, and interspecies entanglements—a series of threads that this conclusion demonstrates is vital to imagining future trajectories of the queerness of water as it mediates human and nonhuman spheres.

In an eighteenth-century prehistory, Carl Linnaeus positioned Sirenia alongside the order Proboscidea, of which elephants are the only extant species. The connection is predicated on cranial and dental fossil records. Dugongs were one of two subgroups of Dugongidae. Only dugongs, which reside in the Pacific and Indian Oceans, exist today. Steller's sea cow, the other, was driven to extinction in the eighteenth century, around 1768, as a result of overfishing, poaching, and the animal's supposed amiability towards sailors in the Bering Sea. Patrik Svensson rhapsodizes, "They didn't try to escape when approached, and their only response when the starving members of the expedition caught them with large iron hooks and cut meat out of them while they were still alive was to sigh quietly."[3] Svensson depicts the sea cow as somberly resigned to its own torturous ends. A sigh mediates the boundary between humans and nonhumans.

Steller's sea cow bears the name of the German naturalist Georg Wilhelm Steller, whose 1741–42 voyage to the Bering Strait documented the sea cows' behavior. Steller's *Journal* remains, by Svensson's assessment, the singular firsthand account of the sea cow—a species that would perish only two decades after their natural-historical "discovery." Like the popularized natural histories that precede and follow Steller's, his *Journal* reads as if literary fiction. In chapter 2, when I approached natural histories of eighteenth-century simians, I further explained how these ostensibly disparate genres become mutually informative throughout the eighteenth century and beyond. Such a case is reiterated here. For instance, interspersed between descriptions of breeding, mobility, and epidermal structure, with illustrative flair Steller describes the sea cow as possessing a "wonderful intelligence" (perhaps foreshadowed by the sigh) and an "uncommon love for one another."[4] He continues: "When one of them was hooked, all the others were intent upon saving him. Some tried to prevent the wounded comrade from [being drawn on] the beach by [forming] a closed circle [around him]; some attempted to upset the yawl; others laid themselves over the rope or tried to pull the harpoon out of [his] body, in which indeed they succeeded several times. We also noticed, not without astonishment, that a male came two days in succession to its female lying dead on the beach, as if he would inform himself about her condition."[5] Steller's ethological observations of the sea cow account for what Svensson pinpoints as "touching displays of empathy."[6] Svensson's use of *touching* operates doubly: as an adjective that denotes the induction of positive, unitive emotional states and as a gerund that realizes the tactical nonhuman realities of empathy. To empathize is to touch. This empathy extends between fellow sea cows, whose sufferings and tortures are enacted by the barbs of greedy expedition crews. And in its most striking form, the invocation of empathy confers heteronormative, monogamous coupledom. The male sea cow enacts grief-filled care work—perhaps palliative in nature—to "its female lying dead on the beach."

Empathy is a tricky category, especially when we exploit it to characterize nonhuman animals. Svensson's deployment of empathy to describe Steller's sea cow projects a benevolent affective state and emotional capacity that effaces difference between species—which is to say nothing of the vexed cultural and biological constructions of cognitive, physiological, psychological, and affective differences that might separate human capacities from those of nonhuman animals such as Steller's sea cows. The sigh likewise corroborates this effacement. Lori Gruen has long advocated for an "alternative ethic" to frameworks of empathy that are often carelessly or sanctimoniously prescribed to nonhuman animals. Gruen's conception of "entangled empathy" accounts for a feminist-oriented ethics of care wherein "attention is directed to individual animals of course, but also to the differences between animals, as well as to the larger structural forces that separate and maintain distance between us and them."[7] Entangled empathy, by Gruen's handling, is care work that recognizes and appreciates difference. This conclusion, in correspondence, revisits textures of care between and among species. How do we intimately care for the nonhuman? this chapter asks. Is there queerness in care? And how might the nonhuman care for us back?

The sirens I navigate here, though, are not strictly from the family Sirenia. They likewise are recognized as mermaids: human-aquatic hybrids that I have addressed in various places throughout this book. Sirens and mermaids of mythic lore operate synonymously, and artistic depictions of them often demonstrate their shared enmeshedness. Consider another eighteenth-century example: Louis Renard's second edition of *Poisson, Ecrevisses et Crabs* (1754), which illustrates aquatic invertebrates and vertebrates alike in 460 kaleidoscopic copper engravings. The first edition, of only sixteen copies, was published in Amsterdam in 1719. Though visually stunning and a landmark compendium when released, *Poisson, Ecrevisses et Crabes* has been repeatedly decried from the nineteenth century forward. Renard's whimsical, creative license overstepped the truth claims implied by his illustrations. He additionally violated the putatively objective disciplinarity of a budding marine biology by authoring some neon-colored hallucination that rivals Lewis Carroll's Wonderland. Theodore Pietsche's trenchant fourth edition of Renard, and the only English translation, resuscitates the polychromatic encyclopedia, which includes 415 tropical fish, 41 crustaceans, two insects, a dugong, and, unbelievably, a siren. In some translations, the siren is a mermaid.[8] Indeed the French *sirène,* which develops from the Latin *sirēna* meaning "alarm," is likewise connected to the French cognate *sereine,* from which English-speakers get "serene." Sirens and mermaids reveal strange and surprising worlds of etymology in which mixed affective states—to be alarmed, to be aroused, to be serene—float together.

Renard's siren, however, stands out. The siren does not conform to the exquisite kaleidoscopic optics of the other engravings. The crawfish illustrated beneath her reveals the stark juxtaposition of color, detail, and representation that characterizes the other images. As the last plate, the brown-skinned siren is Renard's most demure depiction. In plate 57—the largest in the work—she is described thusly:

> *Monstre semblable à une Sirenne pris à la côte de l'isle de Bourné ou Boeron dans le Departement d'Amboïe. Il était long de 59. pounces gros à proportion comme une Anguille. Il a vecu à terre dans une Cuve pleine d'eau quatre jours et sept heurs. Il poussoit de temps en temps des petits cris comme ceux d'une Souris. Il ne voulut point manger, quoy qui'on luy offrit des petits poissons, des coquillages, des Crabes, Ecrevisses, etc. On trouva dans sa Cuve apres qu'il fut mort quelques excrements semblables à des crottes de chat.*

> This monster, resembling a siren, was caught off the coast of Bourné or Boeron in the province of Ambon [Indonesia]. It was fifty-nine inches long and of eel-like proportions. It lived on shore in a tank of water for four days and seven hours. From time to time, it made small cries like a mouse. It would not eat, though it was offered small fishes, mollusks, and crabs. Upon her death, something that resembled cat feces remained at the bottom of the tank.[9]

Renard's extravagant description sizzles with a dizzying admixture of animal and nonhuman metaphors that in their comparison intend to make the siren legible. Her (its?) monstrosity extends from the coalesced nature of an eel's body, a mouse's voice, no appetite, and a cat's excretory system. She is, then, both familiar and unfamiliar. She is uncanny. The unsettling piecemealing of various nonhuman forms is both cause for alarm—as her sirenic qualities corroborate—but also, as the *Oxford English Dictionary* reports for the word *monster*'s antiphrastic use during the first half of the eighteenth century, an "especially attractive thing."[10] Renard's siren approximates domestic familiarity (cat, mouse), a delicious repast (eel-like), and an alluring attraction (monster). She is abject.

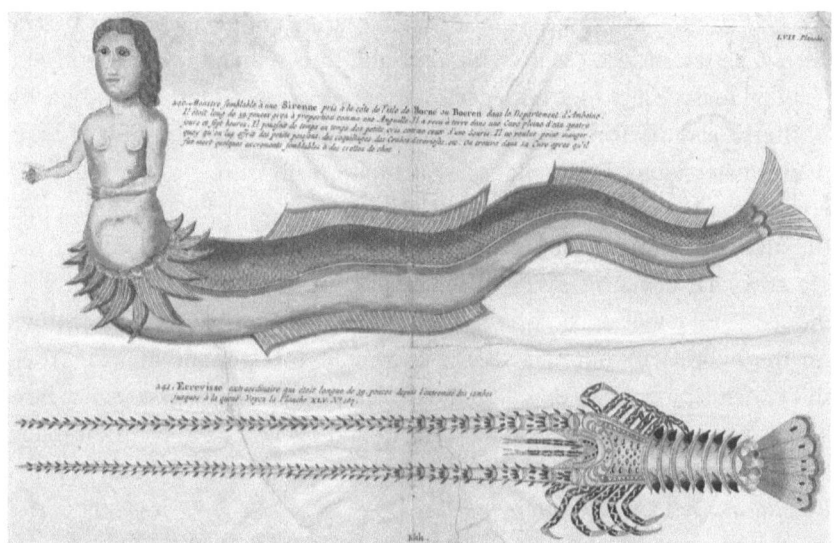

Louis Renard's illustration of the *sirenne* from *Poisson, Ecrevisses et Crabes* (1754). (Utretcht University Library)

If the queerness of water demands and makes available opportunities for unlearning and forced reckonings of relearning, then this book closes with textures of intimacy that enable us to reconsider how violent and utopian eroticisms are mediated by tentacular sensuality and loving kindness—all of which find a home in troubled ecologies. Sirens and mermaids attract me because of their hybrid embodiments and forms that mesh the aquatic, the human, the animal, and the nonhuman. There are, to echo Donna Haraway, "promises in monsters."[11] By way of conclusion, I attach sirenic ways of knowing to eighteenth-century afterlives: first, Ben Winters's fanciful parody of Jane Austen's *Sense and Sensibility* (1811). By Winters's creative handling, Austen's first novel mutates into *Sense and Sensibility and Sea Monsters* (2009). Winters's imaginative revisioning of Austen reanimates the canonicity of the long eighteenth century in its (unintendedly) queerest, most aqueously monstrous form. Second, I pair this submarine spin-off alongside Guillermo del Toro's Oscar-winning film, *The Shape of Water* (2015). I thus extend what Brandi Bushman and I have elsewhere called "hydro-eroticism," which envisages how interspecies intimacies and queer relationships with water conjoinedly flourish—ultimately revising the notion of the mermaid/siren femme fatale and querying manifestations of care between human and aquatic hybrid embodiments.[12]

The siren is not female-embodied in either the novel or film I trace here. The sea monster is masculinized and thus reimagines the genres of colonial masculinity I see besieged by aqueous contact. Human women, by Winters's and del Toro's wielding, fall into the aquamarine tendrils of male sea monsters: Colonel Brandon, a part-octopus hybrid, and the film's sea creature, a bipedal Amazonian god–spectacle readied for slaughter upon the altar of biomedicine, respectively. If Steller's documentation of the sea cow that bears his eponym records one mode of the affective rigors induced and experienced by the nonhuman, and Renard's siren accounts for the hybrid embodiment that is knowable, foreign, and alluring, then this conclusion doubles down on those collective illustrations to query how sea monsters—aqueous hybrids—reform and reshape notions of intimacy, sexuality, and violence in the eighteenth century and beyond. *In sea monsters lives the queerest form of water.*

TENTACULAR INTIMACY

The cover of *Sense and Sensibility and Sea Monsters* features an unsettling sea monster. Marianne Dashwood gazes beyond the frame of the cover. Her face reflects mixed emotional states that are difficult to pinpoint: bemusement, ennui, woe, uncertainty, resignation. Colonel Brandon, the aforementioned sea monster and Marianne's foretold husband, studies her face. Beneath his gray locks extend the tentacles that characterize the parodic sea monster inclusions. His angular nose is grafted with attachments to his hybrid form. The tentacular arms extend down his cheeks in rosy, textured curls. One coyly rests itself on Marianne's left shoulder as if to comfort her uncertain countenance. One reaches out to her left chin. Three others pet her neck, just above the ruffled neckline of her cream gown. Still others enfold themselves atop Marianne's right hand, which the Colonel grasps strongly against his chest. She is beheld.

In chapter 1, "Teaching Wreckage in Rising Waters," and the intermezzo "Freeze!," I pointed to the environmental corollaries that literary archives, perhaps unintentionally, bespeak. These, I suggested, were *closet climate fictions*—a term that recognizes the queer capacities of climate narratives but also locates fictional narratives that superficially appear to have nothing to do with climate change realities. Uncloseting these fictions serves to elucidate these realities with a generous queer invitation that welcomes with open arms/tentacles, hospitality, and an opportunity to be heard.

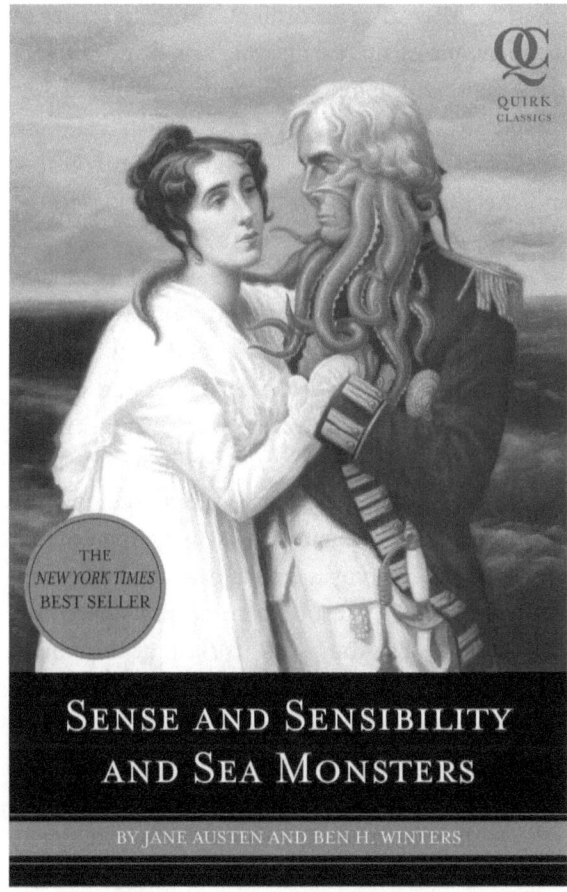

Cover of *Sense and Sensibility and Sea Monsters* (2009), illustration by Eugene Smith. (Quirk Publishing)

Indeed, Winters's retelling of Austen frames the swashbuckling journeys of the Dashwood sisters as part of and in reaction to an anthropogenically altered environment and climate. *Sense and Sensibility and Sea Monsters* thus recasts Austen's beloved novel with a penchant for imagining interspecies intimacies and environmental ruination. Interspecies hybridities and their accordant intimacies result from environmental ruination. In so doing, Winters's prescient retelling of a world ravaged by environmental havoc provides opportunities for us, as I concluded with Rich's poetry, to imagine our queer, interspecies becomings.

What we might read as an Anthropocene future—one that repeatedly and ironically dispatches with the human—in Winters's rewriting is dubbed, "The Alteration." Henry Dashwood, whose own embodiment has metamorphosed, describes The Alteration accordingly: "the creatures of the ocean [pitted] against the people of the earth; which made even the tiniest darting minnow and the gentlest dolphin into aggressive, blood-thirsty predators, hardened and hateful towards our bipedal race; which had given foul birth to whole new races of man-hating, shape-shifting ocean creatures, sirens and sea witches and mermaids and mermen; which rendered the oceans of the world naught but great burbling salt-cauldrons of death."[13] Henry Dashwood's illustration of "sirens and sea witches and mermaids and mermen," who are transformed by The Alteration, notices the siren and mermaid's femme fatale nature as emergent from and in correspondence with their affinities with nature. As Carolyn Merchant, Greta Gaard, Val Plumwood, and other writers of the early waves of ecofeminism have taught us: the domination of a feminine nature by masculinist science is a hallmark of early modernity. So too does this pattern reinforce how the siren and mermaid become enshrouded in a narrative by which their feminine wiles and destruction of masculine voyagers stem from their placement in nature.[14] The siren and mermaid must be domineered, overcome, and reined in by a masculine ethos that they seek to slash at the knees. Winters's parody extends this motif: men, such as John Dashwood, voluntarily subject themselves to experimental modifications "with the goal of creating improvements in human anatomy that would allow our bedeviled species decisive advantage over the chordate races."[15] An army of human men resign themselves to the faith of biomedical science, to commandeer a feminized, violent nature once again. Ironically though, these experiments demand that John Dashwood and the other guinea pigs become thoroughly hybridized. The human no longer proves sufficient to dispossessing animalized others. Also ironically, human-nonhuman hybridity becomes the skeleton key by which to remedy Anthropocene violence. These hybrids, epitomized by John Dashwood, must abnegate their humanity for the sake of, well, humanity.

The Alteration animates an environmentally destroyed, submerged realm whose overthrow has resulted from the contamination of water worlds: "the headwaters of a noxious stream that fed a virulent flow into every sea, every lake and estuary, poisoning the very well of the world."[16] Henry unwittingly positions these hybrid aqueous forms and other "hydrophilic malevolencies," not as naturalized because of their placement in a waterscape but as a perverse ramification of virulent headwaters maligned by human intervention, pollution, and fecklessness.[17] If sirens, mermaids, and sea monsters repulse us, then we are to blame. These are, as *Frankenstein* elucidates, monsters we have begotten. Winters thus aligns the Austen parody with the environmental advocacy spearheaded by Rachel Carson, whose *The Sea Around Us* (1951) and subsequent *Silent Spring* (1963) synthesize how ecological toxicity invariably pours into water sources and, in their invisibility, poison the flora, fauna, and human environment altogether. While Carson opens *The Sea Around Us* with an appeal to "the great mother of life, the sea," Mrs. John Dashwood ventriloquizes the inversion. She cuttingly depicts the waters left in the wake of The Alteration as "Hateful Mother Ocean."[18] Mrs. John Dashwood's remark visualizes a new materialist realm by which the animation of the maternal ocean as hateful, and thereby prepossessed with human antagonism, is ironically a result of the Anthropocene. The Anthropocene not only perverts life as we know it but reframes the cultural narratives that might approach the ocean as feminized, maternal care. We have not only diluted oceanic and arterial waters with toxicity, but this toxicity has returned to enact a mighty revenge. *Sense and Sensibility and Sea Monsters,* then, implicitly takes up Carson's cause, to realize the conjoined water fictions and realities birthed by Anthropocene-induced climate change, the dereliction of responsibility by industrial corporate greed and its collusion with the military, and poisoned proverbial and literal wells.

Whereas John Dashwood's consent to forestall his human form to fight hydrophilic malevolency surfaces later in Winters's tale, Colonel Brandon's introduction into the storyline spotlights his hybridity. The narrator observes, "Colonel Brandon, the friend of Sir John, suffered from a cruel affliction, the likes of which the Dashwood sisters had heard of, but never seen firsthand. He bore a set of long, squishy tentacles protruding grotesquely from his face, writhing this way and that, like hideous living facial hair of slime green."[19] Eugene Smith, the novel's illustrator, however, does not render Brandon's tentacles "slime green" on the cover—since the rest are black and white, the cover is the only color image provided. His tentacles are pink, mauve even. Such a revision seems to ineluctably humanize Brandon's appearance given that what remains of his untransformed face shares the same ruddy color. The use of color thus plays with approximations of humanness deployed to further consolidate the Marianne-Brandon love plot. Slime-green tentacles would, otherwise, further the nonhuman affinities of Colonel Brandon, making him look, at best, as some cousin of the Hulk or Shrek and at worst, gangrenous.

No matter the color-coding and its multitudinous signals, the narration reminds us, ad nauseum, of Colonel Brandon's physical monstrosity; he is "grotesque" and "hideous." Later he is described as possessing a "lunatic's nightmare of a face."[20] These descriptions seem in tension with the fact that "he was very pleasant. His appearance, besides the twitching tentacles that overhung his chin, was not unpleasing, despite being an absolute old bachelor; for he was on the wrong side of five and thirty."[21] Marianne's implicit criticism of Brandon in Austen's *Sense and Sensibility* is his boorish plainness and age; he is the safe choice. Winters amplifies those tensions that initially make impossible any affection Marianne might have towards Brandon. In *Sense and Sensibility and Sea Monsters*, it's not just the residue of boorish plainness; instead Winters imbues Brandon with a physical deformity that inhibits attraction. Boorishness, the parody reasons, is akin to monstrosity. Sea monsters, it would appear, justify Marianne's coldness to Colonel Brandon and thus become the central obstacle to their presaged marriage. But how boorish and plain can a sea monster be?

Marianne's only interest in Brandon, besides polite company, is the cause of his "deformity," and thus our attention remains steadied on his hybrid figuration. The allure of Brandon as hybrid-siren-by-another-name recurs. "Elinor," we read, "leveled a silencing glance at her sister when she sensed Marianne's intention to indecorously enquire of their new acquaintance how he came to bear his peculiar facial stigmata. Such physiognomic eccentricities were variously whispered to result from one's mother drinking sea-water while confined, or a hex, laid upon the bearer by a sea witch."[22] Yet again, the novel evidences the plight caused by unhygienic, toxic waters that instill congenital birth defects. Whereas Carson crusaded against the reckless, widespread use of pesticides like DDT, which invariably plagued avian reproduction and induced cancerous effects in fish and humans, here the comic seawaters relay additional perils. The lack of readily available drinking water—a climate change reality palpably felt by those in desert or archipelagic geographies without access to aquifers—as well as the poisonous infrastructure of seawater serve as possible catalysts of sea-monstrous birth. The sea becomes, once again, embodied by, and bodies forth, monsters aplenty. Colonel Brandon does not elucidate the history of his "curse," and the novel recirculates both of these conspiracy theories. The origin mythos by which sea creatures like Brandon populate the text is not vital information; his tentacles very well might be the result of ensorcelling or something congenital. As with *The Shape of Water*, the repeated conjuring of "deformity"—an eighteenth-century dog-whistle for disability—is an opportunity to realize alternative modes of being that invariably bubble forth interspecies affections and intimacies. The interspecies deformity, in other words, introduces utopic spaces wherein the "deformed" do not live outside economies of desire and sexuality, but become ineluctably enfolded within—consider especially the neat marriage plot with which both Austen and Winters conclude their conversant tales.

Winters's parodic impulses are not entirely innocent: the constant narrative attention to tentacles still rings with crude jokes and covert criticisms of gendered performance. Though much of Brandon's history is muddled, what he does reveal to Elinor, in Austenian fashion, is that his ward Eliza (kismet given that the protagonist in *The Shape of Water* is also called Elisa), jilted and spoiled by Willoughby, would seem to bear a similar facial deformity. Brandon recounts, "I am well aware of rumours that [Eliza] has my same unfortunate facial misfortune. Nothing could be further from the truth; she has only an unwomanly tendency to sprout hair 'pon her lip, an inheritance from the crinite cake-vendor who was her natural parent."[23] Though Brandon and Eliza share no consanguinity, the recurrence of facial protuberances here becomes a sexist joke in that Eliza's facial hair (crinite genetics) is recognized, akin to Brandon's affliction, as monstrous. Some hair on a young woman's lip is cause for accusations of monstrosity. So too is this the case for Brandon's tentacles, which are perpetually the butt of the joke. Willoughby, for example, states, "Brandon is just the kind of man, if man he truly be . . . whom everybody speaks well of and nobody cares about; whom all are delighted to see, and everybody is sort of mildly afraid to look at directly."[24] Just as Eliza's face is derided as being implicitly unfeminine, Brandon's tentacles question his masculine comportment. Willoughby's insult, only mildly flourished here based on Austen's original description, functions doubly: it first serves, more abstractly, to invalidate Brandon's humanity in that his tentacles evict him from notions of the human, and second, it undercuts the idea of "man" as tethered to masculinity. The "squidishness of his visage" doubly binds Brandon as existing outside the parameters of humanity and masculinity, which, while an exciting possibility of queer affiliation, endeavors to expunge him from circles of familiarity and affection.[25] Sea-monstrosity becomes yet another creaturely habit subtended by lonely resignation.

Contrastingly, the concluding marriage of Marianne and Brandon subverts this notion and, as with the communion of Eliza and the creature in

The Shape of Water, telegraphs queer becomings wherein the heteronormative institution of marriage is beset and undone by a sea creature and his beloved. The queer possibility of Marianne's marriage to Brandon involves both her evaporated loathing for his physical appearance as well as the recuperation of those tentacles in an aside unimagined by Austen: the sexual compatibility between a hybrid sea monster and his wife. The close of *Sense and Sensibility and Sea Monsters* animates Haraway's invocation of "tentacular thinking," which conjures any number of interspecies entanglements. Haraway waxes poetic: "The tentacular ones tangle me in SF. Their many appendages make string figures; they entwine me in the poiesis—the making—of speculative fabulation, science fiction, science fact, speculative feminism, *soin de ficelle,* so far. The tentacular ones make attachments and detachments; they make cuts and knots; they make a difference; they weave paths and consequences but not determinisms; they are both open and knotted in some ways and not others."[26] For Haraway, the reminder of tentacular thinking accompanies its etymology, wherein the Latin roots *tentaculum* and *tentare* mean "feeler" and "to feel or try," respectively.

Sea monsters make available new modes of haptic connection that are captured by tentacularity, which implicitly effaces strictures of heteronormativity, and likewise harken back to the textures of touching-empathic attunement with which I opened this chapter. To be tentacled, as Colonel Brandon is, forces one to be constantly feeling (emotively and physically), constantly trying. Austen's Brandon, revised by Winters, magnifies how tentacular embodiment allows for new modes of attachment. What might it mean, Winters seems to ask, if the hybrid sea monster reaches out to touch you? What happens to touch in the aquatic zone? What does it mean to feel a tentacle feel you back, as the cover of the parody portrays?

Brandon's tentacles ultimately win Marianne over, and the revisionist novel suggests that Brandon's hybridity accompanies polymorphic eroticisms. Winters's retelling contends that to feel a tentacle—for a tentacle to feel you back—is to embrace worlds of sexual pleasure unavailable to nonhybridized men. In yet another recuperation, The Alteration's literary imagining of the Anthropocene corresponds with new pleasurable modes of being—a signal tie to Joanna Zylinska's recuperative efforts in *The End of Man.*[27] The tentacles, read this way, no longer stand as obstacles to connubial life. They instead become powerful protuberances imparting erogenous touching that enriches Marianne's marriage to a sea monster. The narrator reveals, "She [Marianne] found, in the event, that his face [Brandon's] was not the only region of his physiognomy that could be described as multi-appendaged, and she found that fact to carry with it certain marital satisfactions."[28] Though coy and inconspicuous in its revelations, Winters's Brandon is an Austen-fied version of Japanese tentacle porn, wherein young women assume mostly octopuses or squid as their sexual partners. This seed is planted earlier in the novel when Elinor observes that "his appendages at times seemed to stiffen a bit when he chanced to glance upon Marianne, as if excess blood were flowing into them."[29] While Elinor reads this as a dispiritedness begat by Marianne's rejection of Brandon (he stiffens in fear), read with the ending it's clear that upon Brandon's face blossom phallic tentacles that engorge with visual attachment to Marianne. In *Sense and Sensibility and Sea Monsters,* multilimbed sea monsters promote an interspecies intimacy wherein hybridization fosters worlds of pleasures that queerly subvert the marriage plot and foster eroticism in hybrid haptics.

LOVING KINDNESS IN WATER

Whereas Winter bequeaths one narrative of interspecies eroticisms, Guillermo del Toro's *The Shape of Water* (2017) offers alternative opportunities to visualize romantic attachments and pleasurable sex among disparate species. *Sense and Sensibility and Sea Monsters* forges a literary mode; *The Shape of Water* casts these full-frontal scenes of intimacy on the big screen. Interspecies intimacy thus manifests as a mode that bends/blends genres, embodiments, and notions of the human. At the same time, the film responds to concerns over rising waters—what we might brand as troubled ecologies—which are not waylaid by queer attachments but manifest as sites redolent with queer attachment.

Nominated for thirteen Academy Awards and recipient of four, including Best Picture, *The Shape of Water* has become an international and commercial success in its interweaving of fairy tale, horror, Cold War thriller, and monster movie genres. Set in an early 1960s Baltimore, a mute custodial worker, Elisa Esposito (Sally Hawkins), falls helplessly in love with *The Creature from the Black Lagoon*'s doppelganger (Doug Jones), who is given no name and likewise cannot speak. He doesn't, perhaps to Renard's dismay, make murine noises either. Acknowledging their shared disability, Elisa relays through sign language, "What am I? I move my mouth like him. I make no sound like him. The way he looks at me, he doesn't know what I lack or that I'm incomplete . . . He sees me as I am."[30] Yet again, the interspecies connection is recast through the lens of disability. As with Colonel Brandon, the sharing of similar disabilities inspires forms of authentic being rather than tired notions of disability as lack or exclusion.

Rumored to be a god to the Amazonians (because of his curative touch), the creature is shackled and held hostage by the United States military—headed up by Strickland (Michael Shannon)—to weaponize his alleged magical powers in hopes of upstaging the Russians' space-race triumphs. When the magical weapons cannot be harnessed, the military seeks to vivisect the creature. To free her lover from this fate, and bring their sex acts to fruition, Elisa recruits her tokenized friends—Zelda (Octavia Spencer), her Black companion and translator, and Giles (Richard Jenkins), her gay neighbor, who is also the film's omniscient narrator and translator—to manumit the creature from the laboratory prison.[31] The triad steals the creature from the lab, and he takes up residence in Elisa's bathtub. It is in her impossibly flooded bathroom where Elisa and the creature consummate their interspecies sex. Whereas Disney's Ariel, the little mermaid, belts out "Part of Your World" to imagine the possibility of connubial bliss on land, *The Shape of Water* evidences that it is only underwater where sexual compatibility is conferred. In other words, *The Shape of Water* endows water with two powerful didacticisms: one, that water is the sole medium wherein consensual, sexual intimacy is realized, and two, water provides an elemental opportunity by which to queerly unify human and nonhuman relations.

The film opens submerged. We tread our way through the aquamarine rays of Baltimore deluged: del Toro envisages a revived Atlantis, a settled Titanic wreck, or a Baltimore of the future in which sea level rise has wrought what has been prophesized by climate scientists. Possibilities of terrestrial inversion and aquatic fantasy abound. Elisa buoyantly floats above her sofa asleep. She is, the narratorial voice-over notes, "the princess without voice."[32] The cacophonous ring of the alarm breaks Elisa's literally wet dream, and she commences her nocturnal routine (she works the midnight shift). In repeated pattern, Elisa promptly starts the bath, sets an egg timer, drops her eggs into boiling water, and then immerses herself in the bathtub, where she masturbates. Elisa's routine includes this hygienic-masturbatory practice (perhaps ironically so), calling both backwards to the fantasy of the submarine dream, which both comforts and exhilarates her, and forward to the consummation of her relationship with her fish lover. The water-filled bathtub—which is noticeably aged, cracked, and paved by robin's-egg-blue tiles—and, later, the flooded bathroom become aquatic sites rife for water's masturbatory potential. Water, here, participates as both medium and actor in the autoerotic gratification. The creature's aquarium prison features identically colored tiles thus suggesting the tank and bathroom as fluid spheres that signal the eroticism between Elisa and the creature, especially given that following their introduction, Elisa's masturbatory praxis is dedicated to the creature.

Del Toro's deft handling of the troubled ecologies that reside within aquamarine worlds reveals a hydroconnective tissue that might unite sexual, intimate bonds, especially given that the relationships that exist outside of water are doomed to fail: Giles is condemned to loneliness when his flirtation with the waiter is homophobically rejected; Zelda's browbeaten husband proves effete when confronted with Strickland's menacing assault; and Strickland's own perfunctory marriage is consummated only through sadistic sexual violence in which he muffles his wife's mouth with his necrotic hand. The comparative failures of these relationships spotlight Elisa's relationship with the creature as one in which aqueous futures facilitate a loving kindness otherwise absent on land.

Elisa's engagement with water and her entangled intimacy with her fish lover epitomize the reshuffling and blending of various bodies that characterize transcorporeality's unceasing erotic and queer potentiality. Water constitutes their unmistakable, ineffable co-constitution. In Astrida Neimanis's words, "Our own embodiment . . . is never really autonomous. Nor is it autochthonous, nor autopoietic; we require other bodies of other waters (that in turn require other bodies and other waters) to bathe us into being."[33] The use of "to bathe" is, of course, poetically figurative, but Elisa's recurrent bathtub moments allow us to take these words at face value. It is both the nonhuman lover and the medium of water that bathes Elisa into being, resonating with a freedom and intimate reunification that the film's final scene assures we never forget. Elisa's quotidian and aqueous masturbatory praxis rejects both the sanctimonious projection that masturbation is somehow unhygienic and the procreative model of a heteronormative sexual relation, which is further maligned when she begins to fantasize about the creature, who is implicitly understood as male but not human. While Eliza and the creature ostensibly operate within a heteronormative nexus, their queer entanglement results from their displacements from corporeal normativity: she is mute, and he does not possess the capability of human language, in addition to his physiology that is more fish than human despite his bipedalism. Eliza and the creature thus embolden Dana

Luciano and Mel Chen's question as to whether the queer has ever been human—and how queer, disabled, and racial identifications invariably hold such stalwart conceptions in abeyance.[34]

But the bathtub is not only home to Eliza's autoeroticism, it is also the site of an impossible sexual congress with the nonhuman. Sex between the two conjures up considerations of an off-brand bestiality that rejects a stifling heteronormativity and invites readings of mutually pleasurable experiences between animals and humans. Even more powerfully, it has been fetishized by the film's die-hard fans, who were quick to imagine what the creature's erect penis might look like and literalize such an imagination in dildos made of silicone.[35] Ithyphallic/ichthyphallic, indeed. First, a caveat: I am not conflating queer affection or eroticism with bestial affection or eroticism—itself a homophobic, animalizing conflation wielded against queer individuals—and the main difference, as offered by the film, is the issue of consent. If the West Indian manatee who reaches out to you offers one paradigm for consensual contact, then sex with a sea monster in *The Shape of Water* and *Sense and Sensibility and Sea Monsters* registers others.

Prior to the cinematic splendor that is the flooded bathroom, interspecies flirtation accompanies Elisa's feeding of the creature. Their interspecies intimacy is then reliant upon the care work that accompanies feeding and nurturing: these are, as María Puig de la Bellacasa observes, matters of care.[36] For the two, the hard-boiled egg exemplifies a shared food staple that allows for community and fosters this nurturing lovingness. In fact, the first shared sign Elisa teaches the creature is "egg." To sign "egg" in American Sign Language (ASL), the pointer and middle fingers on both hands touch and separate downward as if to replicate the process of cracking eggs. The same two fingers on both hands tapped together twice is the ASL word for "name" as in "my name is . . ." While many words employ similar gestural modes in ASL, I point to these connections, not because the creature somehow misinterprets Elisa's name as "egg," but rather to demonstrate that like "my name is," Elisa's use of "egg" functions as an introduction between two individuals who do not share a common language, frame of reference, or embodiment. Eggs somehow dissipate the impossible boundaries by which different species are incommunicable, forging bridges by which those boundaries are forded.

The egg, in turn, signals alternative modes of queer reproduction and sexual intimacy. Though fish species reproduce in a variety of ways—and reproductive sex is neither discussed in, nor the point of, the film—a common

Elisa shares an egg with the creature. *The Shape of Water* (2017). (Fox Searchlight)

reproductive mode is that of ovuliparity, which does not require penetrative insemination. Egg-laying fish species, like salmon, goldfish, and eels (perhaps sirens too, if we believe Renard) who reproduce by way of ovuliparity lay eggs and await the semen of fish from the same species to fertilize those eggs; this entire process is conducted externally. While it is difficult to discern the creature's ichthyo-background, we can read Elisa's offering of the hard-boiled eggs as an index both of their sexual compatibility and of her sexual readiness. Eggs thus masquerade as a burlesque food exchanged between Elisa and the creature, ultimately situating a loving kindness predicated on the sharing of meals and sustenance.

Despite this ichthyological Easter egg, Eliza and the creature *do* engage in penetrative sex—she describes this to Zelda with humorous reaction—which may, on the surface, disregard ovuliparity. However, given that the creature is a CGI'd pastiche of different nonhuman aquatic species, the process of laying and leaving eggs is one that would be recognizable to ichthyologists and perhaps the fish lover. The presentation of the eggs may initially invoke reproductive capability between the two, and yet the fact that both ingest the eggs engenders a kronistic reading in which the potential young are consumed as an aphrodisiac. Such delicacies continue to foster interspecies connections in which human, nonhuman (chicken), and sea monster are enveloped. To partake in the meal is to recognize how Elisa and the creature float among various human, nonhuman, and suprahuman worlds with erotic zeal. The hard-boiled egg as a nonreproductive gift offers an additional layer to their queer entanglement that rejects the reproductive narrative that otherwise might be imposed given their ostensible heteronormative arrangement.

Their queer arrangement is further mired by the fact that both Elisa and the creature are visualized as amphibious and aquatic hybrids, respectively. While for the creature this is explicit, Elisa's own hybrid form is hinted at through a trail of visual breadcrumbs that become fully realized only in the film's closing shot. Each morning, in addition to setting the egg timer and masturbating in the tub, Elisa traces her fingers along three parallel scars on either side of her neck. These become fully fledged gills when she accepts the submarine life offered to her by the creature. The cicatrices remain a mystery alongside Elisa's origin story—yet a further connection between the lovers. Zelda reveals under duress to Strickland, "they found her by the river in the water."[37] Strickland observes that Elisa's surname, Esposito, derives from the Italian word meaning "orphan." The Italian use of *esposito* transliterates the Latin word *expositus*, which means to "place outside." But Elisa is found "in the water" along the river's littoral, and the scars on both sides of her neck reason that despite her human body, she bears the mark of an evolved amphibian state. Elisa the orphan thus realizes that being placed outside is not strictly about interior and exterior space, but rather about modes of amphibious and aquatic belonging that reject the stifling strictures of terrestrial being. Elisa epitomizes the shifting embodiments that fluidity endows. Though the film is sold as imagining what happens when a human woman falls in love with a sea creature, *The Shape of Water*, as this visual semaphore telegraphs, is committed to recognizing that the love story is not strictly human on either side.

Baltimore's Inner Harbor homes the film's concluding scenes, which further demonstrate that terrestrial modes of life are predicated on grief, separation, and violence and that intimate attachment and care are possible only in blue utopias. The endeavor to free the creature into the harbor—which underscores an implicit connectivity of aqueous sites, especially in recognition of the creature's Amazonian home—is derailed by Strickland, who represents the unrepentant, militaristic arm that might harness the creature's powers and obliterate loving connection. Elisa and the creature embrace a final time upon the industrial littoral before the two are wounded by gunshots. The ending, so near the water's edge, would seem to potentially introduce an immersive bathos in which the possibility of emancipation is foiled, only a body's length from the overfilled channel. The film refuses such disappointment. The creature's powers, which were unsuccessfully harnessed in the laboratory, spring to photoluminescent éclat as the cast is inundated by rain.

In a previous iteration of these exercised powers, the creature heals the wound unintentionally inflicted upon Giles's forearm and turns back the gay-best-friend's biological clock: he miraculously regrows his hair, and with it, the masculine confidence that comes with the obsession with youthfulness. The power of the creature emanates from this haptic connection: as with the West Indian manatee, there are licit pleasures that unfold when the nonhuman touches first. Giles and the creature touch heads—a sort of cerebral, tactile overlap—and the electric blue that signals photoluminosity sparks from the creature's skin. Within the creature's grasp lie reparative, restorative, and curative properties, which can only be passed through the creature's consent to caress.

The visuality of loving, reparative touch is captured by the film's advertising materials, and remains contingent on proximity to—here, immersion in—water. The thunderstorms that induce Baltimore's rainy season trigger the effusion of the creature's powers, which preempt yet another interconnection of watery bodies. Strickland's gunshots prove ineffective, and with the spread of his webbed claw across the wounds, the creature counteracts Strickland's attempt to further possess his body through mechanized, militarized control. He heals himself. "You *are* a god," Strickland whispers before the creature slits his throat.[38] In an unsettling irony, Strickland's erotic obsession (weaponized against his wife) with Elisa's muteness becomes a self-fulfilled prophesy in which he gasps for air as he exsanguinates. He makes no sound. Only the patter of the raindrops on the pavement fills the soundwaves. Water overcomes.

Having defeated the film's antagonist, the creature retrieves Elisa's bullet-punctured body and they dive into the riparian waters. This moment reinforces an understanding of water as life: it is a creaturely home that facilitates the creature's return to an aquatic environment and Elisa's fully realized metamorphosis into an amphibious being. Water fosters their intimate state of togetherness. The camera follows the two underwater, as if

Poster for *The Shape of Water* (2017). (Fox Searchlight)

to join the underwater fantasy with which the film opens. The two passionately embrace and the creature presses his lips against Elisa's. Whereas the touching of heads with Giles prompts the creature's curative bioluminescence, in this final moment it is the touching of lips and mouths—mouths that are equally mute—that incites restorative property. The creature's kiss does not set out to instill voices in either; they have long nurtured alternative forms of embodied language by which to communicate. Instead, the healing allows Elisa to transform into her aqueous form. The gill-like scars she bears throughout the film become operational, and we are led to believe that she is not beholden to the gunshot wounds that puncture her body either. The gunshots open her body to one form of violation; the creature's kiss and his claws open another, in which the physical incision of Eliza's body is the portal to communal belonging. In water, we can be together.

If the queerness of water maintains that bodies of water entangle histories and futures of queer opportunity, then monstrous (in both its eighteenth-century and contemporary parlance) aquatic beings enliven these opportunities to relish literary, artistic, and filmic instantiations, especially as we peer over the water's edge to witness our own aqueous belonging and becoming. In the words of the voice-over by Giles with which the film concludes—a re-created mash-up of Islamic poetry that has long stayed with del Toro—"Unable to perceive the shape of you, I find you all around me. Your presence fills my eyes with your love. It humbles my heart, for you are everywhere."[39] *Let us welcome our queer becomings in troubled waters.*

Notes

INTRODUCTION

1. William Falconer, *The Shipwreck* (London: W. Miller, 1762), 9.
2. Ibid., 9.
3. Ibid., 101.
4. Scott Juengel, "What Is Orientation in Sinking?," *European Romantic Review* 30, no. 3 (2019): 267.
5. Falconer, *Shipwreck*, 102.
6. Mel Chen, *Animacies: Biopolitics, Racial Mattering, and Queer Affect* (Durham: Duke University Press, 2012), 11.
7. Other terms include Elizabeth DeLoughrey's "oceanic turn," Peter Miller's "thalassography," Stefanie Hessler's "tidalectics," Karin Amimoto Ingersoll's "seascape epistemology," Laura Winkiel's "hydro-criticism," and Margaret Cohen and Killian Quigley's "submarine aesthetics." Steve Mentz, "Towards a Blue Cultural Studies: The Sea, Maritime Culture, and Early Modern English Literature," *Literature Compass* 6, no. 5 (2009): 997–1013; John Gillis, "The Blue Humanities," *Humanities: The Magazine for the National Endowment for the Humanities* 34, no. 4 (2013), https://www.neh.gov/humanities/2013/mayjune/feature/the-blue-humanities; Hester Blum, "The Prospect of Oceanic Studies," *PMLA* 125, no. 3 (2010): 670–77; Elizabeth DeLoughrey, "Submarine Futures of the Anthropocene," *Comparative Literature* 69, no. 1 (2017): 32–44; Peter Miller, ed., *The Sea: Thalassography and Historiography* (Ann Arbor: University of Michigan Press, 2013); Stefanie Hessler, ed., *Tidalectics: Imagining an Oceanic Worldview through Art and Science* (Cambridge, MA: MIT Press, 2018); Karin Amimoto Ingersoll, *Waves of Knowing: A Seascape Epistemology* (Durham, NC: Duke University Press, 2016); Laura Winkiel, "Introduction: Hydro-criticism," *English Language Notes* 57, no. 1 (2019): 1–10; Margaret Cohen and Killian Quigley, "Submarine Aesthetics," *The Aesthetics of the Undersea*, ed. Margaret Cohen and Killian Quigley (New York: Routledge, 2019), 1–13.
8. See, for example, Jenia Mukherjee, *Blue Infrastructures: Natural History, Political Ecology and Urban Development in Kolkata* (Singapore: Springer, 2020); Sugata Ray and Venugopal Maddipati, eds., *Water Histories of South Asia: The Materiality of Liquescence* (New York: Routledge, 2021); Alex Bolding and Rossella Alba, "Viewpoint—IWRM and I: A Reflexive Travelogue of the Flows and Practices Research Team," *Flows and*

Practices: The Politics of Integrated Water Resources Management in Eastern and Southern Africa, ed. Lyla Mehta, Bill Derman, and Emmanuel Manzungu (Zimbabwe: Weaver Press, 2017): 345–67. Thanks to Sritama Chatterjee for this helpful reminder.

9. Steve Mentz, "Ice/Water/Vapor," in *The Cambridge Companion to Environmental Humanities*, ed. Jeffrey Jerome Cohen and Stephanie Foote (Cambridge, UK: Cambridge University Press, 2021), 193.

10. Stefan Helmreich, *Alien Ocean: Anthropological Voyages in Microbial Seas* (Berkeley: University of California Press, 2009), 17.

11. See Dan Brayton, *Shakespeare's Ocean* (Charlottesville: University of Virginia Press, 2012); Steve Mentz, *Shipwreck Modernity: Ecologies of Globalization, 1550–1719* (Minneapolis: University of Minnesota Press, 2015); Lowell Duckert, *For All Waters: Finding Ourselves in Early Modern Wetscapes* (Minneapolis: University of Minnesota Press, 2017); Christopher Pastore, *Between Land and Sea: The Atlantic Coast and the Transformation of New England* (Cambridge, MA: Harvard University Press, 2014); Jonathan Lamb, ed., *A Cultural History of the Sea in the Age of Enlightenment*, vol. 4 of *A Cultural History of the Sea*, ed. Margaret Cohen (New York: Bloomsbury, 2021).

12. Margaret Cohen, *The Novel and the Sea* (Princeton, NJ: Princeton University Press, 2010), 3–4.

13. Cohen, *Novel and the Sea*, 14. All italics original unless indicated otherwise.

14. Jayne Lewis, *Air's Appearance: Literary Atmosphere in British Fiction, 1660–1794* (Chicago: University of Chicago Press, 2012); John Durham Peters, *The Marvelous Clouds: Toward a Philosophy of Elemental Media* (Chicago: University of Chicago Press, 2015); Melody Jue, *Wild Blue Media* (Durham: Duke University Press, 2020).

15. Siobhan Carroll, *An Empire of Air and Water: Uncolonizable Space in the British Imagination, 1750–1850* (Philadelphia: University of Pennsylvania Press, 2015), 6.

16. Cohen and Quigley, "Submarine Aesthetics," 7.

17. Ibid., 7; Mona Narain, "Oceanic Intimacies," *Eighteenth-Century Fiction* 34, no. 2 (2022): 147–65.

18. Philip Steinberg and Kimberly Peters, "Wet Ontology, Fluid Spaces: Giving Depth to Volume through Oceanic Thinking," *Environment and Planning D: Society and Space* 33, no.2 (2015): 256.

19. Cecilia Chen, Janine MacLeod, and Astrida Neimanis, *Thinking with Water* (Montreal, QU: McGill-Queen's University Press, 2013), 3.

20. Donna Haraway, *Staying with the Trouble: Making Kin in the Chthulucene* (Durham, NC: Duke University Press, 2016), 1.

21. Eve Sedgwick, *Touching Feeling: Affect, Pedagogy, Performativity* (Durham, NC: Duke University Press, 2003), 8.

22. Samuel Taylor Coleridge, *The Rime of the Ancient Mariner*, in *The Poetical Works of S. T. Coleridge*, ed. Henry Nelson Coleridge (London, UK: Pickering, 1834), line 413.

23. Catriona Sandilands and Bruce Erikson, eds., *Queer Ecologies* (Bloomington: Indiana University Press, 2010); Nicole Seymour, *Strange Natures: Futurity, Empathy, and the Queer Ecological Imagination* (Champaign-Urbana: University of Illinois Press,

2013); Greg Garrard, "How Queer Is Green?," *Configurations* 18, nos. 1–2 (2010): 73–96; Greta Gaard, "Toward a Queer Ecofeminism," *Hypatia* 12, no. 1 (1997): 114–37; Chen, *Animacies*; Stacy Alaimo, *Exposed: Environmental Politics and Pleasures in Posthuman Times* (Minneapolis: University of Minnesota Press, 2018); Omise'eke Natasha Tinsley, "Black Atlantic, Queer Atlantic: Queer Imaginings of the Middle Passage," *GLQ: A Journal of Lesbian and Gay Studies* 14, nos. 2–3 (2008): 191–215; Timothy Morton, "Queer Ecology," *PMLA* 125, no. 2 (2010): 273–82.

24. Catriona Sandilands and Bruce Erikson, "A Genealogy of Queer Ecologies," in Sandilands and Erikson, *Queer Ecologies*, 5.

25. Daniel Defoe, *Robinson Crusoe*, ed. Thomas Keymer (Oxford, UK: Oxford University Press, 2003), 39.

26. Roderick Ferguson's *One-Dimensional Queer* adroitly unravels this monolithic thinking to imagine how queerness and its imbrication in social justice and sexual liberation is not a single-issue polemic. Roderick Ferguson, *One-Dimensional Queer* (New York: Polity, 2018).

27. Kadji Amin, *Disturbing Attachments: Genet, Modern Pederasty, and Queer History* (Durham, NC: Duke University Press, 2017), 115.

28. Catriona Sandilands, "Into This Blue: Betsy Warland's Queer Ecopoetics," *Interdisciplinary Studies in Literature and Environment* 25, no. 1 (2018): 198.

29. Astrida Neimanis, *Bodies of Water: Posthuman Feminist Phenomenology* (New York: Bloomsbury, 2017), 3.

30. Elizabeth Povinelli, "The Kinship of Tides," in Hessler, *Tidalectics*, 167.

31. Amin Ghaziani and Matt Brim, "Queer Methods: Four Provocations for an Emerging Field," in *Imagining Queer Methods*, eds. Amin Ghaziani and Matt Brim (New York: New York University Press, 2019), 15.

32. José Esteban Muñoz, *Cruising Utopia: The Then and There of Queer Futurity* (New York: New York University Press, 2009), 1.

33. Alaimo, *Exposed*, 1.

34. William Diaper, *Nereides: Or Sea-Eclogues* (London, 1712), x.

35. Rachel Carson, *The Sea Around Us* (Oxford, UK: Oxford University Press, 2018), 3.

36. Killian Quigley, "The Pastoral Submarine: William Diaper and Eclogue's Marine Frontier," *Eighteenth-Century Studies* 53, no. 1 (2019): 122.

37. Quigley, "Pastoral Submarine," 113.

38. Diaper, *Nereides*, "Eclogue III," lines 11–14.

39. Ibid., lines 19–20.

40. Ibid., lines 29–34.

41. Of the end of the eighteenth century, Samuel Baker writes, "politically and geopolitically, the sea provides them [literary governmental strategies] with a field of compatibility in which to reconcile the demands of the ancien régime and bourgeois nation, and in which to envision the integration of pastoral, agricultural, and martial ways of like into modern commercial society." Samuel Baker, *Written on the Water: British Romanticism and the Maritime Empire of Culture* (Charlottesville: University of Virginia Press, 2010), 3.

42. Gaston Bachelard employs "violent water" differently than I do. For Bachelard, violent water is a psychological diagnostic that enables even more than materiality, a type of therapy. While evocative and founded in readings of literature, Bachelard's strictly symbolic interpretation of water decries the material power of water traversed here. Gaston Bachelard, *Water and Dreams: An Essay on the Imagination of Matter*, trans. Edith R. Farrell (Dallas, TX: Dallas Institute, 1983).

43. William Boelhower, "Reframing Oceanic Violence: The Pax Britannica and Wild Weather during the Nineteenth Century," in *A Cultural History of the Sea in the Age of Empire*, vol. 5 of *A Cultural History of the Sea*, ed. Margaret Cohen (New York: Bloomsbury, 2021), 122, 105, 106.

44. Rob Nixon, *Slow Violence and the Environmentalism of the Poor* (Cambridge, MA: Harvard University Press, 2011), 2.

45. Nixon, *Slow Violence*, 11.

46. Greta Gaard, "Where Is Feminism in the Environmental Humanities?," in *Environmental Humanities: Voices from the Anthropocene*, eds. Serpil Oppermann and Serenella Iovino (New York: Rowman & Littlefield, 2017), 93.

47. Greta LaFleur's *Natural History of Sexuality in Early America* articulates how these Enlightenment knowledges, especially through taxonomy, represent an epiphenomenal production of sexual difference as a science of racial difference. Greta LaFleur, *The Natural History of Sexuality in Early America* (Baltimore, MD: Johns Hopkins University Press, 2018).

48. Steve Mentz, *Break Up the Anthropocene* (Minneapolis: University of Minnesota Press, 2019), 5.

49. See, for example, Megan A. Woodward, *Eighteenth-Century Women Writers and the Gentlemen's Liberation Movement: Independence, War, Masculinity, and the Novel, 1778–1818* (Farnham, UK: Ashgate, 2011); Jason Solinger, *Becoming the Gentleman: British Literature and the Invention of Modern Masculinity, 1660–1815* (New York: Palgrave Macmillan, 2012); Susan Broomhall and Jacqueline Van Gent, eds., *Governing Masculinities in the Early Modern Period: Regulating Selves and Others* (Farnham, UK: Ashgate, 2011); Declan Kavanagh, *Effeminate Years: Literature, Politics, and Aesthetics in Mid-eighteenth-century Britain* (Lewisburg, PA: Bucknell University Press, 2017).

50. David Kutcha, *The Three-Piece Suit and Modern Masculinity: England, 1550–1850* (Berkeley: University of California Press, 2002), 11.

51. Hans Turley, *Rum, Sodomy, and the Lash: Piracy, Sexuality, and Masculine Identity* (New York: New York University Press, 1999); Tim Hitchcock and Michèle Cohen, eds., *English Masculinities 1660–1800* (New York: Longman, 1999); Katherine Arens, "When Performing Gender Is Nonconforming: The Need for Archives in the Practice of Theory," in *Castration, Impotence, and Emasculation in the Long Eighteenth Century*, ed. Anne Greenfield (New York: Routledge, 2020), 201–36; Mary Beth Harris, "Masculinity, Performance Anxiety, and Literary Impotence in Charlotte Charke's *The History of Henry Dumont*," in Greenfield, *Castration, Impotence, and Emasculation*, 168–84.

52. Julia Banister, *Masculinity, Militarism and Eighteenth-Century Culture, 1689–1815* (Cambridge, UK: Cambridge University Press, 2020), 3.

53. Neimanis, *Bodies of Water*, 2.
54. I am grateful to Katie Adkison for assistance with this lucid phrase.
55. Ana de Freitas Boe and Abby Coykendall, Eds. *Heteronormativity in Eighteenth-Century Literature and Culture* (New York: Routledge, 2015).
56. Michel Foucault, *The History of Sexuality*, vol. 1, trans. Robert Hurley (New York: Vintage, 1978); Michel Foucault, *Security, Territory, Population: Lectures at the Collège de France 1977–1978* (New York: Picador, 2004).
57. Pamela Cheek, *Sexual Antipodes: Enlightenment Globalization and the Placing of Sex* (Stanford, CA: Stanford University Press, 2003); Felicity Nussbaum, *Torrid Zones: Maternity, Sexuality, and Empire in Eighteenth-Century English Narratives* (Baltimore, MD: Johns Hopkins University Press, 1995); Joseph Massad, "Re-Orienting Desire: The Gay International and the Arab World," *Public Culture* 14, no. 2 (2002): 361–85; Jasbir Puar, *Terrorist Assemblages: Homonationalism in Queer Times* (Durham, NC: Duke University Press, 2007).
58. Eve Tuck and K. Wayne Yang, "Decolonization Is Not a Metaphor," *Decolonization: Indigeneity, Education & Society* 1, no. 1 (2012): 1–40.
59. Max Liboiron, *Pollution Is Colonialism* (Durham, NC: Duke University Press, 2021), 26.
60. Tuck and Yang, "Decolonization," 7.
61. Kate Rigby and Emily Sun have recently considered what decolonizing Romanticism might entail. For Rigby, Romantic poetry "harbours potentials for decolonial praxes, pitched against both human domination and nonhuman others, especially, in the case for settler nations, Indigenous and enslaved peoples by colonial powers" (4). Sun, however, proposes that decolonizing Romanticism might best be realized by accommodating (viz. Dipesh Chakrabarty) a type of "provincialization" that moves "in the direction of cosmopolitan multiplicity" (163). Kate Rigby, *Reclaiming Romanticism: Towards an Ecopoetics of Decolonization* (New York: Bloomsbury, 2021). Emily Sun, "Romanticism, Decolonization, Provincialization," *Keats-Shelley Journal* 70 (2021): 157–65.
62. Ami Yoon, "Imagining Decolonial Futures in William Gilbert's *The Hurricane*," in *Eighteenth-Century Environmental Humanities*, ed. Jeremy Chow (Lewisburg, PA: Bucknell University Press, 2022), 174.
63. Catherine Walsh and Walter Mignolo, *On Decoloniality: Concepts, Analytics, Praxis* (Durham, NC: Duke University Press, 2018); Aníbal Quijano, "Coloniality of Power, Eurocentrism, and Latin America," *Nepantla: Views from the South* 1, no. 3 (2000): 533–80; María Lugones, "Toward a Decolonial Feminism," *Hypatia* 25, no. 4 (2010): 742–59; Frantz Fanon, *The Wretched of the Earth*, trans. Richard Philcox (New York: Grove, 1963); Achille Mbembe, *Necropolitics* (Durham, NC: Duke University Press, 2011).
64. Édouard Glissant, *The Poetics of Relation*, trans. Betsy Wing (Ann Arbor: University of Michigan Press, 1990); Macarena Gómez-Barris, *The Extractive Zone: Social Ecologies and Decolonial Perspectives* (Durham, NC: Duke University Press, 2017).
65. Walsh and Mignolo, *On Decoloniality*, 7.
66. Michel Serres, *The Parasite*, trans. Lawrence R. Schehr (Minneapolis: University of Minnesota Press, 2007), 6.

67. Ibid., 7.
68. Ibid., 10.
69. Mbembe, *Necropolitics*, 77. Recent trends in Black animal studies are especially useful to this end; see Zakiyyah Iman Jackson and Joshua Bennett. Zakiyyah Iman Jackson, *Becoming Human: Matter and Meaning in an Antiblack World* (New York: NYU Press, 2020); Joshua Bennett, *Being Property Once Myself: Blackness and the End of Man* (Boston: Beacon, 2020).
70. On queer decoloniality see Gómez-Barris, *Extractive Zone;* Pedro Paulo Gomes Pereira, "Reflecting on Decolonial Queer," *GLQ A Journal of Lesbian and Gay Studies* 25, no. 3 (2019): 403–29.
71. Tiffany Lethabo King, *The Black Shoals: Offshore Formations of Black and Native Studies* (Durham, NC: Duke University Press, 2019), 16.
72. Walsh and Mignolo, *On Decoloniality*, 154–55.
73. Ibid., 138.
74. The tensions between queer studies and Fanon do not escape me. See, for example, Keguro Macharia's "Frantz Fanon's Homosexual Territories" for a careful consideration of queerness, Blackness, and coloniality. Keguro Macharia, *Frottage: Frictions of Intimacy across the Black Diaspora* (New York: NYU Press, 2019): 31–60.
75. Philip Steinberg, *The Social Construction of the Ocean* (Cambridge, UK: Cambridge University Press, 2001), 109.
76. James Thomson, "Rule Britannia," *The Longman Anthology of Poetry*, ed. Averill Curdy and Lynne McMahon (New York: Longman, 2006), line 6.
77. Carroll, *Empire of Air and Water*, 74.
78. Jonathan Groff, "You'll Be Back," *Hamilton: The Musical*, Atlantic Records, 2015.
79. Ariella Aïsha Azoulay, *Potential History: Unlearning Imperialism* (New York: Verso, 2019), 8.
80. I will not get on my high horse about these alleged crises and the consequent effect in which humanities scholars must further justify their existence, though the *Chronicle of Higher Education*, the *Atlantic, Inside Higher Ed*, and the *New Yorker* have repeatedly taken the bait. I do however take to task the scandalizing, polemical nature of these "crises" elsewhere. See Jeremy Chow, "Eighteenth Century + Environmental Humanities," in *Eighteenth-Century Environmental Humanities*, ed. Jeremy Chow (Lewisburg, PA: Bucknell University Press, 2023), 1–20.
81. Chen, MacLeod, and Neimanis, *Thinking with Water*, 11.
82. Blum, "Prospect of Oceanic Studies," 670.
83. Steve Mentz, "After Sustainability," *PMLA* 127, no. 3 (2012): 590.
84. Mentz, "After Sustainability," 590.
85. Diana Coole and Samantha Frost, *New Materialisms: Ontology, Agency, and Politics* (Durham, NC: Duke University Press, 2010), 7.
86. Neimanis, *Bodies of Water*, 1.
87. Ibid., 2.
88. Stacy Alaimo, "States of Suspension: Trans-corporeality at Sea," *Interdisciplinary Studies in Literature and the Environment* 19, no. 3 (2012): 477.

89. Margaret Cohen, "The Chronotopes of the Sea," in *The Novel: Forms and Themes*, vol. 2 of *The Novel*, ed. Franco Moretti (Princeton, NJ: Princeton University Press, 2007): 647–66.

90. William Beckford, *Vathek*, trans. Frank L. Marzials (London, UK: Chapman & Dodd, 1922), xviii.

91. Cudworth employs the concept to consider the networked predominance of the human in mediating environments for exclusive anthropocentric benefit, which of course benefits particular "humans" more than others. Erika Cudworth, *Developing Ecofeminist Theory: The Complexity of Difference* (New York: Palgrave Macmillan, 2005).

92. Bachelard, *Water and Dreams*, 6.

1. TAKEN BY STORM

1. Richard Hamblyn, introduction to *The Storm* (New York: Penguin, 2005), x.

2. Robert Markley, "'Casualties and Disasters': Defoe and the Interpretation of Climatic Instability," *Journal for Early Modern Cultural Studies* 8, no. 2 (2008): 103.

3. Jeremy Chow, "Taken by Storm: Aqueous Violence and Robinson Crusoe," *Robinson Crusoe after 300 Years*, eds. Glynis Ridley and Andreas Mueller (Lewisburg, PA: Bucknell University Press, 2021), 108–34.

4. Dagomar Degroot, "Climate Change and Society in the 15th to 18th Centuries, *Wiley Interdisciplinary Reviews (WIREs): Climate Change* 9, no. 5 (2018): 5; David Zhang, "Climate Change and War Frequency in Eastern China over the Last Millennium," *Human Ecology* 35 (2007): 403–14; Phillip Slavin, "Climate and Famines: A Historical Reassessment," *WIREs: Climate Change* 7, no. 3 (2016): 433–47.

5. Degroot, "Climate Change and Society," 5.

6. Alaimo, "States of Suspension," 478.

7. Astrida Neimanis, "Water, a Queer Archive of Feeling," in Hessler, *Tidalectics*, 196.

8. Defoe, *Robinson Crusoe*, 39. Emphasis added.

9. Ibid., 12. Emphasis added.

10. Juengel, "What Is Orientation," 270.

11. Priscilla Wald, Nancy Tomes, and Lisa Lynch, "Introduction: Contagion and Culture," *American Literary History* 14, no. 4 (2002): 617–24. See also Cynthia Davis, "Contagion as Metaphor," *American Literary History* 14, no. 4 (2002): 828–36.

12. For an eighteenth-century investigation of disease contagion and its association with reading, see Annika Mann, who pinpoints contagion in Defoe's *Journal of a Plague Year*. Annika Mann, *Reading Contagion: The Hazards of Reading in the Age of Print* (Charlottesville: University of Virginia Press, 2018).

13. Steve Mentz, "'We Split,'" in *The Routledge Companion to Marine and Maritime Worlds, 1400–1800*, ed. Claire Jowitt, Craig Lambert, and Steve Mentz (New York: Routledge, 2020): 580–97.

14. Fanon, *Wretched of the Earth*, 36.

15. Absolute violence for Fanon is a part of the totality of violence that constitutes both the colonizer and the colonized. It also responds to the "absolute evil of the native," which colonizers use to justify imperialism (50).

16. Jesse Molesworth, "Introduction: The Temporal Turn in Eighteenth-Century Studies," *The Eighteenth Century* 60, no. 2 (2018): 135; Elizabeth Freeman, *Time Binds: Queer Temporalities, Queer Histories* (Durham, NC: Duke University Press, 2010).

17. Elizabeth Freeman, *Beside You in Time: Sense Methods and Queer Sociabilities in the American Nineteenth Century* (Durham, NC: Duke University Press, 2019), 8.

18. Peter Miller, "Introduction: The Sea is the Land's Edge Also," *The Sea: Thalassography and Historiography*, ed. Peter Miller (Ann Arbor: University of Michigan Press, 2013).

19. Defoe, *Robinson Crusoe*, 9; 11.

20. Cohen, *Novel and the Sea*.

21. Defoe, *Robinson Crusoe*, 9.

22. P. N. Furbank and W. R. Owen, "Defoe and the 'Improvisatory' Sentence," *English Studies* 67, no. 2 (1987): 157–66; Cynthia Wall, introduction to *Journal of a Plague Year* (New York: Penguin, 2003), xvii–xxxiii.

23. Paul K. Alkon, *Defoe and Fictional Time* (Athens: University of Georgia Press, 1979), 39.

24. Sara Ahmed, *Queer Phenomenology: Orientations, Objects, Others* (Durham, NC: Duke University Press, 2006).

25. Ahmed, *Queer Phenomenology*, 157.

26. Defoe, *Robinson Crusoe*, 9.

27. Nixon, *Slow Violence*, 2.

28. David S. Jones and Stefan Helmreich, "The Shape of Epidemics," *Boston Review*, 26 June 2020, https://bostonreview.net/science-nature/david-s-jones-stefan-helmreich-shape-epidemics. For a critique of fluid metaphors and the extents of globalization, see Warwick Anderson, "Looking for Newton: From Hydraulic Societies to the Hydraulics of Globalization," in *Force, Movement, Intensity: The Newtonian Imagination in the Humanities and Social Sciences*, ed. Ghassan Hage and Emma Kowal (Melbourne: Melbourne University Publishing, 2011): 106–11.

29. Steinberg, *Social Construction of the Ocean*; Helen Rozwadowski, *Vast Expanses: A History of the Oceans* (London, UK: Reaktion Books, 2018).

30. Heather Love, *Feeling Backward: Loss and the Politics of Queer History* (Cambridge, MA: Harvard University Press, 2007).

31. Ibid., 9.

32. Defoe, *Robinson Crusoe*, 11

33. Ibid.

34. Ibid., 14–15.

35. Jane Bennett, *Vibrant Matter: A Political Ecology of Things* (Durham, NC: Duke University Press, 2009).

36. Defoe, *Robinson Crusoe*, 14.

37. Ibid., 15.

38. Neimanis, *Bodies of Water*, 2.

39. Bruno Latour, "Agency at the Time of the Anthropocene," *New Literary History* 45 (2014): 5.
40. Defoe, *Robinson Crusoe*, 9.
41. Ian Watt, *The Rise of the Novel* (Los Angeles: University of California Press, 2001), 63.
42. Caitlin Charman, "'Newfoundland's Robinson Crusoe?': Mobility, Masculinity, and the Failure of Ecological Management in Michael Crummey's *Sweetland*," in *Negotiating Waters: Seas, Oceans, and Passageways in the Colonial and Postcolonial Anglophone World*, ed. André Dodeman and Nancy Pedri (Wilmington, DE: Vernon Press, 2020): 41–58.
43. Peter Hulme, *Colonial Encounters: Europe and the Native Caribbean, 1492–1797* (New York: Routledge, 1986), 215.
44. Defoe, *Robinson Crusoe*, 35.
45. Ibid., 39.
46. *Oxford English Dictionary*, s.v., "swallow," https://oed.com/view/Entry/195387.
47. Defoe, *Robinson Crusoe*, 39.
48. David Marshall, "Autobiographical Acts in *Robinson Crusoe*," *ELH* 71, no. 4 (2004): 916.
49. Ibid., 904.
50. Marilyn Francus, *Monstrous Motherhood: Eighteenth-Century Culture and the Ideology of Domesticity* (Baltimore, MD: Johns Hopkins University Press, 2013), 25.
51. Steve Mentz and Matha Elena Rojas, "The Hungry Ocean," in *The Sea and Nineteenth-Century Anglophone Literary Culture*, ed. Steve Mentz and Martha Elena Rojas (New York: Routledge, 2016), 2.
52. Defoe, *Robinson Crusoe*, 39.
53. Ibid., 40.
54. Ibid., 40.
55. Ibid., 41.
56. Ibid., 147.
57. Ibid., 154.
58. Ibid., 193.
59. Ibid., 118.
60. Ingersoll, *Waves of Knowing*, 6.
61. Ibid.
62. Defoe, *Robinson Crusoe*, 140.
63. Ibid., 140.
64. Jeremy Chow, "Crusoe's Creature Comforts," *Digital Defoe* 10, no. 1 (2017): 1–17.
65. Defoe, *Robinson Crusoe*, 155.
66. Katherine Quinsey, "'Little Lives in Air': Animal Sentience and Sensibility in Pope," in *Animals and Humans: Sensibility and Representation, 1650–1820*, ed. Katherine Quinsey (Oxford, UK: Oxford University Press, 2017), 4.
67. Defoe, *Robinson Crusoe*, 156.

68. Ibid., 156.
69. Ibid., 161.
70. Ibid., 161.
71. Ibid., 242.
72. Ibid., 242.
73. Ibid., 242–23.
74. A. T. Mahan, *Influence of Sea Power Upon History, 1660–1783* (Boston, MA: Little, 1894), 1.
75. Steinberg, *Social Construction of the Ocean*; Alan James, "Commanding the World Itself: Sir Walter Raleigh, La Popelinière, and the Huguenot Influence on Early English Sea Power," in *The Maritime World of Early Modern Britain*, ed. Richard Blakemore and James Davey (Amsterdam, Netherlands: Amsterdam University Press, 2020), 67–80; Christopher Storrs, "Fleets and States in a Composite Catholic Monarchy: Spain c. 1500–1700," in *Ideologies of Western Naval Power c.1500–1815*, ed. J. D. Davis, Alan James, and Gijs Rommelse (New York: Routledge, 2019), 85–105.
76. Phillipa Hellawell, "Systematizing the Sea: Knowledge, Power and Maritime Sovereignty in Late Seventeenth-Century Science," *The Maritime World of Early Modern Britain*, ed. Richard Blakemore and James Davey (Amsterdam, Netherlands: Amsterdam University Press, 2020), 258.
77. Defoe, *Robinson Crusoe*, 243.

INTERMEZZO: TEACHING WRECKAGE IN RISING WATERS

1. Amy Ohlheiser, "Why a Smallmouth Bass with a Rare, Cancerous Tumor Has Pa. Officials Worried," *Washington Post*, 5 May 2015, https://www.washingtonpost.com/news/speaking-of-science/wp/2015/05/05/a-susquehanna-river-angler-caught-a-smallmouth-bass-with-a-rare-cancerous-tumor/.
2. Adrienne Rich, "Diving into the Wreck," *Diving into the Wreck: Poems 1971–1972* (New York: W. W. Norton, 1973), lines 22–35.
3. Union of Concerned Scientists, *Climate Change in Pennsylvania* (Cambridge, MA: UCS Publications, 2008), 11, https://www.nrc.gov/docs/ML0913/ML091390883.pdf.
4. Ibid.
5. Rich, "Diving into the Wreck," lines 35–44.
6. Ibid., lines 53–61.
7. Ibid., lines 71–94.

2. SEE MONKEYS

1. For those unconvinced of the framing of Gulliver as colonist, I refer you to the character Elizabeth Costello's discussion of Gulliver in J. M. Coetzee's *The Lives of Animals*, wherein she prefigures Gulliver as the potential impetus for colonial

intervention in Lilliput and Houyhnhnmland. J. M. Coetzee, *The Lives of Animals* (Princeton, NJ: Princeton University Press, 1999).

2. Rebekah Mitsein's work serves as an important reminder that this attention is in fact ongoing and important to eighteenth-century examinations of the novel and its racial and colonial imaginaries. Rebekah Mitsein, "Upon a Voyage and No Voyage: Mapping Africa's Waterways in Defoe's *Captain Singleton*," *Digital Defoe* 11, no. 1 (2019): 1–19.

3. Robert James Merrett, "Natural History and the Eighteenth-Century Novel," *Eighteenth-Century Studies* 25, no. 2 (Winter 1991–1992), 145.

4. For indispensable readings of the historical mythos of apes and simians in Western culture, see H. W. Hanson, *Apes and Ape Lore in the Middle Ages and Renaissance* (London, UK: Studies of the Warburg Institute, 1952); and William McDermott, *The Ape in Antiquity* (Baltimore, MD: Johns Hopkins University Press, 1938).

5. LaFleur, *Natural History of Sexuality*, 7.

6. Jeffrey Jerome Cohen, *Prismatic Ecologies: Ecotheory Beyond Green* (Minneapolis: University of Minnesota Press, 2013), xxvii.

7. John Gabriel Stedman, *Narrative of a Five Years Expedition against the Revolted Negroes of Surinam*, ed. Richard Price and Sally Price (Baltimore, MD: Johns Hopkins University Press, 1988), 560. All citations are to this edition.

8. Bachelard, *Water and Dreams*, 6.

9. Thomas Bewick and Ralph Beilby, *A General History of Quadrupeds* (Newcastle Upon Tyne, 1790), 390.

10. Edward Long, *The History of Jamaica* (London, 1774), 36. Gary Taylor has located the early sixteenth-century origination of these racially and ethnically motivated myths: Spanish writer, Antonio de Torquemada who suggests that a Portuguese woman was the survivor of simian sexual violence. Gary Taylor, "'White Like Us': Early Modern King Kongs and Calibans," in *Racism and Modernity*, ed. Iris Wigger and Sabine Ritter (Munster, Germany: Lit-Verlag, 2012): 31–54.

11. Stedman, *Narrative*, 141.

12. Juno Salazar Parreñas, *Decolonizing Extinction: The Work of Care in Orangutan Rehabilitation* (Durham, NC: Duke University Press, 2018), 6.

13. Richard Nash, *Wild Enlightenment: The Borders of Human Identity in the Eighteenth Century* (Charlottesville: University of Virginia Press, 2002), 18.

14. Nash writes that the term "primate" only came into common parlance in 1758 and was only then "distinguished from another set of fellow primates designated as 'nonhumans.'" Nash, *Wild Enlightenment*, 15.

15. Edward Tyson, *Orang-outang, sive homo sylvestris* (London, 1699), 2.

16. Primatologists today still employ a four-pronged ordering system (great apes, lesser apes, monkeys, and prosimians), but have abandoned some of Linnaeus's initial categorizations. For example, Linnaeus presumptively grouped bats (*Vespertilio*) into this order.

17. Laura Brown, *Homeless Dogs and Melancholy Apes: Humans and Other Animals in the Modern Literary Imagination* (Ithaca, NY: Cornell University Press, 2010).

18. Londa Schiebinger, *Nature's Body: Gender in the Making of Modern Science* (New Brunswick, NJ: Rutgers University Press, 1993), 78.

19. Robert Crib, Helen Gilbert, and Helen Tiffin, *Wild Man from Borneo: A Cultural History of the Orangutan*, (Honolulu: University of Hawai'i Press, 2014), 59.

20. Voltaire, *Candide; or Optimism*, ed. Nicholas Cronk (New York: Norton, 2016), 21.

21. Ibid., 22.

22. Stedman, *Narrative*, 502. See my essay, "Simian Sexuality" for an exploration of how the eighteenth-century simian configures interspecies intimacies in literature and art. Jeremy Chow, "Simian Sexuality: Interspecies Intimacies in the Long Eighteenth Century," *Studies in the Novel* 53, no. 3 (2021): 209–31.

23. The Prices read this as "Stedman's lack of racialism" because he doesn't pair the lascivious monkey with a Black, female mate, as his literary peers might have. I disagree. Such a statement feels more like a recuperative projection on their part than an accurate representation of Stedman's discussion of race. Stedman, *Narrative*, liii–liv; xciv.

24. Lugones, "Toward a Decolonial Feminism"; Susan Stryker, "My Words to Victor Frankenstein above the Village of Chamounix: Performing Transgender Rage," *GLQ: A Journal of Lesbian and Gay Studies* 1, no. 3 (1994): 244–56.

25. Elizabeth R. Napier suggests that the same characteristics that were "iconographically associated with Hottentots [*sic*], apes, savage Indians, Christian representations of sin, and the Irish poor" are endowed in Swift's depiction of the Yahoos. Elizabeth R. Napier, *Falling into Matter: Problems of Embodiment in English Fiction from Defoe to Shelley* (Toronto, Ontario: University of Toronto Press, 2012), 50.

26. Schiebinger, *Nature's Body*, 78.

27. Ibid., 99.

28. Ingrid Tague, *Animal Companions: Pets and Social Change in Eighteenth-Century Britain* (University Park: Pennsylvania State University Press, 2015), 50–51.

29. George Edwards, *Gleanings of Natural History* (London, 1758), 11, https://www.biodiversitylibrary.org/bibliography/153666.

30. Schiebinger, *Nature's Body*, 95.

31. Paulo Medeiros puts it best: "The way in which Buffon portrays his baboon leaves the reader inclined to believe that the animal was intent in crossing the species barrier out of immoral and inordinate desire towards women, something which of course is more revelatory of the observer than the observed." Paulo Medeiros, "Simian Narratives at the Intersection of Science and Literature," *Modern Language Studies* 23, no. 2 (1993): 64.

32. Erin Spampinato, "Theorizing the New Rape Studies at MLA 2019," https://www.erinspampinato.com/theorizing-the-new-rape-studies.

33. Frances Ferguson, "Rape and the Rise of the Novel," *Representations* 20 (1987); Melissa Sanchez, *Erotic Subjects: The Sexuality of Politics in Early Modern English Literature* (New York: Oxford University Press, 2011). See also my extended discussion of this theme in the Gothic, to which I will turn in the next chapter, especially as sexual violence is configured alongside figurations of the succubus.

Jeremy Chow, "Succubus Matters," *ABO: Interactive Journal for Women in the Arts* 12, no.1 (2022): 1–30.

34. Declan Kavanagh and Ula Klein, "Swift's Queerness," *Journal for Eighteenth-Century Studies* 43, no. 4 (2020): 276.

35. Michael F. Suarez, "Swift's Satire and Parody," *The Cambridge Companion to Jonathan Swift*, ed. Christopher Fox (Cambridge, UK: Cambridge University Press, 2003), 112.

36. Ibid., 116.

37. In both *Ends of Empire* and *Fables of Modernity,* Brown aligns the female Yahoo with historical depictions of Khoikhoi ("Hottentots" [sic]), which is an "intersection of alterities" (*Ends of Empire,* 241). Brown's reading coincides with Haraway's articulation of "simian orientalism," in *Primate Visions,* in which the simian prefigures issues of race and gender. I am concerned, though, about the implications of such a reading, if only because they may further racialist thinking in the present. Laura Brown, *Fables of Modernity: Literature and Culture in the English Eighteenth Century* (Ithaca, NY: Cornell University Press, 2001); Donna Haraway, *Primate Visions: Gender, Race, and Nature in the World of Modern Science* (New York: Routledge, 1989).

38. Haraway, *Staying with the Trouble,* 4. Emphasis added.

39. John Bullitt, *Jonathan Swift and the Anatomy of Satire* (Cambridge, MA: Harvard University Press, 1954), 24–30.

40. Laura Baudot, "What Not to Avoid in Swift's 'In the Lady's Dressing Room,'" *Studies in English Literature 1500–1900* 49, no. 3 (2009): 640.

41. Jonathan Swift, *Gulliver's Travels,* ed. Robert DeMaria Jr. (New York: Penguin, 2003), 113. All citations are to this edition. James Wood historicizes this incident and suggests that Swift included it to goad the 19th Earl of Kildare, upon whose relative the mythic anecdote is allegedly based. James O. Wood, "Gulliver and the Monkey of Tralee," *Studies in English Literature 1500–1900* 9, no. 3 (1969): 415–26.

42. Ann Cline Kelly reads this relationship of pet and pet-keeper as one that reverberates throughout the visit to Houyhnhnmland and as a growing cultural practice akin to our own contemporary obsession with pet-keeping, which is similarly located by Brown's *Homeless Dogs and Melancholy Apes.* Ann Cline Kelly, "Gulliver as Pet and Pet Keeper: Talking Animals in Book 4," *ELH* 72, no. 2 (2007): 323–49.

43. Swift, *Gulliver's Travels,* 94.

44. Mark Blackwell suggests that it-narratives "emphasize richly characterized, psychologically complex novels as the terminus ad quem of eighteenth-century narrative evolution," which "complicates the history of prose fiction." Mark Blackwell, ed., *The Secret Life of Things: Animals, Objects, and It-Narratives in Eighteenth-Century England,* (Lewisburg, PA: Bucknell University Press, 2007), 14.

45. Swift, *Gulliver's Travels,* 113.

46. Harriet Ritvo, "Species," *Critical Terms for Animal Studies,* ed. Lori Gruen (Chicago, IL: University of Chicago Press, 2018), 383–94.

47. In the process of being gifted, Gulliver is often placed in dangerous erotic situations (in bed with his mistress, beholder to the nakedness of the maids of honor, as a plaything on a maid of honor's breast, etc.), which he summarily rejects because

they conjure up no other feelings than "Horror and Disgust" (111). His misogyny is palpable.

48. Swift, *Gulliver's Travels*, 95.
49. Ibid., 113.
50. Jean-Jacques Rousseau, "Discours sur l'origine et les fondements de l'inégalité parmi les homess," *Oeuvres Complètes*, ed. Bernard Gagnebin and Marcel Raymond (Paris: Gallimard, 1959), 211.
51. Kelly, "Gulliver as Pet," 328.
52. Swift, *Gulliver's Travels*, 113.
53. Though space does not permit here, Gulliver exhibits mastrophobia throughout the narrative, this moment with the monkey being only one of his adverse reactions to breasts and breastfeeding.
54. Schiebinger addresses naturalist observations of the female ape's deft abilities to nurse, which connected her to chastity and a sense of modesty. Schiebinger, *Nature's Body*, 105.
55. Margaret Anne Doody suggests that in this scene and for Swift, "the baboon or ape is replacing an absent parent and seems to act chiefly the mother's part, in compensation for loss of attendants or paternal parent . . . The monkey as adoptive parent acts the kind of rescuing role that was congenial to Swift's own notion of his relation to other people—more especially people of the opposite sex." Margaret Anne Doody, "Swift and Women," *The Cambridge Companion to Jonathan Swift*, ed. Christopher Fox (Cambridge, UK: Cambridge University Press, 2003), 101.
56. Swift, *Gulliver's Travels*, 114.
57. The abjection of emesis is not lost on me, and I explore this moment within a Kristevan framework elsewhere. Jeremy Chow, "Prime Mates: The Simian, Maternity, and Abjection in Brobdingnag," *Journal for Eighteenth-Century Studies* 43, no. 3 (2020): 315–25.
58. Swift, *Gulliver's Travels*, 114.
59. Ibid., 115.
60. Ibid., 207.
61. Cohen, "Chronotopes of the Sea," 655. Cohen, borrowing from Bakhtin, employs "chronotope" to think through how space, time, and movement are bound in different genres of water—that is, how water of different colors (for Cohen, blue, white, brown, etc.) extend the narrative of the novel and what types of time and space accompany that movement.
62. Charles Darwin, *On the Origin of Species* (New York: Appleton & Co, 1861), 425.
63. Swift, *Gulliver's Travels*, 213.
64. Ibid., 220.
65. Laura Brown, *Fables of Modernity*, 240.
66. Swift, *Gulliver's Travels*, 245.
67. *Oxford English Dictionary*, s.v., "fulsome," http://www.oed.com/view/Entry/75389.
68. Donna Haraway, *When Species Meet* (Minneapolis: University of Minnesota Press, 2008), 36.

69. Michael Franklin, "Lemuel Self-Translated; Or, Being an Ass in Houyhnhnmland," *Modern Language Review* 100, no. 1 (2005): 2.

70. Swift, *Gulliver's Travels*, 242–43. There is no possible way for Swift to have observed this, but, very strangely, Jane Goodall, whose life work has been spent with chimpanzees in Tanzania, describes chimpanzee mating rituals nearly identically. Jane Goodall, *Through a Window* (Boston: Houghton Mifflin, 1990).

71. Goodall describes an eerily similar mating ritual—one that occurs on a riverbank—between chimpanzees Evered and Winkle. See chapter 9, "Sex," in Goodall, *Through a Window* (Boston, MA: Houghton Mifflin, 1990).

72. Darwin, *On the Origin of Species*, 425. Two important rivers in the eighteenth century corroborate Darwin's thoughts about the entangled flitting of species: at home, the Thames—famously exalted and anthropomorphized by Pope's "Windsor Forest" (1713)—and, abroad, the Oroonoque. The latter is the contact zone for the turbulent violence in Aphra Behn's *Oroonoko* (1688), a geographic locator for the first-edition title page of *Robinson Crusoe* (1719), and like Behn's sojourn before him, the ingress to Suriname for Stedman.

73. Swift, *Gulliver's Travels*, 245.

74. Kelly suggests that Gulliver realizes this but then spends the rest of his time in Houyhnhnmland attempting to prove otherwise: "Gulliver establishes his difference and his dominion by skinning Yahoos to make himself clothing and a canoe." Kelly, "Gulliver as Pet," 331.

75. Franklin, "Lemuel Self-Translated," 2.

76. Stedman, *Narrative*, 141.

77. Emily Senior, "'Perfectly Whole': Skin and Text in John Gabriel Stedman's *Narrative of a Five Years Expedition against the Revolted Negroes of Surinam*," *Eighteenth-Century Studies* 44, no. 1 (2010): 52.

78. Haraway, *When Species Meet*, 36.

79. Stedman, *Narrative*, xvii.

80. See, for example, Lori Gruen, *Entangled Empathy: An Alternative Ethic for Our Relationship with Animals* (New York: Lantern Publishing, 2014); Suzanne Keen, *Empathy and the Novel* (Oxford, UK: Oxford University Press, 2007); Paul Bloom, *Against Empathy: A Case for Rational Compassion* (New York: Ecco, 2018); and Fritz Breithaupt, *The Dark Sides of Empathy*, trans. Andrew B. B. Hamilton (Ithaca, NY: Cornell University Press, 2019).

81. Stedman, *Narrative*, xvii.

82. Elaine Scarry's *The Body in Pain* offers important consideration into the world-destroying abilities of pain and, specifically, torture. While I take up this work more carefully in the next chapter, I find that pain and torture constitute worlds built as much as destroyed, keeping in mind that not all world construction is positive or Eutopic.

83. Debbie Lee, *Slavery and the Romantic Imagination* (Philadelphia: University of Pennsylvania Press, 2002), 73.

84. Stedman does not illustrate the monkey murder, but Blake draws similar monkeys frolicking above the river, perhaps awaiting their doom. Hanging is an

important characterization of Blake's engravings. Like the monkeys perched over the river, Blake similarly illustrates the hanging of an anaconda, and, even more viscerally, the hanging of "disobedient" enslaved peoples and failed revolutionaries.

85. Stedman, *Narrative*, 141.
86. Ibid.
87. A nearly identical encounter is accounted for under the title "Odd Story of a Monkey at the Brazils; From Pernety's Journal." To avoid a "chattering" monkey from recruiting his simian kin to pillage fruits and corn, a "freed negro" borrows a loaded rifle and shoots the monkey dead. It takes three bullets to successfully kill the monkey who—and here is where the odd story reaches its pinnacle—is missing an eyeball and has fashioned a prosthesis from "a gum which was unknown to us, of rotten wood and some very fine moss, the whole mixed up together." *The Annual Register, or a View of the History, Politics, and Literature, for the Year 1771* (London, 1772), 102.
88. *Oxford English Dictionary*, s.v. "mortal," http://www.oed.com/view/Entry/122438.
89. Gordon Williams, *A Dictionary of Sexual Language and Imagery in Shakespearean and Stuart Literature* (London, UK: Athlone, 1994), 902.
90. Steven Bruhm, *Reflecting Narcissus: A Queer Aesthetic* (Minneapolis: University of Minnesota Press, 2001), 13.
91. Swift, *Gulliver's Travels*, 225.
92. Jean Baudrillard, *Seduction*, trans. Brian Singer (London, UK: Macmillan, 1990), 69.
93. Stedman, *Narrative*, 141.
94. Heather Keenleyside, *Animals and Other People: Literary Forms and Living Beings in the Long Eighteenth Century* (Philadelphia: University of Pennsylvania Press, 2016).
95. Ibid., 134.

INTERMEZZO: READING SWIFT ON THE PLANET OF THE APES

1. I assign the 1968 film version, though my students much prefer the 2011 reboot trilogy, so we watch that too.
2. Pierre Boulle, *Planet of the Apes*, trans. Xan Fielding (New York: Ballantine Books, 1963), 24–25.
3. Franklin Schaffner, dir., *Planet of the Apes* (Burbank: 20th Century Fox, 1968).
4. Boulle, *Planet of the Apes*, 28–29.
5. Swift, *Gulliver's Travels*, 245.
6. Boulle, *Planet of the Apes*, 29.
7. Swift, *Gulliver's Travels*, 245.
8. Boulle, *Planet of the Apes*, 29.
9. My use of *china doll* is deliberate. At novel's end, and this is corroborated in the original film, an unearthed china doll dressed in human clothing and that can also

speak becomes the "missing link" by which to understand the evolutionary chain of ape supremacy in Soror.

10. Boulle, *Planet of the Apes*, 33–34.
11. Ibid., 34.
12. Ibid., 221.
13. Their nakedness pushes the limits of the "G" rating determined by the Motion Picture Association (MPA), which again seems to suggest that only female nudity (of which there is none in the film, although countless moments in Boulle's novel—Nova, for example, is meant to never wear clothing) incurs the wagging finger of the MPA.
14. Schaffner, *Planet of the Apes*.
15. Ibid.
16. Ibid.

3. AQUEOUS PUNISHMENT

1. Kenneth Graham, introduction to *Vathek with The Episodes of Vathek*, ed. Kenneth W. Graham (Orchard Park, NY: Broadview, 2001), 17.
2. William Beckford Sr. was Mayor of London twice and held considerable clout given the success of his Jamaican plantations. He allegedly bequeathed his son £1 million cash, which did not include the value of the plantations. In today's currency, the cash inheritance is equivalent to more than £180 million. Alexander Boyd, *England's Wealthiest Son* (New York: Centaur Press, 1962). My article "Go to Hell: William Beckford's Skewed Heaven and Hell" elaborates on the Powderham Scandal while also considering, more carefully, the first episode that was meant to accompany *Vathek*'s publication: "The History of Alasi and Firouz." Jeremy Chow, "Go to Hell: William Beckford's Skewed Heaven and Hell," in *TransGothic in Literature and Culture*, ed. Jolene Zigarovich (New York: Routledge, 2017), 53–76.
3. Graham, introduction, 20. George Haggerty has also written extensively on Beckford's same-sex and pedophilic predilections. George Haggerty, "Beckford's Pæderasty," in *Illicit Sex: Identity Politics in Early Modern Culture*, ed. Pat Gill and Thomas DiPiero (Athens: University of Georgia Press, 1997); George Haggerty, "Literature and Homosexuality in the Late Eighteenth Century: Walpole, Beckford, and Lewis," in *Homosexual Themes in Literary Studies*, ed. Wayne Dynes and Stephen Donaldson (New York: Garland, 1992).
4. William Beckford, *Vathek with The Episodes of Vathek*, ed. Kenneth W. Graham (Orchard Park, NY: Broadview, 2001), 45. All citations are to this edition.
5. Ibid., 45.
6. Ibid., 47.
7. Max Fincher, *Queering Gothic in the Romantic Age* (New York: Palgrave Macmillan, 2007), 87.
8. Kristina Gupta, "Compulsory Sexuality: Evaluating an Emergent Concept," *Signs* 41, no. 5 (2015): 131–54; Eunjung Kim, "Asexuality in Disability Narratives," *Sexualities* 14, no. 4 (2011): 479–93.

9. Ela Przybylo, *Asexual Erotics: Intimate Readings of Compulsory Sexuality* (Columbus: Ohio State University Press, 2019).

10. Max Fincher reads Ambrosio as a queer figure because of the historical reception of deviant clerics: "The anti-clericalism of *The Monk* encourages us to read Ambrosio as queer by the suspicion that surrounds the nature of his sexuality. *The Monk* dramatizes the possibility of a close spiritual relationship reflecting 'lower passions' in its opening chapter with Ambrosio as a pedagogue and confidant of Rosario's emotions. This is an endorsement of the link between same-sex desire and Catholicism in the metonym of the closer or the cloister, or the priest-hole." Fincher, *Queering Gothic*, 100. See also George Haggerty's chapter "The Horrors of Catholicism: Religion and Sexuality in Gothic Fiction" for an overview of Catholicism's connection with plural sexualities. George Haggerty, *Queer Gothic* (Urbana: University of Illinois Press, 2006).

11. Michel Foucault, *Discipline and Punish* (New York: Vintage, 1995), 33.

12. By James Simpson's assessment, such a rationale was deployed from at least the late Medieval period through George W. Bush—it undoubtedly continues today. James Simpson, "No Brainer: The Early Modern Tragedy of Torture," *Religion & Literature* 43, no. 3 (2011): 1–23.

13. Steven Bruhm, *Gothic Bodies: The Politics of Pain in Romantic Fiction* (Philadelphia: University of Pennsylvania Press, 1994), 93.

14. Foucault, *Discipline and Punish*, 46.

15. Cesare Beccaria, *On Crimes and Punishments and Other Writings*, ed. Aaron Thomas (Toronto, ON: University of Toronto Press, 2008), 26.

16. In his jeremiad, Beccaria writes, "the death penalty is not a *right*, but the war of a nation against a citizen, which has deemed the destruction of his being to be necessary or useful." Beccaria, *On Crimes and Punishments*, 52. This sentiment would largely be responsible for the disavowal of capital punishment in Tuscany in 1786 and influential to the American founding fathers.

17. Beccaria, *On Crimes and Punishments*, 32.

18. Julie A. Carlson, "Torture on Stage," in *The Encyclopedia of Romantic Literature*, ed. Frederick Burwick, Nancy Moore, and Diane Long Hoeveler (New York: Wiley-Blackwell, 2012), 1404.

19. Gerard Cohen-Vrignaud, *Radical Orientalism: Rights, Reform, and Romanticism* (Cambridge, UK: Cambridge University Press, 2015), 24–25.

20. Ibid., 61.

21. Simpson, "No Brainer," 2–3.

22. Rictor Norton, *Mother Clap's Molly House: The Gay Subculture in England 1700–1830* (London, UK: GMP Publishers, 1992), 67.

23. Foucault, *Discipline and Punish*, 39.

24. Stephen F. Eisenman, *The Abu Ghraib Effect* (London, UK: Reaktion Books, 2007). Laura Henderson evaluates the recurrence of waterboarding imagery in the media and the ways in which this generates judicial independence for the state. She defines waterboarding as the deliberate attempt to make the victim feel like they are drowning. This is enacted by: "(1) placing a cloth or plastic wrap over the face of the victim and pouring water over the cloth or plastic wrap; (2) pouring water directly

into the mouth and nose of the victim; (3) placing a stick between the victim's teeth and pouring water into his or her mouth, often until the victim's stomach becomes distended, then forcing the water back out of the victim's mouth, and (4) dunking and holding the victim's head under water." Laura Henderson, *Tortured Reality: How Media Framing of Waterboarding Affects Judicial Independence* (The Hague: Eleven International Publishing, 2012), 86.

25. Stephen F. Eisenman, "Waterboarding: Political and Sacred Torture," in *Speaking about Torture*, ed. Julie A Carlson and Elisabeth Weber (New York: Fordham University Press, 2012), 135.

26. Beccaria and other anti–capital punishment philosophers note that for a confession to be deemed legitimate, it must be offered twice: once under the ensigns of torture and again, identically, outside of such an environment.

27. Srinivas Aravamudan, *Enlightenment Orientalism: Resisting the Rise of the Novel* (Chicago, IL: University of Chicago Press, 2011). After *Vathek*, this obsession is perhaps best immortalized in Fonthill Abbey—a structure in line with Walpole's Strawberry Hill—which was built on a deserted convent site that emulated orientalized architecture. Beckford lost his inherited fortune in building Fonthill, and, as Stephen Clarke details, "the splendors of Fonthill Abbey were, of course, short-lived, but its spectacular effects were not inextricably linked to the structural shortcomings that destroyed them, and could have been achieved and maintained with durable materials and adequate foundations." In short, shoddy materials and labor were to blame for its ephemerality. Stephen Clarke, "The Ruin of Fonthill: The Reputation and Influence of Beckford's Abbey," *William Beckford and the New Millennium*, ed. Kenneth W Graham (New York: AMS Press, 2004), 181.

28. John Beynon, "'Mr. Beckford's Favourite Propensity': The Erotics of Boyhood and the Emergence of a Sexual Self in Late-Eighteenth-Century England," in Graham, *William Beckford and the New Millennium*, 15.

29. Graham, introduction, 33.
30. Ibid., 36.
31. Aravamudan, *Enlightenment Orientalism*, 5.
32. Cohen-Vrignaud, *Radical Orientalism*, 41.
33. Beckford, *Vathek*, 62.
34. Ibid.
35. Ibid., 65.
36. Jeffrey Masten, *Queer Philologies: Sex, Language, and Affect in Shakespeare's Time* (Philadelphia: University of Pennsylvania Press, 2016); Thomas A. King, *The Gendering of Men, 1600–1750: The English Phallus* (Madison: University of Wisconsin Press, 2004).

37. Anja Müller, *Framing Childhood in Eighteenth-Century English Periodicals and Prints, 1689–1789* (Farnham: Ashgate, 2009), 35.

38. Beckford, *Vathek*, 66.
39. Ibid.
40. Ibid.
41. Andrew Elfenbein reads the maw as an anus that epitomizes the erotic excesses of Beckford's orientalist vision. The boys would then seem to participate in

a variety of anal pleasures. Andrew Elfenbein, *Romantic Genius: The Prehistory of a Homosexual Role* (New York: Columbia University Press, 1999).

42. Beckford, *Vathek*, 67.
43. Ibid.
44. In Beckford's first Episode, "The History of the Two Princes and Friends, Alasi and Firouz," an erotic bath becomes the prerequisite before entering "The Temple of Fire," and a cascading waterfall and its pool become the site for Firouz to attempt to murder his sexual competition.
45. Beckford, *Vathek*, 68.
46. Ibid.
47. Ibid., 69.
48. Ibid.
49. Ibid.
50. Ibid.
51. Ibid., 94.
52. Ibid.
53. Graham, introduction, 61.
54. Richard Wassersug and Thomas Johnson, "Modern Day Eunuchs: Motivations for and Consequences of Contemporary Castration," *Perspectives in Biology and Medicine* 50, no. 4 (2007): 544–56.
55. Jeremy Chow, "Showing the Eunuch: Disability, Sexuality, and Dryden's All for Love," in Greenfield, *Castration, Impotence, and Emasculation*, 105–24.
56. In analyzing the eunuchs in Montesquieu's *The Persian Letters* (1721), Aravamudan states, "The eunuchs realize that because of their castration, they possess a quotidian physical intimacy with the women that no real men could ever be allowed to have. Yet their position derives from being able to represent one half of the absent master. The master is aware that his sexual authority has to be implemented by these managerial surrogates, whose enjoyment of the women takes on a vicarious intimacy." Aravamudan, *Enlightenment Orientalism*, 84.
57. Beckford, *Vathek*, 94.
58. Ibid., 94–95.
59. Ibid., 95.
60. Katharine Binhammer, "The 'Single Propensity' of Sensibility's Extremities: Female Same-Sex Desire and the Eroticization of Pain in Late-Eighteenth-Century British Culture," *GLQ: A Journal of Lesbian and Gay Studies* 9, no. 4 (2003): 490.
61. Beckford, *Vathek*, 95.
62. Ibid.
63. Ibid.
64. Ibid.
65. Ovid, *Metamorphoses*, Book IV, ed. Charles Martin (New York: Norton, 2009), 450.
66. Ibid., 668–69. After repenting, Tereus is also transformed into a bird: "Tereus swift in his grief and desire for revenge, is himself changed to a bird, with a feathered

crest on its head. An immoderate, elongated, beak juts out, like a long spear. The name of the bird is the hoopoe, and it looks as though it is armed" (671–74).

67. Beckford, *Vathek*, 96.

68. Ibid.

69. Ibid.

70. Samuel Taylor Coleridge, "Review of Matthew G. Lewis, *The Monk*," *Critical Review* 2, no. 19 (1797): 195.

71. Ibid., 198.

72. Matthew Gregory Lewis, *The Monk*, ed. Nick Groom (Oxford, UK: Oxford University Press, 2016), 219. All citations are to this edition.

73. Lewis, *Monk*, 219.

74. A. W. Barnes, *Post-Closet Masculinities in Early Modern England* (Lewisburg, PA: Bucknell University Press, 2009); Haggerty, *Queer Gothic*; Fincher, *Queering Gothic*; Diane Long Hoeveler, *The Gothic Ideology: Religious Hysteria and Anti-Catholicism in British Popular Fiction, 1780–1880* (Cardiff, UK: University of Wales Press, 2014); Goran Stanivukovic, "Between Men in Early Modern England," in *Queer Masculinities, 1550–1800*, eds. Katherine O'Donnell and Michael O'Rourke (New York: Palgrave, 2006).

75. Hoeveler, *Gothic Ideology*, 13.

76. Lewis, *Monk*, 223.

77. Ibid.

78. Ibid., 225.

79. Ibid.

80. Ibid.

81. Ibid.

82. Scarry, *Body in Pain*, 6.

83. In *Queer Gothic*, Haggerty locates sexual violence within heteronormativity as essential to the "patriarchal law of the father upon which Catholicism insists" (64).

84. Lewis, *Monk*, 326.

85. Scarry, *Body in Pain*, 55.

86. Michael Richardson, *Gestures of Testimony: Torture, Trauma, and Affect in Literature* (New York: Bloomsbury, 2016), 4.

87. Lewis, *Monk*, 332.

88. Ibid., 333. Mr. Zero will make a similar appeal to Batman and Robin in the final intermezzo, "Freeze!"

89. Ibid., 334.

90. Lewis, *Monk*, 335–36.

91. Jeremy Chow, "Snaking into the Gothic: Serpentine Sensuousness in Lewis and Coleridge," *Humanities* 10, no. 52 (2021): 1–20. Daniel Robinson likewise attends to how *The Monk*'s interpolated poems influence Coleridge's prosody, although it is "Alonzo the Brave and Fair Imogine" on which Robinson's argument hinges. Daniel Robinson, "Gothic Prosody: Monkish Perversity and the Poetics of Weird Form," in *Transnational Gothic: Literary and Social Exchanges in the Long Nineteenth Century*, ed. Monika Elbert and Bridget Marshall (New York: Routledge, 2013): 155–71.

92. Lewis, *Monk*, 336.
93. Ibid., 338.
94. Ibid., 339.
95. Ibid.
96. Ibid.
97. Ibid.
98. Ibid., 338.
99. Foucault, *Discipline and Punish*, 82.
100. Ibid., 34.

INTERMEZZO: OFF WITH HER HEAD

1. Mel Chen offers a provocative queer ecological examination of *Ponyo* and its various hybridities. See "The Spill and the Sea" in Chen, *Animacies*, 225–37. In late 2022, Disney found itself in the throes of a political quagmire when it was announced that the live action remake of *The Little Mermaid* (2023) would feature African American actress and chanteuse, Halle Bailey.
2. Hans Christian Andersen, "The Little Mermaid," trans. H. B. Paull (Lexington, KY: Hythloday Press, 2014), 67–68. All citations are to this edition.
3. Ibid., 70–71.
4. Ibid., 73.
5. Ibid., 44.
6. Ibid., 49.
7. Ibid., 49–50.
8. Ibid., 47.
9. Ibid., 46.
10. Ibid.
11. Ibid., 74.

4. SACRIF-ICE

1. For a more detailed publication history, see Charles Robinson, *The Frankenstein Notebooks* (New York: Garland, 1996).
2. Jessica Richard, "'A Paradise of My Own Creation': *Frankenstein* and the Improbable Romance of Polar Exploration," *Nineteenth-Century Contexts* 25, no. 4 (2003): 295–314; Siobhan Carroll, "Crusades against Frost: *Frankenstein*, Polar Ice, and Climate Change in 1818," *European Romantic Review* 24, no. 2 (2013): 211–30; Jen Hill, *White Horizon: The Arctic in the Nineteenth-Century British Imaginary* (Albany: State University of New York Press, 2008); Adriana Craciun, *Writing Arctic Disaster: Authorship and Exploration* (Cambridge, UK: Cambridge University Press, 2016); Hester Blum, *The News at the Ends of the Earth* (Durham, NC: Duke University Press, 2019).
3. I have opted for "creature" rather than "daemon" or "monster," all of which are used interchangeably by Dr. Frankenstein to refer to his creation. Each of these words has pejorative etymologies, but the use of "creature" throughout the novel

demonstrates that it is often used to bridge human communities, especially with the repeated use of "fellow-creatures."

4. René Girard, *Violence and the Sacred*, trans. Patrick Gregory (Baltimore, MD: Johns Hopkins University Press, 1977), 14.

5. René Girard, *Sacrifice*, trans. Matthew Pattillo and David Dawson (East Lansing: Michigan State University Press, 2011), x.

6. Mary Shelley, *Frankenstein*, ed. Johanna M. Smith, 2nd ed. (New York: Bedford/St. Martin's, 2000), 188. Emphasis added. All quotations are from this edition.

7. Ibid., 115.

8. Francis Spufford, *I May Be Some Time: Ice and the English Imagination* (Boston, MA: Faber and Faber, 1996), 60.

9. Ibid., 61.

10. Duckert, *For all Waters*, 107–8.

11. Jack Halberstam, *The Queer Art of Failure*, (Minneapolis: University of Minnesota Press, 2011), 3.

12. Ibid., 186.

13. Shelley, *Frankenstein*, 188.

14. Lugones, "Toward a Decolonial Feminism," 742.

15. M. Jacqui Alexander, *Pedagogies of Crossing: Meditations on Feminism, Sexual Politics, Memory, and the Sacred* (Durham, NC: Duke University Press, 2005).

16. Ahmed uses "to path with" to pinpoint an antiracist and feminist coalitional politics of support and desired community. Sara Ahmed, *Living a Feminist Life* (Durham, NC: Duke University Press, 2017), 17.

17. See. for example, Eve Kosofsky Sedgwick, *Between Men: English Literature and Male Homosocial Desire* (New York: Columbia University Press, 1985); James Holt McGraven, "'Insurmountable Barriers to Our Union': Homosocial Male Bonding, Homosexual Panic, and Death on Ice in *Frankenstein*," *European Romantic Review* 11, no. 1 (2000): 46–67; Christopher Nagle, *Sexuality and the Culture of Sensibility in the British Romantic Era* (New York: Palgrave Macmillan, 2007); Mair Rigby, "'Do You Share My Madness?': *Frankenstein*'s Queer Gothic," *Queering the Gothic*, eds. William Hughes and Andrew Smith (Manchester, UK: Manchester University Press, 2009), 36–54; Harlan Weaver, "Monster Trans: Diffracting Affect, Reading Rage," in *TransGothic in Literature and Culture*, ed. Jolene Zigarovich (New York: Routledge, 2018): 119–38.

18. Stryker, "My Words to Victor Frankenstein," 248. I am also mindful of the fact that the term "transsexual" is no longer preferred though perhaps a historical artifact still invested in trans liberation.

19. Ibid., 249.

20. Ibid., 251.

21. These motifs also find a home in the queer cult-classic film, *The Rocky Horror Picture Show* (1975), where Frank-N-Furter, the "sweet transvestite" mad scientist, animates Rocky with iridescent waters in a rainbow aquarium. Their mutual death at film's end also takes place in a pool.

22. Stryker, "My Words to Victor Frankenstein," 252.

23. See, for example, Benjamin Bragg's *A Voyage to the North Pole*, published just months prior to *Frankenstein*. Benjamin Bragg, *A Voyage to the North Pole* (London, UK: G. Walker, 1817).

24. Shelley, *Frankenstein*, 28.

25. Burke observes, "Having considered terror as producing an unnatural tension and certain violent emotions of the nerves; it easily follows, from what we have just said, that whatever is fitted to produce such a tension must be productive of a passion similar to terror, and consequently must be a source of the sublime, though it should have no idea of danger connected with it." Edmund Burke, *A Philosophical Enquiry into the Origin of Our Ideas of the Sublime and Beautiful* (Oxford, UK: Oxford University Press, 2008), 121.

26. Shelley, *Frankenstein*, 32–3.

27. Ibid., 28.

28. Defoe, *Robinson Crusoe*, 5.

29. Shelley, *Frankenstein*, 33.

30. Ibid., 29.

31. Ibid., 31.

32. Ibid.

33. George Haggerty, *Queer Friendship: Male Intimacy in the English Literary Tradition* (Cambridge, UK: Cambridge University Press, 2018), 109.

34. Ibid.

35. Craciun, *Writing Arctic Disaster*, 31.

36. Ibid.

37. Girard, *Sacrifice*, ix.

38. In *Sacrifice* Girard details, "Sacrifice is not then merely an instrument of peace; it sets in motion a process of repetition that engenders, no doubt very gradually, what we call our social and political institutions. The more sacrifices are repeated, the more they tend to become what we call funerals, marriages, rites of passage, initiations of sorts, and likewise royalty—political power is always suffused with the sacred—all the institutions, in short, of our culture" (32).

39. Shelley, *Frankenstein*, 35. This description is similarly mirrored in Frankenstein's description of his creation, who is "horrid," "dun," "shriveled," and a "demoniacal corpse" (60–61).

40. Ibid., 34.

41. Ibid., 37.

42. Ibid.

43. Ibid., 36.

44. Ibid., 38. Italics added.

45. Ibid.

46. Jennifer Airey, *Religion around Mary Shelley* (University Park: Pennsylvania State University Press, 2019), 67.

47. Girard, *Violence*, 4.

48. Shelley, *Frankenstein*, 38.

49. Ibid.

50. Miranda Joseph, *Against the Romance of Community* (Minneapolis: University of Minnesota Press, 2002), vii. *Oxford English Dictionary*, s.v. "common," https://oed.com/view/Entry/37217.

51. Eric G. Wilson, *The Spiritual History of Ice: Romanticism, Science, and the Imagination* (New York: Palgrave Macmillan, 2003), 94.

52. For an overview of Shelley's and the Enlightenment's relationship with mountaineering as a form of active science, see Jane Nardin, "A Meeting on the Mer de Glace: Frankenstein and the History of Alpine Mountaineering," *Women's Writing* 6, no. 3 (1999): 441–49. Eric G. Wilson also takes up the glacier's significance for the Shelleys. Eric G. Wilson, "Shelley and the Poetics of Glaciers," *The Wordsworth Circle* 36, no. 2 (2005): 53–56.

53. Duckert, *For all Waters*, 112.

54. Shelley, *Frankenstein*, 131.

55. Ibid., 92–93.

56. Ibid., 95.

57. Ibid., 93.

58. Ibid.

59. Girard, *Sacrifice*, 27.

60. Shelley, *Frankenstein*, 129. The line "we shall be monsters" has perhaps resonated the most loudly with queer-identified audiences given the recuperation of monstrosity as that which characterizes non-heteronormativity. Stryker exemplifies this.

61. Adrienne Rich, "Compulsory Heterosexuality and Lesbian Experience," in *Powers of Desire: The Politics of Sexuality*, ed. Ann Stinow, Christine Stansell, and Sharon Thompson (New York: Monthly Review Press, 1983): 177–205.

62. Shelley, *Frankenstein*, 129–30.

63. Ibid., 145.

64. Ibid., 147. Italics original.

65. Girard, *Sacrifice*, 73.

66. Girard acknowledges in *Sacrifice* the illogical paradox of the scapegoat: "It [the scapegoat] is not an ordinary concept. Instead, it is something paradoxical, a principle of illusion whose efficacy requires complete ignorance of it. To have a scapegoat is not to know that one has one. As soon as the scapegoat is revealed and named as such, it loses its power" (72).

67. Jacqueline Labbe, "A Monstrous Fiction: Frankenstein and the Wifely Ideal," *Women's Writing* 6, no. 3 (1990): 353.

68. Ibid.

69. Shelley, *Frankenstein*, 147.

70. Girard, *Sacrifice*, 22.

71. Shelley, *Frankenstein*, 183.

72. Ibid., 186.

73. Ibid., 188.

74. Ibid., 189.

75. Ibid., 188.

76. Jacques Derrida, "'Eating Well,' or the Calculation of the Subject," in *Who Comes after the Subject?*, ed. Eduardo Cadava, Peter Connor, and Jean-Luc Nancy (New York: Routledge, 1991), 114.

77. In *I May Be Some Time*, Spufford suggests that the polar world (or at least how it was imagined in the nineteenth century) also participates in sealing this loneliness, as well as in a knot that might bind Walton and Shelley as author (62–63).

78. Stryker, "My Words to Victor Frankenstein," 251. Italics original.

INTERMEZZO: FREEZE!

1. Bill Finger and Sheldon Moldoff, "The Ice Crimes of Mr. Zero," *Batman*, vol. 1, no. 121 (Burbank, CA: DC Comics, 1959), 9.

2. Ibid.

3. In "Just Keep Swimming?: Queer Pooling and Hydropoetics," Maite Urcaregui and I locate other forms of hydronarratology in film and graphic narrative. Jeremy Chow and Maite Urcaregui, "Just Keep Swimming?: Queer Pooling and Hydropoetics," *Angelaki: A Journal of the Theoretical Humanities* 27, no. 1 (2023, forthcoming).

4. Finger et al., "The Ice Crimes," 9.

5. Ibid., 13.

6. In Frederic Wertham's censorious *Seduction of the Innocent: The Influence of Comic Books on Today's Youth* (New York: Rinehart, 1954), which indubitably launched the Comics Code Authority, Batman is psychoanalyzed as possessing homosexual traits. Wertham noted this, not as praise but to set in motion a congressionally supported censorship of the comic arts. Andy Medhurst and Will Brooker have also addressed why Batman appeals to gay men—an analysis largely predicated on modes of desirable masculinity. And gay rumors surfaced more palpably in Schumacher's *Batman and Robin* precisely because Schumacher is openly gay. Fan fiction sites, such as Wattpad, FanFiction.net, and ArchiveOfOurOwn.org, are replete with user-requested pieces that exploit these queer resonances with a variety of fetishistic flavors. Andy Medhurst, "Batman, Deviance, and Camp," in *The Many Lives of the Batman: Critical Approaches to a Superhero and His Media*, ed. Roberta Pearson (New York: Routledge, 1991): 149–63; Will Brooker, *Batman Unmasked: Analyzing a Cultural Icon* (New York: Continuum, 2013).

7. Finger et al., "The Ice Crimes," 14.

8. Ibid.

9. Paul Dini and Mark Buckingham, *Batman: Mr. Freeze* (Burbank, CA: DC Comics, 1997), 102.

10. Ibid., 103.

11. Ibid.

12. Ibid., 102.

13. Ibid., 108.

14. Shelley, *Frankenstein*, 188.

15. Joel Schumacher, dir., *Batman and Robin* (Los Angeles, CA: Warner Bros., 1997).

16. Ibid.

17. Dini and Buckingham, *Batman: Mr. Freeze*, 114.
18. Ibid., 122.
19. Ibid., 108.
20. Schumacher, *Batman and Robin*.
21. Ibid.
22. Nicole Starosielski, "The Materiality of Media Heat," *International Journal of Communication* 8 (2014): 2506.
23. Schumacher, *Batman and Robin*.

CONCLUSION

1. Ian Simpson, "Manatees Taken Off U.S. Endangered List, Conservationists Cry Foul," *Reuters*, 30 March 2017, https://www.reuters.com/article/us-usa-manatee/manatees-taken-off-u-s-endangered-list-conservationists-cry-foul-idUSKBN17200Z.
2. "Chapter 68C-22: The Florida Manatee Sanctuary Act," *Florida Department of State* (Tallahassee: State of Florida, 2010), 5.
3. Patrik Svensson, *The Book of Eels: Our Enduring Fascination with the Most Mysterious Creature in the Natural World*, trans. Agnes Broomé (New York: Ecco, 2019), 216.
4. Georg Wilhelm Steller, "Steller's Journal of the Sea Voyage from Kamchatka to America and Return on the Second Expedition, 1741–1742," *Bering's Voyages*, trans. Leonhard Stejneger (New York: American Geographical Society, 1925), 232.
5. Ibid., 233.
6. Svensson, *Book of Eels*, 216.
7. Gruen, *Entangled Empathy*, 35.
8. Theodor Pietsch, ed., *Fishes, Crayfishes, and Crabs: Louis Renard's Natural History of the Rarest Curiosities of the Seas of the Indies* (Baltimore. MD: Johns Hopkins University Press, 1995).
9. Louis Renard, *Poisson, Ecrevisses et Crabs* (Amsterdam: Reinier & Josué Ottens, 1754), plate LVII, https://www.biodiversitylibrary.org/page/50095135#page/7/mode/1up. The translation, and any errors within, are my own.
10. *Oxford English Dictionary*, s.v. "monster," https://www-oed-com/view/Entry/121738.
11. Donna Haraway, "The Promises of Monsters: A Regenerative Politics for Inappropriate/d Others," *The Monster Theory Reader*, ed. Jeffrey Andrew Weinstock (Minneapolis: University of Minnesota Press, 2020), 459–521.
12. Jeremy Chow and Brandi Bushman, "Hydro-Eroticism," *English Language Notes* 57, no. 1 (2019): 96–115.
13. Jane Austen and Ben Winters, *Sense and Sensibility and Sea Monsters* (Philadelphia, PA: Quirk Books, 2009), 8.
14. Carolyn Merchant, *The Death of Nature: Women, Ecology, and the Scientific Revolution* (New York: Harper, 1980); Gaard, "Where Is Feminism?"; Val Plumwood, *Feminism and the Mastery of Nature* (New York: Routledge, 1993).
15. Austen and Winters, *Sense*, 155.
16. Ibid., 8.

17. Ibid., 44.
18. Carson, *Sea around Us*, 3; Austen and Winters, *Sense*, 11.
19. Austen and Winters, *Sense*, 37.
20. Ibid., 39.
21. Ibid., 37.
22. Ibid.
23. Ibid., 191.
24. Ibid., 55.
25. Ibid., 37.
26. Haraway, *Staying with the Trouble*, 31.
27. Zylinska rejects the all-is-lost narratives that populate theories of apocalypse to imagine a feminist revision in which visualities are not foreclosed but instead reopened. Joanna Zylinska, *The End of Man: A Feminist Counterapocalypse* (Minneapolis: University of Minnesota Press, 2018).
28. Austen and Winters, *Sense*, 339.
29. Ibid., 158.
30. Guillermo del Toro, dir., *The Shape of Water* (Century City, CA: Fox Searchlight Pictures, 2017).
31. Representation matters; it matters less when Hollywood typecasts Black and gay characters as stereotypes of domineering, henpecking Black womanhood and perpetually lonely, unsuccessful, and detached queerness, respectively.
32. Del Toro, *The Shape of Water*.
33. Neimanis, *Bodies of Water*, 3.
34. Dana Luciano and Mel Chen, "Has the Queer Ever Been Human?," *GLQ: A Journal of Lesbian and Gay Studies* 21, nos. 2–3 (2015): 182–207.
35. XenoCat Artifacts, a vendor on kitsch-proprietor Etsy, mass-reproduced two versions of a silicone sex toy, "The Asset," that are meant to replicate the fish lover's genitalia. According to *The Wrap*, the dildos sold out even before the telecast of the Academy Awards had finished. Tony Maglio, "'Shape of Water' Dildo Sales Surge over Oscars Weekend," *The Wrap*, March 6, 2018, https://www.thewrap.com/the-shape-of-water-dildo-amphibian-man-asset-movie/.
36. Puig de la Bellacasa's ethical quandary simultaneously reclaims and disrupts notions of care in acknowledgment that such a praxis "requires engaging with situated recognitions of care's importance that operate displacements in established hierarchies of value and understanding how divergent modes of valuing care coexist and co-make each other in non-innocent ways." María Puig de la Bellacasa, *Matters of Care: Speculative Ethics in More Than Human Worlds* (Minneapolis: University of Minnesota Press, 2017), 12.
37. Del Toro, *The Shape of Water*.
38. Ibid.
39. Ibid.

Bibliography

Ahmed, Sara. *Living a Feminist Life.* Durham, NC: Duke University Press, 2017.
———. *Queer Phenomenology: Orientations, Objects, Others.* Durham, NC: Duke University Press, 2006.
Airey, Jennifer. *Religion around Mary Shelley.* University Park: Pennsylvania State University Press, 2019.
Alaimo, Stacy. "States of Suspension: Trans-corporeality at Sea." *Interdisciplinary Studies in Literature and the Environment* 19, no. 3 (2012): 476–93.
———. *Exposed: Environmental Politics and Pleasures in Posthuman Times.* Minneapolis: University of Minnesota Press, 2016.
Alexander, M. Jacqui. *Pedagogies of Crossing: Meditations on Feminism, Sexual Politics, Memory, and the Sacred.* Durham, NC: Duke University Press, 2005.
Alkon, Paul. *Defoe and Fictional Time.* Athens: University of Georgia Press, 1979.
Amin, Kadji. *Disturbing Attachments: Genet, Modern Pederasty, and Queer History.* Durham, NC: Duke University Press, 2017.
Andersen, Hans Christian. "The Little Mermaid." Translated by H. B. Paull. Lexington, KY: Hythloday Press, 2014.
Anderson, Warwick. "Looking for Newton: From Hydraulic Societies to the Hydraulics of Globalization." In *Force, Movement, Intensity: The Newtonian Imagination in the Humanities and Social Sciences,* edited by Ghassan Hage and Emma Kowal, 106–11. Melbourne: Melbourne University Publishing, 2011.
The Annual Register, or a View of the History, Politics, and Literature, for the Year 1771. London, 1772.
Aravamudan, Srinivas. *Enlightenment Orientalism: Resisting the Rise of the Novel.* Chicago, IL: University of Chicago Press, 2011.
Arens, Katherine. "When Performing Gender Is Nonconforming: The Need for Archives in the Practice of Theory." In *Castration, Impotence, and Emasculation in the Long Eighteenth Century,* edited by Anne Greenfield, 201–36. New York: Routledge, 2020.
Austen, Jane, and Ben Winters. *Sense and Sensibility and Sea Monsters.* Philadelphia, PA: Quirk Books, 2009.
Azoulay, Ariella Aïsha. *Potential History: Unlearning Imperialism.* New York: Verso, 2019.

Bachelard, Gaston. *Water and Dreams: An Essay on the Imagination of Matter.* Translated by Edith R. Farrell. Dallas, TX: Dallas Institute, 1983.
Baker, Samuel. *Written on Water: British Romanticism and the Maritime Empire of Culture.* Charlottesville: University of Virginia Press, 2010.
Banister, Julia. *Masculinity, Militarism and Eighteenth-Century Culture, 1689–1815.* Cambridge, UK: Cambridge University Press, 2020.
Barnes, A. W. *Post-Closet Masculinities in Early Modern England.* Lewisburg, PA: Bucknell University Press, 2009.
Baudot, Laura. "What Not to Avoid in Swift's 'In the Lady's Dressing Room.'" *Studies in English Literature 1500–1900* 49, no. 3 (2009): 637–66.
Baudrillard, Jean. *Seduction.* Translated by Brian Singer. London: Macmillan, 1990.
Beccaria, Cesare. *On Crimes and Punishments and Other Writings.* Edited by Aaron Thomas. Toronto, ON: University of Toronto Press, 2008.
Beckford, William. *Vathek.* Translated by Frank L. Marzials. London: Chapman & Dodd, 1922.
———. *Vathek with the Episodes.* Edited by Kenneth Graham. Petersborough, ON: Broadview, 2001.
Bennett, Jane. *Vibrant Matter: A Political Ecology of Things.* Durham, NC: Duke University Press, 2009.
Bewick, Thomas. *A General History of Quadrupeds.* Newcastle Upon Tyne, 1790.
Beynon, John. "'Mr Beckford's Favourite Propensity': The Erotics of Boyhood and the Emergence of a Sexual Self in Late-Eighteenth-Century England." In *William Beckford and the New Millennium,* edited by Kenneth W Graham, 7–36. New York: AMS Press, 2004.
Binhammer, Katharine. "The 'Single Propensity' of Sensibility's Extremities: Female Same-Sex Desire and the Eroticization of Pain in Late-Eighteenth-Century British Culture." *GLQ: A Journal of Lesbian and Gay Studies* 9, no. 4 (2003): 471–98.
Blackwell, Mark, ed. *The Secret Life of Things: Animals, Objects, and It-Narratives in Eighteenth-Century England.* Lewisburg, PA: Bucknell University Press, 2007.
Bloom, Paul. *Against Empathy: A Case for Rational Compassion.* New York: Ecco, 2018.
Blum, Hester. *The News at the Ends of the Earth.* Durham, NC: Duke University Press, 2019.
———. "The Prospect of Oceanic Studies." *PMLA* 125, no. 3 (2010): 670–77.
Boe, Ana De Freitas, and Abby Coykendall, eds. *Heteronormativity in the Eighteenth-Century Literature and Culture.* New York: Routledge, 2015.
Boelhower, William. "Reframing Oceanic Violence: The Pax Britannica and Wild Weather during the Nineteenth Century." In *A Cultural History of the Sea in the Age of Empire,* vol. 5 of *A Cultural History of the Sea,* edited by Margaret Cohen, 105–30. New York: Bloomsbury, 2021.
Bolding, Alex, and Rossella Alba. "Viewpoint—IWRM and I: A Reflexive Travelogue of the Flows and Practices Research Team." In *Flows and Practices: The Politics of Integrated Water Resources Management in Eastern and Southern Africa,* edited by Lyla Mehta, Bill Derman, and Emmanuel Manzungu, 345–67. Zimbabwe: Weaver Press, 2017.

Boulle, Pierre. *Planet of the Apes*. Translated by Xan Fielding. New York: Ballantine Books, 1963.
Boyd, Alexander. *England's Wealthiest Son*. New York: Centaur Press, 1962.
Bragg, Benjamin. *A Voyage to the North Pole*. London: G. Walker, 1817.
Brayton, Dan. *Shakespeare's Ocean: An Ecocritical Exploration*. Charlottesville: University of Virginia Press, 2012.
Breithaupt, Fritz. *The Dark Sides of Empathy*. Translated by Andrew B. B. Hamilton. Ithaca, NY: Cornell University Press, 2019.
Brooker, Will. *Batman Unmasked: Analyzing a Cultural Icon*. New York: Continuum, 2013.
Broomhall, Susan, and Jacqueline Van Gent, eds. *Governing Masculinities in the Early Modern Period: Regulating Selves and Others*. Farnham, UK: Ashgate, 2011.
Brown, Laura. *Fables of Modernity: Literature and Culture in the English Eighteenth Century*. Ithaca, NY: Cornell University Press, 2001.
———. *Homeless Dogs and Melancholy Apes: Humans and Other Animals in the Modern Literary Imagination*. Ithaca, NY: Cornell University Press, 2010.
Bruhm, Steven. *Gothic Bodies: The Politics of Pain in Romantic Fiction*. Philadelphia: University of Pennsylvania Press, 1994.
———. *Reflecting Narcissus: A Queer Aesthetic*. Minneapolis: University of Minnesota Press, 2001.
Bullitt, John. *Jonathan Swift and the Anatomy of Satire*. Cambridge, MA: Harvard University Press, 1954.
Burke, Edmund. *A Philosophical Enquiry into the Origin of Our Ideas of the Sublime and Beautiful*. Oxford, UK: Oxford University Press, 2008.
Carlson, Julie A. "Torture on Stage." In *The Encyclopedia of Romantic Literature*, edited by Frederick Burwick, Nancy Moore, and Diane Long Hoeveler. New York: Wiley-Blackwell, 2012. 1403–11.
Carroll, Siobhan. "Crusades against Frost: *Frankenstein*, Polar Ice, and Climate Change in 1818." *European Romantic Review* 24, no. 2 (2013): 211–30.
———. *An Empire of Air and Water: Uncolonizable Space in the British Imagination, 1750–1850*. Philadelphia: University of Pennsylvania Press, 2015.
Carson, Rachel. *The Sea Around Us*. Oxford, UK: Oxford University Press, 2018.
Charman, Caitlin. "'Newfoundland's Robinson Crusoe?': Mobility, Masculinity, and the Failure of Ecological Management in Michael Crummey's Sweetland." In *Negotiating Waters: Seas, Oceans, and Passageways in the Colonial and Postcolonial Anglophone World*, edited by André Dodeman and Nancy Pedri, 41–58. Wilmington, DE: Vernon Press, 2020.
Cheek, Pamela. *Sexual Antipodes: Enlightenment Globalization and the Placing of Sex*. Stanford, CA: Stanford University Press, 2003.
Chen, Cecilia, Janine MacLeod, and Astrida Neimanis, eds. *Thinking with Water*. Montreal, QU: McGill-Queen's University Press, 2013.
Chen, Mel. *Animacies: Biopolitics, Racial Mattering, and Queer Affect*. Durham, NC: Duke University Press, 2012.
Chow, Jeremy. "Crusoe's Creature Comforts." *Digital Defoe* 10, no. 1 (2017): 1–17.

———. "Eighteenth Century + Environmental Humanities." In *Eighteenth-Century Environmental Humanities*, edited by Jeremy Chow, 1–20. Lewisburg, PA: Bucknell University Press, 2023.

———. "Go to Hell: William Beckford's Skewed Heaven and Hell." In *TransGothic in Literature and Culture*, edited by Jolene Zigarovich, 53–76. New York: Routledge, 2017.

———. "Prime Mates: The Simian, Maternity, and Abjection in Brobdingnag." *Journal for Eighteenth-Century Studies* 43, no. 3 (2020): 315–325.

———. "Showing the Eunuch: Disability, Sexuality, and Dryden's All for Love." In *Castration, Impotence, and Emasculation in the Long Eighteenth Century*, edited by Anne Greenfield, 105–24. New York: Routledge, 2020.

———. "Simian Sexuality: Interspecies Intimacies in the Long Eighteenth Century." *Studies in the Novel* 53, no. 3 (2021): 209–31.

———. "Snaking into the Gothic: Serpentine Sensuousness in Lewis and Coleridge." *Humanities* 10, no. 52 (2021): 1–20.

———. "Succubus Matters." *ABO: Interactive Journal for Women in the Arts* 12, no. 1 (2022): 1–30.

———. "Taken by Storm: Aqueous Violence and Robinson Crusoe." In *Robinson Crusoe after 300 Years*, edited by Glynis Ridley and Andreas Mueller, 108–34. Lewisburg, PA: Bucknell University Press, 2021.

Chow, Jeremy, and Brandi Bushman. "Hydro-Eroticism." *English Language Notes* 57, no. 1 (2019): 96–115.

Chow, Jeremy, and Maite Urcaregui. "Just Keep Swimming?: Queer Pooling and Hydropoetics." *Angelaki: A Journal of the Theoretical Humanities* 27, no. 1 (forthcoming).

Clarke, Stephen. "The Ruin of Fonthill: The Reputation and Influence of Beckford's Abbey." In *William Beckford and the New Millennium*, edited by Kenneth W Graham, 181–212. New York: AMS Press, 2004.

Coetzee, J. M. *The Lives of Animals*. Princeton, NJ: Princeton University Press, 1999.

Cohen-Vrignaud, Gerard. *Radical Orientalism: Rights, Reform, and Romanticism*. Cambridge, UK: Cambridge University Press, 2015.

Cohen, Jeffrey Jerome, ed. *Prismatic Ecologies: Ecotheory beyond Green*. Minneapolis: University of Minnesota Press, 2013.

Cohen, Margaret. "The Chronotopes of the Sea." In *The Novel: Forms and Themes*, vol. 2 of *The Novel*, edited by Franco Morretti, 647–66. Princeton, NJ: Princeton University Press, 2007.

———. *The Novel and the Sea*. Princeton, NJ: Princeton University Press, 2010.

Cohen, Margaret, and Killian Quigley. "Submarine Aesthetics." In *The Aesthetics of the Undersea*, edited by Margaret Cohen and Killian Quigley, 1–13. New York: Routledge, 2019.

Coleridge, Samuel Taylor. "Review of Matthew G. Lewis, *The Monk*." *Critical Review*, 19, no. 2 (1797): 194–99.

———. *The Rime of the Ancient Mariner*. In *The Poetical Works of S. T. Coleridge*. Edited by Henry Nelson Coleridge, 101–17. London: Pickering, 1834.

Coole, Diana and Samantha Frost. *New Materialisms: Ontology, Agency, and Politics.* Durham, NC: Duke University Press, 2010.
Craciun, Adriana. *Writing Arctic Disaster: Authorship and Exploration.* Cambridge, UK: Cambridge University Press, 2016.
Crib, Robert, Helen Gilbert, and Helen Tiffin. *Wild Man from Borneo: A Cultural History of the Orangutan.* Honolulu: University of Hawai'i Press, 2014.
Cudworth, Erika. *Developing Ecofeminist Theory: The Complexity of Difference.* New York: Palgrave Macmillan, 2005.
Darwin, Charles. *On the Origin of Species.* New York: Appleton & Co, 1861.
Davis, Cynthia. "Contagion as Metaphor." *American Literary History* 14, no. 4 (2002): 828–36.
Defoe, Daniel. *Robinson Crusoe.* Edited by Thomas Keymer. Oxford, UK: Oxford University Press, 2007.
Degroot, Dagomar. "Climate Change and Society in the 15th to 18th Centuries." *Wiley Interdisciplinary Reviews: Climate Change* 9, no. 5 (2018): 1–20.
DeLoughrey, Elizabeth. "Submarine Futures of the Anthropocene." *Comparative Literature* 69, no. 1 (2017): 32–44.
del Toro, Guillermo, dir. *The Shape of Water.* Century City, CA: Fox Searchlight Pictures, 2017.
Derrida, Jacques. "'Eating Well,' or the Calculation of the Subject." In *Who Comes after the Subject?*, edited by Eduardo Cadava, Peter Connor, and Jean-Luc Nancy, 96–119. New York: Routledge, 1991.
Diaper, William. *Nereides: Or Sea-Eclogues.* London, 1712.
Dini, Paul, and Mark Buckingham. *Batman: Mr. Freeze.* Burbank, CA: DC Comics, 1997.
Doody, Margaret Anne. "Swift and Women." In *The Cambridge Companion to Jonathan Swift*, edited by Christopher Fox, 87–111. Cambridge, UK: Cambridge University Press, 2003.
Duckert, Lowell. *For all Waters: Finding Ourselves in Early Modern Wetscapes.* Minneapolis: University of Minnesota Press, 2017.
Edwards, George. *Gleanings of Natural History.* London, 1758.
Eisenman, Stephen F. "Waterboarding: Political and Sacred Torture." In *Speaking about Torture*, edited by Julie A Carlson and Elisabeth Weber, 129–39. New York: Fordham University Press, 2012.
———. *The Abu Ghraib Effect.* London: Reaktion Books, 2007.
Elfenbein, Andrew. *Romantic Genius: The Prehistory of a Homosexual Role.* New York: Columbia University Press, 1999.
Falconer, William. *The Shipwreck.* London: W. Miller, 1762.
Fanon, Frantz. *The Wretched of the Earth.* Translated by Richard Philcox. New York: Grove Press, 2004.
Ferguson, Frances. "Rape and the Rise of the Novel." *Representations*, no. 20 (1987): 88–112.
Ferguson, Roderick. *One-Dimensional Queer.* New York: Polity, 2018.
Fincher, Max. *Queering Gothic in the Romantic Age.* New York: Palgrave Macmillan, 2007.

Finger, Bill, and Sheldon Moldoff. "The Ice Crimes of Mr. Zero." *Batman*. Vol. 1, no. 121. Burbank, CA: DC Comics, 1959.

Foucault, Michel. *Discipline and Punish*. New York: Vintage, 1995.

———. *The History of Sexuality*. Vol. 1. Translated by Robert Hurley. New York: Vintage, 1978.

———. *Security, Territory, Population: Lectures at the Collège de France 1977–1978*. New York: Picador, 2004.

Francus, Marilyn. *Monstrous Motherhood: Eighteenth-Century Culture and the Ideology of Domesticity*. Baltimore, MD: Johns Hopkins University Press, 2013.

Franklin, Michael. "Lemuel Self-Translated; Or, Being an Ass in Houyhnhnmland." *Modern Language Review* 100, no. 1 (2005): 1–19.

Freeman, Elizabeth. *Beside You in Time: Sense Methods and Queer Sociabilities in the American Nineteenth Century*. Durham, NC: Duke University Press, 2019.

———. *Time Binds: Queer Temporalities, Queer Histories*. Durham, NC: Duke University Press, 2010.

Furbank, P. N., and W. R. Owen. "Defoe and the 'Improvisatory' Sentence." *English Studies* 67, no. 2 (1987): 157–66.

Gaard, Greta. "Toward a Queer Ecofeminism." *Hypatia* 12, no. 1 (1997): 114–37.

———. "Where Is Feminism in the Environmental Humanities?" In *Environmental Humanities: Voices from the Anthropocene*, edited by Serpil Oppermann and Serenella Iovino, 81–98. New York: Rowman & Littlefield, 2017.

Garrard, Greg. "How Queer Is Green?" *Configurations* 18, nos. 1–2 (2010): 73–96.

Ghaziani, Amin, and Matt Brim. "Queer Methods: Four Provocations for an Emerging Field." In *Imagining Queer Methods*, edited by Amin Ghaziani and Matt Brim, 1–27. New York: New York University Press, 2019.

Gillis, John. "The Blue Humanities." *HUMANITIES, The Magazine for the National Endowment for the Humanities* 34, no. 4 (2013). https://www.neh.gov/humanities/2013/mayjune/feature/the-blue-humanities.

Girard, René. *Sacrifice*. Translated by Matthew Pattillo and David Dawson. East Lansing: Michigan State University Press, 2011.

———. *Violence and the Sacred*. Translated by Patrick Gregory. Baltimore, MD: Johns Hopkins University Press, 1977.

Glissant, Édouard. *The Poetics of Relation*. Translated by Betsy Wing. Ann Arbor: University of Michigan Press, 1990.

Gomes Pereira, Pedro Paulo. "Reflecting on Decolonial Queer." *GLQ: A Journal of Lesbian and Gay Studies* 25, no. 3 (2019): 403–29.

Gómez-Barris, Macarena. *The Extractive Zone: Social Ecologies and Decolonial Perspectives*. Durham, NC: Duke University Press, 2017.

Goodall, Jane. *Through a Window*. Boston, MA: Houghton Mifflin, 1990.

Graham, Kenneth. Introduction to *Vathek with The Episodes of Vathek*, edited by Kenneth W. Graham, 17–41. Petersborough, ON: Broadview, 2001.

Groff, Jonathan. "You'll Be Back" (song). *Hamilton: The Musical*. New York: Atlantic Records, 2015.

Gruen, Lori. *Entangled Empathy: An Alternative Ethic for Our Relationship with Animals*. New York: Lantern Publishing, 2014.
Gupta, Kristina. "Compulsory Sexuality: Evaluating an Emergent Concept." *Signs* 41, no. 5 (2015): 131–54.
Haggerty, George. "Beckford's Pæderasty." In *Illicit Sex: Identity Politics in Early Modern Culture*, edited by Pat Gill and Thomas DiPiero, 123–42. Athens: University of Georgia Press, 1997.
———. "Literature and Homosexuality in the Late Eighteenth Century: Walpole, Beckford, and Lewis." In *Homosexual Themes in Literary Studies*, edited by Wayne Dynes and Stephen Donaldson, 167–79. New York: Garland, 1992.
Haggerty, George. *Queer Friendship: Male Intimacy in the English Literary Tradition*. Cambridge, UK: Cambridge University Press, 2018.
———. *Queer Gothic*. Urbana: University of Illinois Press, 2006.
Halberstam, Jack. *The Queer Art of Failure*. Minneapolis: University of Minnesota Press, 2011.
Hamblyn, Richard. Introduction to *The Storm*, edited by Richard Hamblyn, x–xl. New York: Penguin, 2005.
Hanson, H. W. *Apes and Ape Lore in the Middle Ages and Renaissance*. London: Studies of the Warburg Institute, 1952.
Haraway, Donna. *Primate Visions: Gender, Race, and Nature in the World of Modern Science*. New York: Routledge, 1989.
———. "The Promises of Monsters: A Regenerative Politics for Inappropriate/d Others." In *The Monster Theory Reader*, edited by Jeffrey Andrew Weinstock, 459–521. Minneapolis: University of Minnesota Press, 2020.
———. *Staying with the Trouble: Making Kin in the Chthulucene*. Durham, NC: Duke University Press, 2016.
———. *When Species Meet*. Minneapolis: University of Minnesota Press, 2008.
Harris, Mary Beth. "Masculinity, Performance Anxiety, and Literary Impotence in Charlotte Charke's *The History of Henry Dumont*." In *Castration, Impotence, and Emasculation in the Long Eighteenth Century*, edited by Anne Greenfield, 168–84. New York: Routledge, 2020:
Hellawell, Phillipa. "Systematizing the Sea: Knowledge, Power and Maritime Sovereignty in Late Seventeenth-Century Science." In *The Maritime World of Early Modern Britain*, edited by Richard Blakemore and James Davey, 257–82. Amsterdam, Netherlands: Amsterdam University Press, 2020.
Helmreich, Stefan. *Alien Ocean: Anthropological Voyages in Microbial Seas*. Berkeley: University of California Press, 2009.
Henderson, Laura. *Tortured Reality: How Media Framing of Waterboarding Affects Judicial Independence*. The Hague: Eleven International Publishing, 2012.
Hessler, Stefanie, ed. *Tidalectics: Imagining an Oceanic Worldview through Art and Science*. Cambridge, MA: MIT Press, 2018.
Hill, Jen. *White Horizon: The Arctic in the Nineteenth-Century British Imaginary*. Albany: State University of New York Press, 2008.

Hitchcock, Tim, and Michèle Cohen, eds. *English Masculinities 1660–1800*. New York: Longman, 1999.
Hoeveler, Diane Long. *The Gothic Ideology: Religious Hysteria and Anti-Catholicism in British Popular Fiction, 1780–1880*. Cardiff, UK: University of Wales Press, 2014.
Hulme, Peter. *Colonial Encounters: Europe and the Native Caribbean, 1492–1797*. New York: Routledge, 1986.
Ingersoll, Karin Amimoto. *Waves of Knowing: A Seascape Epistemology*. Durham, NC: Duke University Press, 2016.
James, Alan. "Commanding the World Itself: Sir Walter Ralegh, La Popelinière, and the Huguenot Influence on Early English Sea Power." In *The Maritime World of Early Modern Britain*, edited by Richard Blakemore and James Davey, 67–80. Amsterdam, Netherlands: Amsterdam University Press, 2020.
Jones, David S., and Stefan Helmreich. "The Shape of Epidemics." *Boston Review*, 26 June 2020. https://bostonreview.net/science-nature/david-s-jones-stefan-helmreich-shape-epidemics.
Joseph, Miranda. *Against the Romance of Community*. Minneapolis: University of Minnesota Press, 2002.
Jue, Melody. *Wild Blue Media*. Durham, NC: Duke University Press, 2020.
Juengel, Scott. "What Is Orientation in Sinking?" *European Romantic Review* 30, no. 3 (2019): 265–74.
Kavanagh, Declan. *Effeminate Years: Literature, Politics, and Aesthetics in Mid-Eighteenth-Century Britain*. Lewisburg, PA: Bucknell University Press, 2017.
Kavanagh, Declan, and Ula Klein. "Swift's Queerness." *Journal for Eighteenth-Century Studies* 43, no. 4 (2020): 275–80.
Keen, Suzanne. *Empathy and the Novel*. Oxford, UK: Oxford University Press, 2007.
Keenleyside, Heather. *Animals and Other People: Literary Forms and Living Beings in the Long Eighteenth Century*. Philadelphia: University of Pennsylvania Press, 2016.
Kelly, Ann Cline. "Gulliver as Pet and Pet Keeper: Talking Animals in Book 4." *ELH* 72, no. 2 (2007): 323–49.
Kim, Eunjung. "Asexuality in Disability Narratives." *Sexualities* 14, no. 4 (2011): 479–93.
King, Thomas A. *The Gendering of Men, 1600–1750: The English Phallus*. Madison: University of Wisconsin Press, 2004.
King, Tiffany Lethobo. *The Black Shoals: Offshore Formations of Black and Native Studies*. Durham, NC: Duke University Press, 2019.
Kutcha, David. *The Three-Piece Suit and Modern Masculinity: England, 1550–1850*. Berkeley: University of California Press, 2002.
Labbe, Jacqueline. "A Monstrous Fiction: *Frankenstein* and the Wifely Ideal." *Women's Writing* 6, no. 3 (1990): 345–63.
LaFleur, Greta. *The Natural History of Sexuality in Early America*. Baltimore, MD: Johns Hopkins University Press, 2018.
Lamb, Jonathan, ed. *A Cultural History of the Sea in the Age of Enlightenment*. Vol. 4 of *A Cultural History of the Sea*. Edited by Margaret Cohen. New York: Bloomsbury, 2021.

Latour, Bruno. "Agency at the Time of the Anthropocene." *New Literary History*, no. 45 (2014): 1–18.
Lee, Debbie. *Slavery and the Romantic Imagination*. Philadelphia: University of Pennsylvania Press, 2002.
Lewis, Jayne. *Air's Appearance: Literary Atmosphere in British Fiction, 1660–1794*. Chicago, IL: University of Chicago Press, 2012.
Lewis, Matthew Gregory. *The Monk*. Edited by Nick Groom. Oxford, UK: Oxford University Press, 2016.
Liboiron, Max. *Pollution Is Colonialism*. Durham, NC: Duke University Press, 2021.
Long, Edward. *The History of Jamaica*. London, 1774.
Love, Heather. *Feeling Backward: Loss and the Politics of Queer History*. Cambridge, MA: Harvard University Press, 2007.
Luciano, Dana, and Mel Chen. "Has the Queer Ever Been Human?" *GLQ: A Journal of Lesbian and Gay Studies* 21, nos. 2–3 (2015): 182–207.
Lugones, María. "Toward a Decolonial Feminism." *Hypatia* 25, no. 4 (2010): 742–59.
Macharia, Keguro. *Frottage: Frictions of Intimacy across the Black Diaspora*. New York: New York University Press, 2019.
Maglio, Tony. "'Shape of Water' Dildo Sales Surge over Oscars Weekend." *The Wrap*, March 6, 2018. https://www.thewrap.com/the-shape-of-water-dildo-amphibian-man-asset-movie/.
Mahan, A. T. *Influence of Sea Power Upon History, 1660–1783*. Boston, MA: Little, 1894.
Mann, Annika. *Reading Contagion: The Hazards of Reading in the Age of Print*. Charlottesville: University of Virginia Press, 2018.
Markley, Robert. "'Casualties and Disasters': Defoe and the Interpretation of Climatic Instability." *Journal for Early Modern Cultural Studies* 8, no. 2 (2008): 102–24.
Marshall, David. "Autobiographical Acts in *Robinson Crusoe*." *ELH* 71, no. 4 (2004): 899–920.
Massad, Joseph. "Re-Orienting Desire: The Gay International and the Arab World." *Public Culture* 14, no. 2 (2002): 361–85.
Masten, Jeffrey. *Queer Philologies: Sex, Language, and Affect in Shakespeare's Time*. Philadelphia: University of Pennsylvania Press, 2016.
Mbembe, Achille. *Necropolitics*. Durham, NC: Duke University Press, 2011.
McDermott, William. *The Ape in Antiquity*. Baltimore, MD: Johns Hopkins University Press, 1938.
McGraven, James Holt. "'Insurmountable Barriers to Our Union': Homosocial Male Bonding, Homosexual Panic, and Death on Ice in *Frankenstein*." *European Romantic Review* 11, no. 1 (2000): 46–67.
Medeiros, Paulo. "Simian Narratives at the Intersection of Science and Literature." *Modern Language Studies* 23, no. 2 (1993): 59–73.
Medhurst, Andy. "Batman, Deviance, and Camp." In *The Many Lives of the Batman: Critical Approaches to a Superhero and His Media*, edited by Roberta Pearson, 149–63. New York: Routledge, 1991.
Mentz, Steve. "After Sustainability." *PMLA* 127, no. 3 (2012): 585–92.

———. *Break Up the Anthropocene*. Minneapolis: University of Minnesota Press, 2019.

———. "Ice/Water/Vapor." In *The Cambridge Companion to Environmental Humanities*, edited by Jeffrey Jerome Cohen and Stephanie Foote, 185–98. Cambridge, UK: Cambridge University Press, 2021.

———. *Shipwreck Modernity: Ecologies of Globalization, 1550–1719*. Minneapolis: University of Minnesota Press, 2015.

———. "Towards a Blue Cultural Studies: The Sea, Maritime Culture, and Early Modern English Literature." *Literature Compass* 6, no. 5 (2009): 997–1013.

———. "'We Split.'" In *The Routledge Companion to Marine and Maritime Worlds, 1400–1800*, edited by Claire Jowitt, Craig Lambert, and Steve Mentz, 580–97. New York: Routledge, 2020.

Mentz, Steve, and Martha Elena Rojas. "The Hungry Ocean." In *The Sea and Nineteenth-Century Anglophone Literary Culture*, edited by Steve Mentz and Martha Elena Rojas, 1–14. New York: Routledge, 2016.

Merchant, Carolyn. *The Death of Nature: Women, Ecology, and the Scientific Revolution*. New York: Harper, 1980.

Merrett, Robert James. "Natural History and the Eighteenth-Century Novel." *Eighteenth-Century Studies* 25, no. 2 (Winter 1991–92): 145–70.

Miller, Peter. "Introduction: The Sea is the Land's Edge Also." In *The Sea: Thalassography and Historiography*, edited by Peter Miller, 1–26. Ann Arbor: University of Michigan Press, 2013.

Miller, Peter, ed. *The Sea: Thalassography and Historiography*. Ann Arbor: University of Michigan Press, 2013.

Mitsein, Rebekah. "Upon a Voyage and No Voyage: Mapping Africa's Waterways in Defoe's *Captain Singleton*." *Digital Defoe* 11, no. 1 (2019): 1–19.

Molesworth, Jesse. "Introduction: The Temporal Turn in Eighteenth-Century Studies." *The Eighteenth Century* 60, no. 2 (2018): 129–38.

Morton, Timothy. "Queer Ecology." *PMLA* 125, no. 2 (2010): 273–82.

Mukherjee, Jenia. *Blue Infrastructures: Natural History, Political Ecology and Urban Development in Kolkata*. Singapore: Springer, 2020.

Müller, Anja. *Framing Childhood in Eighteenth-Century English Periodicals and Prints, 1689–1789*. Farnham, UK: Ashgate, 2009.

Muñoz, José Esteban. *Cruising Utopia: The Then and There of Queer Futurity*. New York: New York University Press, 2009.

Nagle, Christopher. *Sexuality and the Culture of Sensibility in the British Romantic Era*. New York: Palgrave Macmillan, 2007.

Napier, Elizabeth R. *Falling into Matter: Problems of Embodiment in English Fiction from Defoe to Shelley*. Toronto, ON: University of Toronto Press, 2012.

Narain, Mona. "Oceanic Intimacies." *Eighteenth-Century Fiction* 34, no. 2 (2022): 147–65.

Nardin, Jane. "A Meeting on the *Mer de Glace*: *Frankenstein* and the History of Alpine Mountaineering." *Women's Writing* 6, no. 3 (1999): 441–49.

Nash, Richard. *Wild Enlightenment: The Borders of Human Identity in the Eighteenth Century*. Charlottesville: University of Virginia Press, 2002.

Neimanis, Astrida. "Water, a Queer Archive of Feeling." In *Tidalectics: Imagining an Oceanic Worldview through Art and Science*, edited by Stefanie Hessler, 189–98. Cambridge, MA: MIT Press, 2018.

———. *Bodies of Water: Posthuman Feminist Phenomenology.* New York: Bloomsbury, 2017.

Nixon, Rob. *Slow Violence and the Environmentalism of the Poor.* Cambridge, MA: Harvard University Press, 2011.

Norton, Rictor. *Mother Clap's Molly House: The Gay Subculture in England 1700–1830.* London: GMP Publishers, 1992.

Nussbaum, Felicity. *Torrid Zones: Maternity, Sexuality, and Empire in Eighteenth-Century English Narratives.* Baltimore, MD: Johns Hopkins University Press, 1995.

Ohlheiser, Amy. "Why a Smallmouth Bass with a Rare, Cancerous Tumor Has Pa. Officials Worried." *Washington Post*, 5 May 2015. https://www.washingtonpost.com/news/speaking-of-science/wp/2015/05/05/a-susquehanna-river-angler-caught-a-smallmouth-bass-with-a-rare-cancerous-tumor/.

Ovid. *Metamorphoses.* Edited by Charles Martin. New York: Norton, 2009.

Parreñas, Juno Salazar. *Decolonizing Extinction: The Work of Care in Orangutan Rehabilitation.* Durham, NC: Duke University Press, 2018.

Pastore, Christopher. *Between Land and Sea: The Atlantic Coast and the Transformation of New England.* Cambridge, MA: Harvard University Press, 2014.

Peters, John Durham. *The Marvelous Clouds: Toward a Philosophy of Elemental Media.* Chicago, IL: University of Chicago Press, 2015.

Pietsch, Theodor, ed. *Fishes, Crayfishes, and Crabs: Louis Renard's Natural History of the Rarest Curiosities of the Seas of the Indies.* Baltimore, MD: Johns Hopkins University Press, 1995.

Plumwood, Val. *Feminism and the Mastery of Nature.* New York: Routledge, 1993.

Povinelli, Elizabeth. "The Kinship of Tides." In *Tidalectics: Imagining an Oceanic Worldview through Art and Science*, edited by Stefanie Hessler, 165–76. Cambridge, MA: MIT Press, 2018.

Przybylo, Ela. *Asexual Erotics: Intimate Readings of Compulsory Sexuality.* Columbus: Ohio State University Press, 2019.

Puar, Jasbir. *Terrorist Assemblages: Homonationalism in Queer Times.* Durham, NC: Duke University Press, 2007.

Puig de la Bellacasa, María. *Matters of Care: Speculative Ethics in More Than Human Worlds.* Minneapolis: University of Minnesota Press, 2017.

Quigley, Killian. "The Pastoral Submarine: William Diaper and Eclogue's Marine Frontier." *Eighteenth-Century Studies* 53, no. 1 (2019): 109–27.

Quijano, Aníbal. "Coloniality of Power, Eurocentrism, and Latin America." *Nepantla: Views from the South* 1, no. 3 (2000): 533–80.

Quinsey, Katherine. "'Little Lives in Air': Animal Sentience and Sensibility in Pope." In *Animals and Humans: Sensibility and Representation, 1650–1820*, edited by Katherine Quinsey, 141–72. Oxford, UK: Oxford University Press, 2017.

Ray, Sugata, and Venugopal Maddipati. *Water Histories of South Asia: The Materiality of Liquescence.* New York: Routledge, 2021.

Renard, Louis. *Poisson, Ecrevisses et Crabs.* Amsterdam, Netherlands: Reinier & Josué Ottens, 1754.
Rich, Adrienne. "Compulsory Heterosexuality and Lesbian Experience." In *Powers of Desire: The Politics of Sexuality,* edited by Ann Stinow, Christine Stansell, and Sharon Thompson, 177–205. New York: Monthly Review Press, 1983.
———. "Diving into the Wreck." In *Diving into the Wreck: Poems 1971–1972.* New York: W. W. Norton, 1973.
Richard, Jessica. "'A Paradise of My Own Creation': *Frankenstein* and the Improbable Romance of Polar Exploration." *Nineteenth-Century Contexts* 25, no. 4 (2003): 295–314.
Richardson, Michael. *Gestures of Testimony: Torture, Trauma, and Affect in Literature.* New York: Bloomsbury, 2016.
Rigby, Kate. *Reclaiming Romanticism: Towards an Ecopoetics of Decolonization.* New York: Bloomsbury, 2021.
Rigby, Mair. "'Do You Share My Madness?': *Frankenstein*'s Queer Gothic." In *Queering the Gothic,* edited by William Hughes and Andrew Smith, 36–54. Manchester, UK: Manchester University Press, 2009.
Ritvo, Harriet. "Species." In *Critical Terms for Animal Studies,* edited by Lori Gruen, 383–94. Chicago, IL: University of Chicago Press, 2018.
Robinson, Charles. *The Frankenstein Notebooks.* New York: Garland, 1996.
Robinson, Daniel. "Gothic Prosody: Monkish Perversity and the Poetics of Weird Form." In *Transnational Gothic: Literary and Social Exchanges in the Long Nineteenth Century,* edited by Monika Elbert and Bridget Marshall, 155–71. New York: Routledge, 2013.
Rousseau, Jean-Jacques. "Discours sur l'origine et les fondements de l'inégalité parmi les homes." In *Oeuvres Complètes,* edited by Bernard Gagnebin and Marcel Raymond. Paris: Gallimard, 1959.
Rozwadowski, Helen. *Vast Expanses: A History of the Oceans.* London: Reaktion Books, 2018.
Sanchez, Melissa. *Erotic Subjects: The Sexuality of Politics in Early Modern English Literature.* Oxford, UK: Oxford University Press, 2011.
Sandilands, Catriona. "Into This Blue: Betsy Warland's Queer Ecopoetics." *Interdisciplinary Studies in Literature and Environment* 25, no. 1 (2018): 186–205.
Sandilands, Catriona, and Bruce Erikson. "A Genealogy of Queer Ecologies." In *Queer Ecologies,* edited by Catriona Sandilands and Bruce Erikson, 1–44. Bloomington: Indiana University Press, 2010.
Sandilands, Catriona, and Bruce Erikson, eds. *Queer Ecologies.* Bloomington: Indiana University Press, 2010.
Scarry, Elaine. *The Body in Pain.* Oxford, UK: Oxford University Press, 1985.
Schaffner, Franklin, dir. *Planet of the Apes.* Burbank, CA: 20th Century Fox, 1968.
Schiebinger, Londa. *Nature's Body: Gender in the Making of Modern Science.* New Brunswick, NJ: Rutgers University Press, 1993.
Schumacher, Joel, dir. *Batman and Robin.* Los Angeles, CA: Warner Bros., 1997.
Sedgwick, Eve Kosofsky. *Between Men: English Literature and Male Homosocial Desire.* New York: Columbia University Press, 1985.

———. *Touching Feeling: Affect, Pedagogy, Performativity*. Durham, NC: Duke University Press, 2003.
Senior, Emily. "'Perfectly Whole': Skin and Text in John Gabriel Stedman's *Narrative of a Five Years Expedition against the Revolted Negroes of Surinam*." *Eighteenth-Century Studies* 44, no. 1 (2010): 39–56.
Serres, Michel. *The Parasite*. Translated by Lawrence R. Schehr. Minneapolis: University of Minnesota Press, 2007.
Seymour, Nicole. *Strange Natures: Futurity, Empathy, and the Queer Ecological Imagination*. Urbana: University of Illinois Press, 2013.
Sharpe, Christina. *In the Wake: On Blackness and Being*. Durham, NC: Duke University Press, 2016.
Shelley, Mary. *Frankenstein*. Edited by Johanna M. Smith. 2nd ed. New York: Bedford/St. Martin's, 2000.
Simpson, Ian. "Manatees Taken Off U.S. Endangered List, Conservationists Cry Foul." *Reuters*, 30 March 2017. https://www.reuters.com/article/us-usa-manatee/manatees-taken-off-u-s-endangered-list-conservationists-cry-foul-idUSKBN17200Z.
Simpson, James. "No Brainer: The Early Modern Tragedy of Torture." *Religion & Literature* 43, no. 3 (2011): 1–23.
Slavin, Phillip. "Climate and Famines: A Historical Reassessment." *WIREs: Climate Change*, no. 7 (2016): 433–47.
Solinger, Jason. *Becoming the Gentleman: British Literature and the Invention of Modern Masculinity, 1660–1815*. New York: Palgrave Macmillan, 2012.
Spampinato, Erin. "Theorizing the New Rape Studies at MLA 2019." https://www.erinspampinato.com/theorizing-the-new-rape-studies.
Spufford, Francis. *I May Be Some Time: Ice and the English Imagination*. Boston, MA: Faber and Faber, 1996.
Stanivukovic, Goran. "Between Men in Early Modern England." In *Queer Masculinities, 1550–1800*, edited by Katherine O'Donnell and Michael O'Rourke, 232–51. New York: Palgrave, 2006.
Starosielski, Nicole. "The Materiality of Media Heat." *International Journal of Communication* 8 (2014): 2504–8.
Stedman, John Gabriel. *Narrative of a Five Years Expedition against the Revolted Negroes of Surinam*. Edited by Richard and Sally Price. Baltimore, MD: Johns Hopkins University Press, 1988.
Steinberg, Pilip. *The Social Construction of the Ocean*. Cambridge, UK: Cambridge University Press, 2001.
Steinberg, Philip, and Kimberley Peters. "Wet Ontology, Fluid Spaces: Giving Depth to Volume through Oceanic Thinking." *Environment and Planning D: Society and Space* 33 (2015): 247–64.
Steller, Georg Wilhelm. "Steller's Journal of the Sea Voyage from Kamchatka to America and Return on the Second Expedition, 1741–1742." In *Bering's Voyages*, translated by Leonhard Stejneger, edited by F. A. Golder, 9–188. New York: American Geographical Society, 1925.

Storrs, Christopher. "Fleets and States in a Composite Catholic Monarchy: Spain c. 1500–1700." In *Ideologies of Western Naval Power c.1500–1815*, edited by J. D. Davis, Alan James, and Gijs Rommelse, 85–105. New York: Routledge, 2019.

Stryker, Susan. "My Words to Victor Frankenstein above the Village of Chamounix: Performing Transgender Rage." *GLQ: A Journal of Lesbian and Gay Studies* 1, no. 3 (1994): 237–54.

Suarez, Michael. "Swift's Satire and Parody." In *The Cambridge Companion to Jonathan Swift*, edited by Christopher Fox, 112–27. Cambridge, UK: Cambridge University Press, 2003.

Sun, Emily. "Romanticism, Decolonization, Provincialization." *Keats-Shelley Journal*, no. 70 (2021): 157–65.

Svensson, Patrik. *The Book of Eels: Our Enduring Fascination with the Most Mysterious Creature in the Natural World*. Translated by Agnes Broomé. New York: Ecco, 2019.

Swift, Jonathan. *Gulliver's Travels*. Edited by Robert DeMaria Jr. New York: Penguin, 2003.

Tague, Ingrid. *Animal Companions: Pets and Social Change in Eighteenth-Century Britain*. University Park: Pennsylvania State University Press, 2015.

Taylor, Gary. "'White Like Us': Early Modern King Kongs and Calibans." In *Racism and Modernity*, edited by Iris Wigger and Sabine Ritter, 31–54. Munster, Germany: Lit-Verlag, 2012.

Thomson, James. "Rule Britannia." In *The Longman Anthology of Poetry*, edited by Averill Curdy and Lynne McMahon, 2696. New York: Longman, 2006.

Tinsley, Omise'eke Natasha. "Black Atlantic, Queer Atlantic: Queer Imaginings of the Middle Passage." *GLQ: A Journal of Lesbian and Gay Studies* 14, nos. 2–3 (2008): 191–215.

Tuck, Eve, and K. Wayne Yang. "Decolonization Is Not a Metaphor." *Decolonization: Indigeneity, Education & Society* 1, no. 1 (2012): 1–40.

Turley, Hans. *Rum, Sodomy, and the Lash: Piracy, Sexuality, & Masculine Identity*. New York: New York University Press, 1999.

Tyson, Edward. *Orang-outang, sive homo sylvestris*. London, 1699.

Union of Concerned Scientists. *Climate Change in Pennsylvania*. Cambridge, MA: UCS Publications, 2008. https://www.nrc.gov/docs/ML0913/ML091390883.pdf.

Voltaire. *Candide; or Optimism*. Edited by Nicholas Cronk. New York: Norton, 2016.

Wald, Priscilla, Nancy Tomes, and Lisa Lynch. "Introduction: Contagion and Culture." *American Literary History* 14, no. 4 (2002): 617–24.

Wall, Cynthia. Introduction to *Journal of a Plague Year*, xvii–xxxiii. New York: Penguin, 2003.

Walsh, Catherine, and Walter Mignolo. *On Decoloniality: Concepts, Analytics, Praxis*. Durham, NC: Duke University Press, 2018.

Wassersug, Richard, and Thomas Johnson. "Modern Day Eunuchs: Motivations for and Consequences of Contemporary Castration." *Perspectives in Biology and Medicine* 50, no. 4 (2007): 544–56.

Watt, Ian. *The Rise of the Novel*. Los Angeles: University of California Press, 2001.

Weaver, Harlan. "Monster Trans: Diffracting Affect, Reading Rage." In *TransGothic in Literature and Culture*, edited by Jolene Zigarovich, 119–38. New York: Routledge, 2018.
Wertham, Frederick. *Seduction of the Innocent: The Influence of Comic Books on Today's Youth.* New York: Rinehart & Company, 1954.
Williams, Gordon. *A Dictionary of Sexual Language and Imagery in Shakespearean and Stuart Literature.* London: Athlone, 1994.
Wilson, Eric G. "Shelley and the Poetics of Glaciers." *The Wordsworth Circle* 36, no. 2 (2005): 53–56.
Wilson, Eric G. *The Spiritual History of Ice: Romanticism, Science, and the Imagination.* New York: Palgrave Macmillan, 2003.
Winkiel, Laura. "Introduction: Hydro-criticism." *English Language Notes* 57, no. 1 (2019): 1–10.
Wood, James O. "Gulliver and the Monkey of Tralee." *Studies in English Literature 1500–1900* 9, no. 3 (1969): 415–26.
Woodward, Megan A. *Eighteenth-Century Women Writers and the Gentlemen's Liberation Movement: Independence, War, Masculinity, and the Novel, 1778–1818.* Farnham, UK: Ashgate, 2011.
Yoon, Ami. "Imagining Decolonial Futures in William Gilbert's *The Hurricane*." In *Eighteenth-Century Environmental Humanities*, edited by Jeremy Chow, 170–85. Lewisburg, PA: Bucknell University Press, 2023.
Zhang, David. "Climate Change and War Frequency in Eastern China over the Last Millennium." *Human Ecology*, no. 35 (2007): 403–14.
Zylinska, Joanna. *The End of Man: A Feminist Counterapocalypse.* Minneapolis: University of Minnesota Press, 2018.

Index

Page numbers in italics refer to figures.

aesthetics, 6; of beauty, 133–34; of modernism, 42. *See also* beauty
Ahmed, Sara, 39–40, 45, 140, 209n16
Airey, Jennifer, 146
Alaimo, Stacy, 8, 11, 24, 34
Alexander, M. Jacqui, 140
Algerian independence, 21
Alkon, Paul, 39, 41
allegory, 23
American Sign Language (ASL), 180
Amimoto Ingersoll, Karin, *Waves of Knowing*, 53
Amin, Kadji, 9
Amsterdam, 73
Andersen, Hans Christian, "The Little Mermaid," 29, 130–34
Angola, 72, 80
animals: cats, 81, 155, 168; doves, 120; monkeys, 24, 27, 67–76, *76*, 89–96, *91*, 99–100, 200nn53–54; turtles, 119–20; whales, 2, 6. *See also* mermaids; monkeys
Anne, Queen, 33
anthroparchy, 31, 45, 67, 89
Anthropocene, 11, 15, 21, 29–30, 35, 173; exigency of, 61; future of, 171; literary imagining of, 176; remedy of, 162, 172; remnant of, 163; stakes of, 44–45. *See also* climate change
anthropocentrism, 7, 13, 20, 35, 72; categories of, 57; paradigms of, 45; Western, 24

anticoloniality, 4, 7, 17–20, 37; masculinity and, 14–22; parasitism of, 20; praxis of, 42; queer, 72, 140. *See also* decoloniality
anti-utopianism, 9
Arabian Nights, 111
Aravamudan, Srinivas, 111–12
Arens, Katherine, 15
asexuality, 106, 117. *See also* sexuality
Atlantic Monthly, 97
Austen, Jane, 4, 30; *Sense and Sensibility*, 30, 169, 171, 174–76
Austin, J. L., 124
autobiography, 48–49; failed, 56
autonomy: anthropocentric, 47; anticolonial, 45–46; erotic, 140; masculine, 82; shared, 44–46, 53
Azoulay, Ariella Aïsha, 22

Bachelard, Gaston, 31, 70, 190n42
Baltimore, Inner Harbor of, 182–83
Banister, Julia, 16
Barnes, A. W., 122
Batman (Dozier), 159
Batman and Robin (Schumacher), 29, 157, 160–63, 212n6
Batman: Mr. Freeze (Dini and Buckingham), 159–62
Baudot, Laura, 79–80
Baudrillard, Jean, 95–96
beauty, 133–34. *See also* aesthetics
Beccaria, Cesare, *On Crimes and Punishment*, 108–9, 204n16, 205n26

Beckford, William, 4, 103, 203nn2–3, 205n27; erotic excesses of orientalist vision of, 205n41; *Vathek*, 26–28, 102–4, 108–9, 111–23, 127–29
Behn, Aphra, *Oroonoko*, 201n72
Beilby, Ralph, *A General History of Quadrupeds*, 71, 79
Bennett, Jane, 43
Bentham, Jeremy, 109
bestiality, 74, 78–84, 180; and rape, 86. *See also* sexuality
Bewick, Thomas, *A General History of Quadrupeds*, 71, 74, 79
Beynon, John, 111
Bible, 55
binary: dialectical, 20, 23; gender-performance, 14
Binhammer, Katherine, 119
bioengineering, 163
Black, Jack, 68
Black animal studies, 192n69
Black Lives Matter movement, 131
Blake, William, 69, 90–91, 93, 201n84; *The Mecoo and Kishee Kishee Monkeys*, 90–91
Blum, Hester, 5, 23, 136
body: animal, 68; aqueous, 11, 34–35, 38, 42, 183; Black, 21; brutalized, 86; desexualized, 113–16, 121, 137; environmental, 68; female, 98, 118, 132, 152; Gothic, 47, 102; hegemonic disciplining of, 28; human, 34–35, 38, 47, 54, 86; impenetrable, 80; Indigenous, 21; masculine, 88; maternal, 141; metamorphosis of, 133–35, 171–72; monstrous, 141, 149; oceanic, 47, 50–51, 67; in pain, 124–25, 133; polluted, 65; trans, 141; violent disintegration of sacrificial, 151. *See also* embodiment
Boelhower, William, 13–14
Bontius, Jacob, 75
Botticelli, Sandro, *The Birth of Venus*, 11
Boulle, Pierre, *Planet of the Apes*, 28, 97–101, 203n13
Boyd, William, 103
Brim, Matt, 10
Brooker, Will, 212n6

Brown, Laura, 72, 79, 85; *Ends of Empire*, 199n37; *Fables of Modernity*, 199n37
Bruhm, Steven, 95, 107
Bucknell University, 58, 62–63
Bullitt, John, 79
Burton, Jeff, 100

cannibalism, 51–56, 149, 181; pederastic, 114
Carlson, Julie A., 109
Carroll, Lewis, 167
Carroll, Siobhan, 136; *An Empire of Air and Water*, 6, 22
Carson, Rachel, 58–59; *The Sea Around Us*, 11–12, 173; *Silent Spring*, 58, 173–74
cartography, 6
Catholicism, 104, 121–22; criticism of, 146; Eucharist, 146–47; same-sex desire and, 204n10; sexual violence and, 207n83
Charman, Caitlin, 46–47
Chaucer, Geoffrey, 93
Chen, Cecilia, 7, 23
Chen, Mel, 3–4, 8, 180, 208n1
chromonormativity, 40
Clairemont, Clare, 148
climate change, 25, 60–64; anthropogenic, 31, 162, 173; manipulation of, 162; realities of, 170, 174; sea level rise of, 178. *See also* Anthropocene
Cline Kelly, Ann, 81–82
Clooney, George, 161
closet climate fiction, 26–27, 33–37, 57, 59, 162, 170. *See also* literature
Coetzee, J. M., *The Lives of Animals*, 196n1
Cohen, Jeffrey Jerome, 70
Cohen, Margaret, 84, 200n61; *The Novel and the Sea*, 6, 38, 46
Cohen, Michèle, 15
Cohen-Vrignaud, Gerard, *Radical Orientalism*, 109, 112
Coleridge, Samuel Taylor, 121; *Christabel*, 126; *The Rime of the Ancient Mariner*, 1, 8
colonialism, 7, 17–23, 36; crimes of, 42; destructive queer, 30; as expansion, 136, 141; flattening of ocean as a

central conduit to, 41; gestures of, 21; sea power and, 57; settler, 59; totality of violence of, 194n15. *See also* coloniality; colonization; imperialism
coloniality, 4, 71; exploitation of, 12; global, 140. *See also* colonialism
colonization, 36–37, 54; by biomedicine, 141; United States, 100–101. *See also* colonialism
conquistador humanism, 21
conspiracy theories, 174
Coole, Diana, 24
Copenhagen, 130
Corbin, Alain, *The Lure of the Sea*, 6
Courtenay, Viscount "Kitty," 103
COVID-19, 63
Cowper, William, 2–3
Coykendall, Abby, *Heteronormativity in Eighteenth-Century Literature and Culture*, 16
Craciun, Adriana, 136; *Writing Arctic Disaster*, 144
Creature from the Black Lagoon, The (Arnold), 177
Crib, Robert, 73
Crisp, Quentin, 139
critical water studies, 5, 104
cryocompositionism, 139
cryonarratology, 157. *See also* narratology
Cudworth, Erika, 31, 193n91

Danish whaling, 131
Darwin, Charles, 84, 127, 201n72; *On the Origin of Species*, 87–88
DC comics, 29, 160; "The Ice Crimes of Mr. Zero," 157–59
death, 47, 93; drowning, 122–24, 127; incantatory, 121–24; invocation of, 138, 153; as metaphor for orgasm, 152–54; proximity to, 9; sea cow's response to, 166; singularity of, 145; torture and, 124–25; violation and, 67; virginal, 124
decoloniality, 17–19, 21. *See also* anticoloniality
decolonial theory, 18

Defoe, Daniel, 4; *Journal of a Plague Year*, 193n12; *Robinson Crusoe*, 9, 25–26, 31–57, 63, 83, 98, 113, 127, 143, 149, 201n72; *The Storm*, 31
de Freitas Boe, Ana, *Heteronormativity in Eighteenth-Century Literature and Culture*, 16
Degroot, Dagomar, 34
dehumanization, 74
del Toro, Guillermo, 30, 169–70, 178–79, 185
democracy, 131–32
Derrida, Jacques, "Eating Well," 156
desexuality, 105–8, 113–18, 128–29; of castration, 129. *See also* sexuality
de Torquemada, Antonio, 197n10
Diaper, William, *Nereides: Or Sea-Eclogues*, 11–13
disability, 101, 134, 175, 178
Duckert, Lowell, *For All Waters*, 139, 149
Dutch East Indies, 73

ecocriticism, 10
ecofeminism, 14, 172. *See also* feminism
ecology, 4, 11; oceanic, 13, 37–41, 50; queer, 8–10, 14, 38, 141; ruined, 171; toxicity of, 173; trans, 141; troubled, 7, 11, 30–31, 34–35, 42, 57, 169, 179. *See also* environment
econarratology, 38, 146. *See also* narratology
ecoterrorism, 157, 162
Edwards, George, *Gleanings of Natural History*, 75–76, 76
Eisenman, Stephen, 110–11
Elfenbein, Andrew, 205n41
embodiment, 3–4, 8; autonomous, 179; demonizing feminine, 12; hybrid, 30, 132–35, 169, 172–77, 182; mermaid, 132–35, 169; modes of shared, 57; monstrous, 136–56, 163, 168–69, 173–74, 182; of nereids, 13; of sea, 50; temporality and, 38; violence of metamorphosed, 8; of water, 10, 123. *See also* body
empathy, 90, 166; entangled, 167; as tricky category, 167

England, 57, 80, 83, 109
Enlightenment, 9, 15, 19, 73; and colonial supremacy, 22; heteronormativity of, 140; knowledges of, 190n47; orientalism of, 111–12; science of, 41
enslavement, 21, 36, 74; horrors of, 69; Indigenous peoples and people subject to, 191n61; marooned, 90; violence of, 89, 201n84
environment: anthropogenically altered, 171; body of, 68; degradation of, 162; entangled relationship with, 11, 14; ruination of, 171, 173; separation of human from its, 24; violence of, 10, 26, 35–36, 41, 51, 62. *See also* ecology; environmentalism; nonhuman
environmental humanities, 14, 30
environmentalism, 10, 58. *See also* environment
Environmental Protection Agency, 58
epidemiology, 41
epistemology, 7; classical, 74; colonial, 76, 140; Enlightenment, 19, 21, 23; feminist, 14; seascape, 53, 55. *See also* knowledge
Erickson, Bruce, 8
Eriksen, Edvard, 29; *The Little Mermaid* (statue), 130–32
eroticism, 11, 23, 117; dangerous, 199n47; of human-simian relations, 70, 73–84, 86; hydro-, 169; interspecies, 177–84, 198n22; and pain, 119; in poetry, 60; queer, 154, 180; sybaritic, 115; utopian, 169; and violence, 67, 169; water and, 178–79, 206n44. *See also* sexuality
eschatology, 27
Esteban Muñoz, José, 11
etymology, 13, 20, 26, 36, 48, 51, 93, 107, 113, 118, 124, 137, 146, 176

Falconer, William, *The Shipwreck*, 1–3, 9, 12–13, 22, 41
Fanon, Frantz, 18, 21, 192n74; absolute violence for, 194n15; *The Wretched of the Earth*, 37
femininity, 11. *See also* gender

feminism, 8, 14, 34, 59, 140, 152, 214n27; ethics of care of, 167, 173, 214n36; modes of thinking of, 24; speculative, 176. *See also* ecofeminism; women
Ferguson, Frances, "Rape and the Rise of the Novel," 77
Ferguson, Roderick, *One-Dimensional Queer*, 189n26
Fielding, Xan, 97
Fincher, Max, 105, 204n10
Fossey, Dian, 99
Foucault, Michel, 107–9, 125, 128–29, 139; *Discipline and Punish*, 110; *History of Sexuality*, 17
Francus, Marilyn, 49–50
Franklin, Michael, 87–88
Freeman, Elizabeth, *Beside You in Time*, 37–38
friendship, 143–44; failure of, 145, 147, 160; queer longing for, 144–45, 147; and sex, 119. *See also* relationality
Frost, Samantha, 24
Furbank, P. N., 39
futurism, 29, 39; reproductive, 163

Gaard, Greta, 8, 172; "What Is Feminism in the Environmental Humanities," 14
Galdikas, Biruté, 99
Galenic humoralism, 74
Garrard, Greg, 8
gender: ambiguous, 105; bending of, 104; notions of, 16, 140; performance of, 15; prison of, 142; violence and, 119. *See also* femininity; masculinity; sexuality
genie (jinni), 103, 112
Gentleman's Magazine, 75
geoengineering, 162–63
Ghaziani, Amin, 10
Gilbert, Helen, 73
Gilbert, Sandra, 152
Gilbert, William, *The Hurricane*, 18
Gillis, John, 5
Girard, René: *Sacrifice*, 137, 144, 147, 150, 152, 154, 210n38, 211n66; *Violence and the Sacred*, 137
Glissant, Édouard, 18–19

Global North, 34
Global South, 5
global warming. *See* climate change
Goethe, Johann Wolfgang von, *The Sorrows of Young Werther,* 138
Gómez-Barris, Macarena, 18–19
Goodall, Jane, 99, 201nn70–71
Gothic fiction, 28, 102, 136–56; desexuality in, 105–8; and romantic orientalism, 109; torture in, 109, 127. *See also* literature
graffiti art, 131
Graham, Kenneth, 102–3, 111, 117, 120
Gruen, Lori, 167
Gubar, Susan, 152
Gunner, Robert, 100
Gupta, Kristina, 106

Haggerty, George, 122, 144, 147, 203n3; *Queer Gothic,* 207n83
Halberstam, Jack, 139, 148
Hamblyn, Richard, 33
Hanson, H. W., 79
Haraway, Donna, 86–87, 89–90, 169, 176; *Primate Visions,* 199n37; *Staying with the Trouble,* 7, 79; *When Species Meet,* 99
Harris, Mary Beth, 15
Hellawell, Phillipa, 57
Helmreich, Stefan, 5, 41–42
Henderson, Laura, 204n24
Henley, Samuel, 26
Herder, Johann Gottfried, "Der Wassermann," 122
Heston, Charlton, 97–98, 100
heteronormativity, 8, 11, 16–17, 76; central tenet of, 23; desirability of, 134; of Enlightenment, 140; infatuation with, 134; infrastructures of, 140; limited imaginary of colonial, 139; pairings of, 161, 166; procreative model of, 179; sex acts of, 107, 128; sexual economies of, 28, 102, 104, 106, 121, 137, 151–54, 182; strictures of, 176, 180; value system of, 106. *See also* repro-normativity; sexuality
Hill, Jen, 136

history: colonial, 93; naval, 57; of novel, 68; of water torture, 102
Hitchcock, Tim, 15
homonormativity, 30. *See also* sexuality
Hulme, Peter, 46
Hurricane Agnes, 61
Hurricane Sandy, 62
hypersexuality, 106. *See also* sexuality

identity, 23; borders of human, 72; categories of, 15; colonial knowledge and, 20; hegemonic, 10; masculine, 15, 85; sexual identity politic, 42. *See also* self
imperialism, 2, 13, 15, 36; British, 41; justification by colonizers of, 194n15; technologies of, 22. *See also* colonialism
Indigenous people: Indigenous modes of thinking, 24, 53; subjugation by "conquistador humanism," 21; torture of in Stedman's *Narrative,* 69
individuality: economic, 46; radical, 46–49
intentionality, 36
International Women's Day, 131–32
irony, 84, 88, 121, 126, 138, 145–47, 156, 183
Islam, 111

James, Alan, 57
Johnson, Barbara, 152–53
Johnson, Thomas, 117
Jones, David S., 41–42
Joseph, Miranda, 148
Jue, Melody, 6
Juengel, Scott, 2–3, 35
justice, 10; new regimes of order and, 160; perverse, 145; retributive, 145

Kavanagh, Declan, 78
Keenleyside, Heather, 96
Kelly, Ann Cline, 199n42
Kim, Eunjung, 106
King, Thomas A., 113
Klein, Ula, 78
knowledge: colonial, 20; Indigenous, 53; primatological, 28. *See also* epistemology
Kutcha, David, 15

Labbe, Jacqueline, 152–53
LaFleur, Greta, *The Natural History of Sexuality in Early America*, 68, 190n47
language: alternative forms of embodied, 184; body, 88, 99; capability of human, 179; erasure of, 124; as more-than-human collaboration, 23; performative utterance in, 124; polyglot abilities of, 88. *See also* metaphor; onomatopoeia
Latour, Bruno, "Agency at the Time of the Anthropocene," 44, 46
Leclerc, Georges-Louis (Comte de Buffon), 71
Lee, Debbie, 90–91
Lethabo King, Tiffany, 21
Lewis, Jayne, *Air's Appearance: Literary Atmosphere in British Fiction, 1660–1794*, 6
Lewis, Matthew Gregory, 4; *The Monk*, 28, 102, 104–9, 111, 121–29, 204n10, 207n91
LGBTQIA+ individuals, violence against, 9. *See also* queerness
Liboiron, Max, 18
Linnaeus, Carl, 71, 165, 197n16; *Systema Naturae*, 72
literary criticism, 30; environmental, 14. *See also* literature
literature: censorship in, 77; "it-narrative" in eighteenth-century, 80, 199n44; journal as, 166. *See also* closet climate fiction; Gothic fiction; literary criticism; novel; poetry; satire; science fiction
Little Ice Age, 33–34
Little Mermaid, The (Musker and Clements), 130, 132–33
Locke, John, 96
London Journal, 110
Long, Edward, *A History of Jamaica*, 71, 74, 79
Long Hoeveler, Diane, 122
Louisville Times, 97
Love, Heather, *Feeling Backwards*, 42
Luciano, Dana, 180
Lugones, María, 18, 74, 140
Lynch, Lisa, 36

MacLeod, Janine, 7, 23
Mahan, A. T., *The Influence of Sea Power upon History, 1660–1783*, 56–57
Mann, Annika, 193n12
marine biology, 167
Markley, Robert, 33
Marshall, David, 48–50
masculinity, 4, 20, 23; and anticoloniality, 14–22; colonial, 22, 67, 72, 170; constitution of, 11; construction of, 10, 87; domination of, 14, 94; eighteenth-century, 16; fragility of, 15; gestures of, 16; impenetrable, 10, 80, 87; modes of desirable, 212n6; parameters of humanity and, 175; porosity of, 82–84; queering of, 85; reconsideration of, 14; as symbol, 23; thwarted, 85. *See also* gender
Massad, Joseph, 17
Masten, Jeffrey, 113
materiality: of metaphor, 23; and symbolism, 23–24
Mbembe, Achille, 18, 20
Medhurst, Andy, 212n6
media, 4; print, 6, 76, 97
medicine, 41
Mellor, Anne, 152–53
Melville, Lewis, 111
Mentz, Steve, 5, 24, 37, 50; *Break Up the Anthropocene*, 15
Merchant, Carolyn, 172
mermaids, 29, 130–35, 167–69, 172, 178. *See also* animals; sirens
Merrett, Robert James, 68
metaphor, 23; animal and nonhuman, 168; hydraulic, 41. *See also* language
Miami, 60
Mignolo, Walter, 18–19, 21
Miller, Peter, *The Sea*, 38
Miranda, Lin-Manuel, *Hamilton*, 1, 22
misogyny, 12, 131–32, 151–54, 199n47. *See also* women
Mitsein, Rebekah, 197n2
Molesworth, Jesse, 37
monkeys, 24, 27, 67–76, 76, 89–96, 91, 99–100, 200nn53–54; as adoptive

parent, 200n55; mating rituals of, 201n70; shooting of, 202n87. See also animals; primatology; simian
Montesquieu, *The Persian Letters*, 206n56
Morton, Timothy, 8
Müller, Anja, 113

Napier, Elizabeth R., 198n25
Narain, Mona, 6
narratology, 39. See also cryonarratology; econarratology
Nash, Richard, 72–73
natural history: diaristic, 73; eighteenth-century, 67, 78, 166; literary fiction and, 68–69; and primatology, 72–75; science and, 70, 73. See also science
nature: experience of, 39; sexuality and, 8; violent contagion of, 37
Neimanis, Astrida, 7, 10, 16, 23, 35; *Bodies of Water: Posthuman Feminist Phenomenology*, 24, 44, 179
neocoloniality, 7, 19, 21, 46, 53, 140
Nixon, Rob, *Slow Violence and the Environmentalism of the Poor*, 14, 41
nonhuman: comic villainy as, 29, 157–63; designation of primates as, 197n14; environmental community of, 46–47; environmental degradation of, 58; human and, 3, 7, 13, 30, 34–38, 54–60, 67–96, 165–85, 191n61; hybridity of human and, 130–35, 167–78; intercession of, 17, 25; in interspecies contact zone, 99; parasitism and, 20; sense of self jeopardized by, 48; violence of, 51–52, 54. See also environment
Norton, Rictor, *Mother Clap's Molly House*, 110
novel: decolonial, 141; Gothic, 28, 102, 106–8, 110, 114, 137; rise of, 41; transatlantic maritime culture of, 6. See also literature
Nussbaum, Felicity, 17

ocean: as conduit for merchant capitalism, 21; feminization of, 12; immersive nature of, 6; navigation by cannibals of, 149; origin story of maternal, 11–12; pleasures of, 12; rise in level of, 60, 62–63; river and, 84; romantic lure of, 143; as site of potential erasure, 152–53; violence of, 51–52, 153; waters of, 25, 84, 153. See also sea power; water
O'Donnell, Chris, 161
onomatopoeia, 86. See also language
orientalism, 103, 111–12; simian, 199n37
Ovid, 95, 120, 124
Owen, W. R., 39
Oxford English Dictionary, 93, 112, 124, 168

pain, 124–25; aesthetic elegance and, 133; body in, 124–25, 133. See also torture
Parreñas, Juno Salazar, *Decolonizing Extinction*, 71
pastoral, 11–12
Pennsylvania, 58–62
Peters, Kimberley, "Wet Ontology, Fluid Spaces," 6–7
phenomenology: of experiences of visuality and pain, 35; ocean, 45; wet, 24
photography, 22
physiognomy, 177
Pietsche, Theodore, 167
Planet of the Apes (Schaffner), 97, 100, 101
plantation economy, 36
Plumwood, Val, 172
poetics: marine, 12; swimmer, 24; trans hydropoetics, 142. See also poetry
poetry, 65; Islamic, 185; memoir and, 141; Romantic, 191n61. See also literature; poetics
politics: abolitionist, 91; anticolonial, 20, 71–72; identity, 8; imperial, 6; liberational, 18; and perspective, 7; of touch, 165
Ponyo (Miyazaki), 130
posthumanism, 25
Povinelli, Elizabeth, 10
Powderham Scandal (1784), 103
Price, Richard, 73, 90, 96, 198n23
Price, Sally, 73, 90, 96, 198n23
primatology, 99, 197n16. See also monkeys

Przybylo, Ela, 106
Puar, Jasbir, 17
Puig de la Bellacasa, María, 180, 214n36
punishment: aqueous, 102–29, 132; corporal, 107; desexualized, 113, 128; disavowal of European capital, 109, 204n16; penal reform and, 128; sadistic, 103; and torture, 108–11. *See also* torture; violence

queerness, 3–4, 10, 189n26; art of failure of, 139; of Batman, 212n6; in care, 167; importance of, 30–31; intimacy of, 144, 156; and marriage, 105; notions of, 106; reproduction and, 180–82; of sacrifice, 138, 152; and violence, 9, 11, 16, 114, 139, 152–55; of water, 8–11, 30, 34, 44–45, 67–70, 77, 89, 102, 104, 141–42, 169–70, 185. *See also* LGBTQIA+ individuals; queer theory; sexuality
queer theory, 8, 19, 30, 59, 192n74. *See also* queerness
Quigley, Killian, 6, 12
Quijano, Aníbal, 18
Quinsey, Catherine, 54

racism, 74, 99. *See also* white supremacy
rape, 77–79, 104; attempted by animals in Swift's *Gulliver's Travels*, 82, 86; incestuous, 104; Ovidian, 120. *See also* violence
rationalism, 88
Rejali, Darius, 125
relationality, 43; new genres of being and, 66; queer, 137, 148, 153–56, 169; ruptures of, 150–56; of sea cows, 166; torturous and painful, 129; violent, 136, 151. *See also* friendship
Renaissance, 19
Renard, Louis, *Poissons, Ecrevisses et Crabes*, 167–68, 169, 170, 181
representation: in Hollywood, 214n31; of hybridity, 30; and imagery, 42; and narrative, 68; of sacrifice, 138, 152
repro-normativity, 142, 151, 182. *See also* heteronormativity

revolution, 21
Rich, Adrienne, "Diving into the Wreck," 27, 59–60, 63–65, 142, 151, 171
Richard, Jessica, 136
Richardson, Michael, 125
Rigby, Kate, 191n61
Ritvo, Harriet, 80–82
river, 1, 5, 25–28, 87–91, 95–97. *See also* Susquehanna River; water
Robinson, Daniel, 207n91
Rocky Horror Picture Show, The (Sharman), 209n21
Rojas, Martha Elena, 50
Romanticism, decolonizing, 191n61
Rousseau, Jean-Jacques, 81–82
Royal Society, 75, 82
Rozwadowski, Helen, 41

sacrifice: carnivorous, 156; ice and, 136–56; desexuality as, 118; environmental, 163; killing as, 150, 153; queer potential of, 152–53; representation of, 138, 152; of self, 130, 147–48, 154–56; of statuary of little mermaid, 132; violence and, 137–38, 150–51
Sade, Marquis de, *120 Days of Sodom*, 114
Said, Edward, 111
Sanchez, Melissa, *Erotic Subjects*, 77
Sandilands, Catriona, 8; "Into This Blue: Betsy Warland's Queer Ecopoetics," 9
Sanivukovic, Goran, 122
satire, 78–80, 82–83; eighteenth-century, 97. *See also* literature
Scarry, Elaine, 124–25; *The Body in Pain*, 201n82
Schiebinger, Londa, 72, 74, 76–77, 200n54
Schley, J. V., 75
Schumacher, Joel, 157, 160
Schwarzenegger, Arnold, 29, 160–61
science: biomedical, 172; Enlightenment, 41; environmental, 84; Eurocentric, 72; masculinist, 172; and natural history, 70, 73; sea power and, 57. *See also* natural history; technology
science fiction, 28, 97, 176. *See also* literature

Scotin, Gérard Jean Baptiste, II, "Madame Chimpanzee," 175
sea. *See* ocean
sea monsters, 169–77; sex with, 179–84
sea power, 57. *See also* ocean
Sedgwick, Eve, 7
self: exterior, 54; interior, 54; and other, 54; reconceptualization of, 85; reconfiguration of relationship with, 10; sacrifice of, 130, 147–48, 154–56. *See also* identity; subjectivity
semiotic treading, 24
Senior, Emily, 89
Sense and Sensibility and Sea Monsters (Winters), 30, 169–77
sentimentalism, 108
Serres, Michel, 20
sexuality: animalized gender essentialism and, 77; anti-heteronormative, 105; compulsory, 106; constructions of gender and, 76; economies of desire and, 175; eighteenth-century, 68; gender performance and, 15; liberation of, 189n26; and nature, 8; nonheteronormative, 11, 211n60; nonnormative pleasures of, 122; notions of, 16, 25, 140; pedophilic, 103; and reproduction, 49; same-sex and pedophilic, 203n3; simian, 70, 73–84, 86; sultry invocation of, 60; of women, 74, 119. *See also* asexuality; bestiality; desexuality; eroticism; gender; heteronormativity; homonormativity; hypersexuality; queerness; transsexuality
Seymour, Nicole, 8
Shape of Water, The (del Toro), 30, 169–70, 174–85, *181, 184*
Shelley, Mary, 4; *Frankenstein,* 29, 136–56, 173, 208n3, 210n39, 211n60
Shelley, Percy, 148
shipwreck, 36, 56; early modern, 36–37. *See also* storms
Silverstone, Alicia, 161
simian: eroticism of human relations with, 70, 73–84, 86; orientalism as, 199n37; Swiftian, 80–89; violence of human relations with, 27, 71, 76–84, 86, 89, 197n10; voyeurism as, 81, 85–86, 92. *See also* monkeys
Simpson, James, 109–10
sirens, 165–70, *169,* 172, 181; call of, 47; songs of, 6. *See also* mermaids
Slavin, Phillip, 34
Smith, Eugene, 173
social activism, 131, 133
Spampinato, Erin, 77
species, 73–76, 80–82, 88, 92; endangered, 165–67
Spufford, Francis, 138–39; *I May Be Some Time,* 212n77
Starosielski, Nicole, 162
Stedman, John Gabriel, 4, 17, 24, 31; *Narrative of a Five Years Expedition against the Revolted Negroes of Surinam,* 27–28, 67, 69–74, 85, 89–96, 120, 127, 198n23
Steinberg, Philip, 41, 57; *The Social Construction of the Ocean,* 21; "Wet Ontology, Fluid Spaces," 6–7
Steller, Georg Wilhelm, *Journal,* 166, 170
Steller's sea cow, 165–67, 170
storms, 37–43, 63; violence of, 55, 61–62, 127. *See also* shipwreck; violence
Storrs, Christopher, 57
Stryker, Susan, 74; "My Words to Victor Frankenstein above the Village of Chamounix: Performing Transgender Rage," 141–42, 145, 156
Suarez, Michael F., 78–79
subjectivity: masculine, 3, 9, 15–17, 22, 44; naked, 35; shared, 50; untarnished, 44; violent and violable, 46. *See also* self
Sun, Emily, 191n61
Suriname, 69, 90–91, 201n72
Susquehanna River, 27, 58–65, *61, 62. See also* river
Svensson, Patrik, 166–67
Swift, Jonathan, 4; *Gulliver's Travels,* 27–28, 67–71, 77–89, 92–101, 127, 199n47
symbolism, 23–24

Tague, Ingrid, 75
taxonomy, 75, 165, 190n47
Taylor, Gary, 197n10
technē, 22
technology, 52; advancement of, 163. *See also* science
temporality, 43; and chronology, 41; conditional syntactic structure and, 44; corruptions of, 41; and embodiment, 38; queer, 42. *See also* time
Theirauf, Doreen, 77
Thomson, James, "Rule Britannia," 21
Three Mile Island nuclear disaster, 58
Thurman, Uma, 161
Tiffin, Helen, 73
time: narrative, 38; queer, 42. *See also* temporality
Tinsley, Omise'eke Natasha, 8
Tomes, Nancy, 36
torture: aqueous, 29, 102–29, 204n24; aversion to, 126; carnivalesque, 110; and death, 124–25; human and nonhuman, 89; justification of, 109; pain of, 125, 201n82; punishment and, 108–11, 129; state, 109–10; waterboarding as, 204n24; of women, 104. *See also* pain; punishment; violence
touch, 81–87; disorienting medium of, 89; and empathy, 166; politics of, 165; violent, 89; visuality of reparative, 183
transcorporeality, 24–25, 34, 179
transsexuality, 141, 209n18. *See also* sexuality
Tuck, Eve, 18
Tulp, Nicolaes, *Observationes Medicae*, 75
Turley, Hans, 15
Tyson, Edward, 70; *Orang-Outang*, 72–73

Union of Concerned Scientists, 60
utilitarianism, 109

Verne, Jules, 97
victimhood, 54–55
violence, 4, 11–14, 74, 88; of affliction, 35; anthropocentric, 89; aqueous, 3, 11–17, 20–21, 26, 30–35, 40, 44, 56, 62–63, 69, 95, 132, 190n42; cannibal, 51–56; climate phenomena and, 34; colonial, 37, 89; culture of, 36; cyclical nature of retributive, 150; domestic, 128; early origins of term, 13, 36; ecologies of, 3, 57; emotional, 135; environmental, 10, 26, 35–36, 41, 51, 62; and gender, 119; genealogy of scholarship on, 13; grotesque, 115; human and nonhuman, 13, 26, 89–90, 166; imperial, 36; interrelational, 143; interstate, 34; lascivious, 114; metamorphic, 70; as mimetic, 21, 150; mirrored, 13; misogynistic, 131–32, 151–52; modes of, 29, 52; oceanic, 51–52, 153; orgasmic pleasure in, 153; performance of, 25–26; posturing of, 93; queerness and, 9, 11, 16, 114, 139, 152–55; radical, 21; and sacrifice, 137–38, 150–51; sacrosanct, 137; sexual, 13, 29, 67, 71, 76–79, 97, 104, 107, 179, 198n33, 207n83; simian-human, 27, 71, 76–84, 86, 89, 197n10; slow, 14; social, 15; structural, 14; weaponized, 55–56. *See also* punishment; rape; storms; torture
Voltaire, *Candide*, 73
voyeurism, 7, 105; simian, 81, 85–86, 92

Wald, Priscilla, 36
Wall, Cynthia, 39
Walpole, Horace, *The Castle of Otranto*, 108
Walsh, Catherine, 18–19
Wassersug, Richard, 117
water: availability of drinking, 174; bodies of, 11, 13, 65, 97, 102, 104–5, 107, 113; contamination of worlds of, 172, 174; different genres of, 200n61; embodiment of, 10, 123; and eroticism, 178–79, 206n44; microscopic attention to, 104; queerness of, 8–11, 30, 34, 44–45, 67–70, 77, 89, 102, 104, 141–42, 169–70, 185; (t)reading, 4; violent, 102, 123, 190n42. *See also* ocean; river
"Water-King, The" (Lewis), 105, 121–26, 128

Watt, Ian, 46
Wertham, Frederic, *Seduction of the Innocent: The Influence of Comic Books on Today's Youth*, 212n6
West Indian manatee, 165, 180, 183
white supremacy, 21, 54, 99, 106, 132. *See also* racism
Wilde, Oscar, 102
Wilkes-Barre, 61, *61*
Williams, Gordon, 94
Wilson, Eric G., 148
Winters, Ben, 30; *Sense and Sensibility and Sea Monsters*, 169–77, *171*, 180
Wollstonecraft, Mary, 148
women: Black and Caribbean, 140; bodies of, 98, 118; of color, 74, 78–79; nudity of, 203n13; pregnancy of, 100, 104; quotidian intimacy of eunuchs with, 206n56; sexuality of, 74, 119; subordination of, 15, 74; torture of, 104; violation of bodies of, 152–53. *See also* feminism; misogyny
Wood, James, 199n41
Wynter, Sylvia, 21

Yang, K. Wayne, 18
Yoon, Ami, 18

Zhang, David, 34
Zoroastrianism, 111
Zylinska, Joanna, *The End of Man*, 176, 214n27

Recent books in the series
UNDER THE SIGN OF NATURE: EXPLORATIONS IN ECOCRITICISM

Monica Seger • *Toxic Matters: Narrating Italy's Dioxin*

Taylor A. Eggan • *Unsettling Nature: Ecology, Phenomenology, and the Settler Colonial Imagination*

Samuel Amago • *Basura: Cultures of Waste in Contemporary Spain*

Marco Caracciolo • *Narrating the Mesh: Form and Story in the Anthropocene*

Tom Nurmi • *Magnificent Decay: Melville and Ecology*

Elizabeth Callaway • *Eden's Endemics: Narratives of Biodiversity on Earth and Beyond*

Alicia Carroll • *New Woman Ecologies: From Arts and Crafts to the Great War and Beyond*

Emily McGiffin • *Of Land, Bones, and Money: Toward a South African Ecopoetics*

Elizabeth Hope Chang • *Novel Cultivations: Plants in British Literature of the Global Nineteenth Century*

Christopher Abram • *Evergreen Ash: Ecology and Catastrophe in Old Norse Myth and Literature*

Serenella Iovino, Enrico Cesaretti, and Elena Past, editors • *Italy and the Environmental Humanities: Landscapes, Natures, Ecologies*

Julia E. Daniel • *Building Natures: Modern American Poetry, Landscape Architecture, and City Planning*

Lynn Keller • *Recomposing Ecopoetics: North American Poetry of the Self-Conscious Anthropocene*

Michael P. Branch and Clinton Mohs, editors • *"The Best Read Naturalist": Nature Writings of Ralph Waldo Emerson*

Jesse Oak Taylor • *The Sky of Our Manufacture: The London Fog in British Fiction from Dickens to Woolf*

Eric Gidal • *Ossianic Unconformities: Bardic Poetry in the Industrial Age*

Adam Trexler • *Anthropocene Fictions: The Novel in a Time of Climate Change*

Kate Rigby • *Dancing with Disaster: Environmental Histories, Narratives, and Ethics for Perilous Times*

Byron Caminero-Santangelo • *Different Shades of Green: African Literature, Environmental Justice, and Political Ecology*

Jennifer K. Ladino • *Reclaiming Nostalgia: Longing for Nature in American Literature*

Dan Brayton • *Shakespeare's Ocean: An Ecocritical Exploration*

Scott Hess • *William Wordsworth and the Ecology of Authorship: The Roots of Environmentalism in Nineteenth-Century Culture*

Axel Goodbody and Kate Rigby, editors • *Ecocritical Theory: New European Approaches*

Deborah Bird Rose • *Wild Dog Dreaming: Love and Extinction*

Paula Willoquet-Maricondi, editor • *Framing the World: Explorations in Ecocriticism and Film*

Bonnie Roos and Alex Hunt, editors • *Postcolonial Green: Environmental Politics and World Narratives*

Rinda West • *Out of the Shadow: Ecopsychology, Story, and Encounters with the Land*

Mary Ellen Bellanca • *Daybooks of Discovery: Nature Diaries in Britain, 1770–1870*

John Elder • *Pilgrimage to Vallombrosa: From Vermont to Italy in the Footsteps of George Perkins Marsh*

Alan Williamson • *Westernness: A Meditation*

Kate Rigby • *Topographies of the Sacred: The Poetics of Place in European Romanticism*

Mark Allister, editor • *Eco-Man: New Perspectives on Masculinity and Nature*

Heike Schaefer • *Mary Austin's Regionalism: Reflections on Gender, Genre, and Geography*

Scott Herring • *Lines on the Land: Writers, Art, and the National Parks*

Glen A. Love • *Practical Ecocriticism: Literature, Biology, and the Environment*

Ian Marshall • *Peak Experiences: Walking Meditations on Literature, Nature, and Need*

Robert Bernard Hass • *Going by Contraries: Robert Frost's Conflict with Science*

Michael A. Bryson • *Visions of the Land: Science, Literature, and the American Environment from the Era of Exploration to the Age of Ecology*

Ralph H. Lutts • *The Nature Fakers: Wildlife, Science, and Sentiment*

www.ingramcontent.com/pod-product-compliance
Lightning Source LLC
Chambersburg PA
CBHW020802230426
43666CB00007B/822